DATE DUE

PRINTED IN U.S.A.

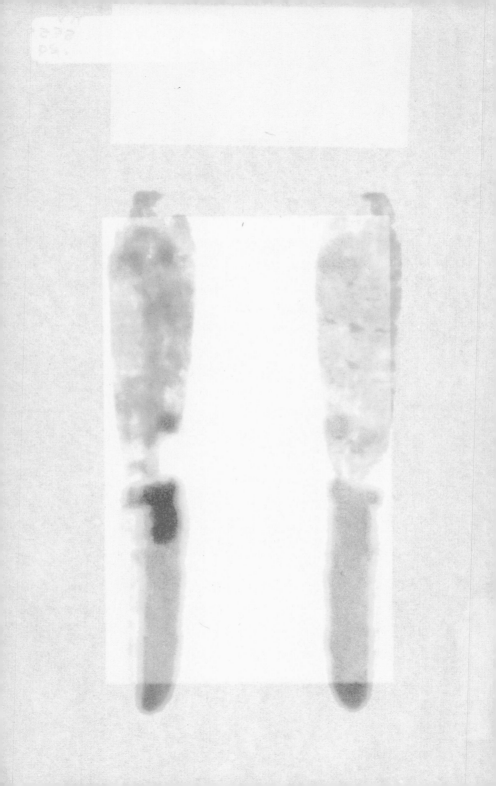

THE 79th SURVIVOR

The author after his release from captivity

THE 79th SURVIVOR

BRONISLAW MLYNARSKI

Foreword by
Arthur Rubinstein

Translated by
Casimir Zdziechowski

BACHMAN & TURNER
LONDON

Bachman & Turner
45 Calthorpe Street
London WC1X 0HH

© Casimir Zdziechowski 1976

ISBN 0 85974 030 7

First Published 1976

Computer typeset by RSB Typesetters, Lightwater Road, Lightwater, Surrey.
Printed in England by Caligraving Ltd., Thetford, Norfolk, and bound by W. J. Rawlinson (Bookbinders) Ltd., Kings Lynn, Norfolk.

CONTENTS

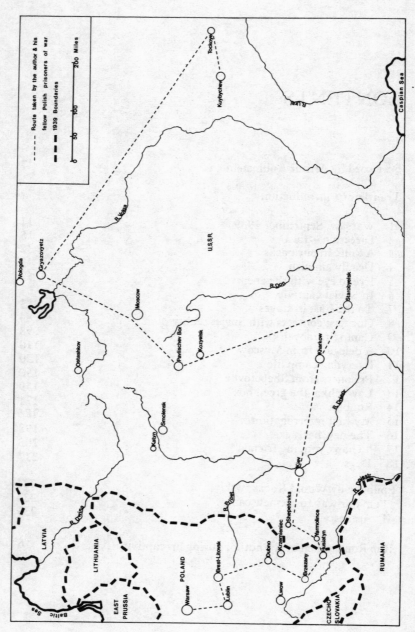

Route taken by the author & his
fellow Polish prisoners of war
1939 Boundaries

0 50 100 200 Miles

6

FOREWORD
ARTHUR RUBINSTEIN

This book needs no introduction. It is the authentic story of my brother-in-law, a Polish officer of the reserve (son of the composer and the well beloved conductor of the Warsaw Opera, Emil Mlynarski), captured at the end of the Polish-German Campaign in 1939 by the invading Red Army and detained in a Soviet camp for officers.

Most of the inmates of these camps, of which there were three, disappeared mysteriously and bodies of over four thousand of them were later found in the Katyn Woods near Smolensk. They were identified and it was established that the victims had been inmates of one camp only, namely that of Kozyelsk.

A similar fate befell officers in the two other camps, most of whom disappeared without trace. Mlynarski was held at the camp of Starobyelsk and for reasons unknown, with 78 other Polish officers, was allowed to survive and to tell his story.

It is a tragic one. First came the treacherous and brutal blow struck by the Red Army in the back of the retreating and unsuspecting Polish troops belonging to a country with whom the Soviet Union not only was not in a state of war but bound by a non-aggression pact. Then came the no less brutal manner by which the prisoners were driven into Central Russia, first on foot, later in box-cars more apt for transporting cattle than human beings. And finally the sojourn in the Starobyelsk Camp. The author's account of his ghastly ordeal is not only gripping but offers an incisive insight into the workings of the secret police, known then as the NKVD, which ran the camp. The way in which, as one can assume, the decision of the ultimate annihilation of the Polish prisoners of war was slowly maturing in Stalin's mind, has the makings of a Greek tragedy of unsurpassed dimensions.

I still remember my brother-in-law, Bronislaw Mlynarski, with strong affection and a deep regret that he is no longer with us. His book will remain as an everlasting document of the inhuman treatment to which he and his fellow prisoners had been subjected.

7

And further a testimony to the courage and endurance as well as their unflagging spirit shown by them in the face of the greatest adversity. I would also like to say that in the darkest hours of his captivity Mlynarski never lost his sense of humour which lends this book a special charm. Mlynarski was a keen observer and a fluent writer. Apart from being a document of importance his book reads at times as the best of thrillers.

Arthur Rubinstein

TRANSLATOR'S INTRODUCTION

The appearance of this book was preceded by the publication in London about two years ago of the original Polish version. I feel that as the one who, apart from having undertaken its translation into English, was also instrumental in editing and publishing the Polish text, I owe a few comments as well as words of explanation.

The story itself, that is the account of falling into Soviet captivity, as well as the sojourn at the Starobyelsk Camp, does not require any special elucidation. The author has seen to that. Told in a clear and precise way it is unequivocal. It has unfortunately however not been brought to an end. After the war, having married and settled in 1947 in California, the author soon commenced working on the book, and with many interruptions slogged along throughout the fifties and sixties. Let me quote here what the widow Mrs. Doris Kenyon-Mlynarski has to say on that subject: ". . . it cost him a lot to write his memoirs – nervously, I mean – they were so subjective and he had to go within himself. Every time he talked or wrote of his massacred friends he would scream in his sleep at night. He wrote more now and then over the next years – through the fifties and sixties. Finally he had determined to finish them in 1971. His health however began to fail. . . ."

There was no doubt that the traumatic experience of the two years spent in Soviet captivity and the still more traumatic experience of having escaped the ghastly lot which befell his closest friends, massacred by the NKVD, left an indelible scar on his consciousness. Although he tended to avoid the subject directly our conversations held during his fairly regular visits to London, before his untimely death in 1971, would always leave me with a feeling that he never really got over the fact of having survived himself while his dearest friends had to perish. The ever nagging question why it was so, to what mysterious cause, eluding any rational explanation, did he owe his life, must have never left his conscience.

And so he could not carry out his resolution to complete the book. The consequence of it was a missing link in an important historical

9

document. His account of the events stops short before the Soviets started to liquidate the Starobyelsk Camp. From April 1940 onwards batches of the 4600 or so camp's inmates would regularly leave for some unknown destination. Their number was therefore dwindling rapidly and in the early part of May there remained the 79 lucky ones only, the author among them. It looked as if the story would have to end at that without disclosing any further events. But then occurred an unexpected event which helped to remedy the situation. When going through the many papers left by the author and kindly sent to me by Mrs. D.K.M., I came across a strange looking copybook of Russian make, of an unbelievable quality. It contained accounts taken down in the Soviet Union, in a pencilled and often illegible handwriting, of the further wanderings of the chosen survivors to other Soviet Camps until their final liberation. My first reaction was that these were the author's notes, but it soon became obvious that they were written by a different person. He happened to be a friend of his and a room-mate at the Gryazovyetz Camp, the last place of their detention in the USSR – Witold Kaczkowski. The epilogue of this book is therefore his. Kaczkowski's death preceded by two years that of his friend Mlynarski. The fact that his notes were found among the latter's papers seems to point to some kind of possible co-operation between the two erstwhile companions.

Their inclusion in the book seemed therefore highly relevant; despite even the fact that the standard of writing in the new text, the narrative and descriptive powers of its author were markedly inferior to those of Mlynarski. A regrettable gap which would have otherwise marred the story could thus be filled in.

One final remark. Mlynarski's descriptions of conditions prevailing then in Soviet Russia were in many cases based on observations made during his nearly two years' captivity in that country. He also had a good knowledge of Russia which went back to his school and university years in Moscow. Relatively little had changed between those two periods and much of what he had to say still holds. After the war however the country underwent a great many changes and some of his comments, such as for instance those relating to the distribution of goods among the population, may therefore appear dated. In my translation some of them I have omitted, some however were left. In the main I have tried to make as few excisions as possible, since the author's eloquent story should be read for its complete honesty.

C.Z.

1. WARSAW, SEPTEMBER 1939

War broke out in Warsaw on the 1st September. At the beginning the people adapted well to the new conditions. With a keen sense of civic responsibility they proceeded to carry out instructions learned during many weeks of anti-air-raid, anti-gas and fire training courses. Although there were few air-raid shelters, the people of Warsaw, on hearing the sound of the first sirens as they travelled to work, obediently left their trams, buses and cars to scurry alongside the walls of the buildings in search of a refuge among the porches of the more solid-looking houses. After the "all clear" signal, a welcome tonic to strained nerves, people continued their interrupted pursuits.

But this disciplined behaviour was not to last long. As the Luftwaffe intensified its activities people began to experience real danger. Faced by collapsing walls and burning buildings their instinct of self-preservation gradually gained the upper hand over any acquired instructions or guidelines. It was to stay and serve as a protective shield against the terrors of war.

I was one of the Warsaw commuters on the 1st September. That day my journey to work at the Gdynia-America shipping line took me a whole hour instead of the usual fifteen minutes. On arrival I found the staff in a state of great agitation. Those living in the more remote districts of the city were relating with much animation their adventures of that morning. From them I learned about the first German bombs, fires and casualties. The staff consisted now mainly of women. Most of the men had already joined the forces, some after receiving unofficial, private call-up papers, others by reporting to their units. My rank being that of a Reserve Lieutenant I was expecting my call-up papers any day.

My work at the office, interrupted incessantly by air-raids, consisted mainly of dashing up and down to the basement in order to bring down what seemed to me the most important files. I later went home in a black mood.

The first night of the war, a sultry, suffocating and sleepless one, soon arrived. On the radio weird air-raid signals alternated with military songs. Stories of heroic deeds by our soldiers and airmen, broadcasted in the news bulletins, were supposed to cheer up the listeners and raise their morale.

More and more worried by the non-arrival of my call-up papers, which I put down to the disrupted postal service, and after some unsuccessful attempts to contact my unit over the telephone, I set off next morning – it happened to be a Saturday – to the headquarters of the Recruiting Centre for Reserve Officers. It was situated in Praga, one of the districts of Warsaw across the Vistula river. On arriving there I could see that chaotic conditions were already badly affecting the military machine. Long queues of several thousands of privates and officers were trying to push their way into the recruiting office either to report for duty or to seek information. Surrounded by stacks of files and documents the staff seemed to be oblivious of the hordes of people around them. One would frequently see depressed or angry applicants, eager to join up, leaving rooms without any firm order or proper instructions. I happened to be one of them.

On the same day I succeeded in getting through on the telephone to Gdynia, our harbour on the Baltic. Things there were deteriorating hour by hour. Fortunately, on the eve of the war, almost all units of the Polish Navy as well as the Merchant Marine had managed to leave for the open seas and were now in British waters. The Hel peninsula was under heavy artillery fire from the German Navy. The tiny Polish garrison at Westerplatte, an arms depot in the Free City of Gdansk (Danzig) which was completely encircled and being bombarded by the Germans, was putting up a heroic resistance. Soon, however, all telephone connections with the Baltic area and the province of Pomorze became severed. German troops, having reached East Prussia, had cut the lines.

In every flat, no matter what size, whether in modern blocks in the centre of the city or in working class districts, people were safeguarding their dwellings according to general orders. All windows, including the smallest ones, in attics as well as big shops, had to be taped vertically and horizontally and blacked out. Every household had to stock a room or closet with an adequate provision of dried or tinned food. The room was to serve as a shelter for every living being, including dogs and other pets, in case of poisonous gas being used by the enemy. Doors and windows had to be kept sealed tight and in order to save oxygen no candles were to be used.

But despite these precautions many people stocked up provisions – in the expectation of a short war, a war which would, after all, be won by the Allies. However, bombing continued and increased in severity and frequency. A gigantic suffocating ring of fire was slowly enveloping Warsaw. Here and there in the centre of the city the first flames could already be seen and a pall of dark choking smoke pervaded the area. As there was little wind the smoke screened the city from the rays of the sun.

Instead of bringing much needed relief to shattered nerves, the nights proved to be even more trying than days. It was only after the first light of dawn that, ignoring the sirens, people took a chance and fell asleep for a few hours.

In the last few months preceding the war, thanks to constant persuasion by the authorities, the population had come to believe that in modern warfare gas presented the biggest threat to human life. Putting aside all the dangerous effects of conventional bombing, all propaganda literature harped on and stressed the dangers of gas. People could not shake off this erroneous belief. Hearing even a distant bomb explode in broad daylight, they would sniff to make sure that no gas could be detected. I have a vivid recollection of a night when after the explosion of a bomb a woman scrambled her way down screaming "Gas!" This happened on a staircase and the acoustics carried the sound of her shrill voice right through the five storey building, causing complete chaos. Terrified women in a state of utter hysteria, dressed in night clothes, carrying children and all kinds of bundles, pets and buckets filled with water were rushing to the gasproof shelters. With clumsy trembling hands they then proceeded to don the hideous gas masks. Later, in deadly silence, holding their breath – breathing uses up oxygen – they sat in their macabre head gear, their hearts beating furiously in expectation of not so much God's mercy but of a slow death in the shape of a creeping trail of gas. After some fifteen minutes, when a somewhat more reassuring male voice announced the "All Clear" and that there was no gas, the spectre of death vanished, but the fear still remained.

At last, on the 5th September my call-up papers arrived. My unit had already left Warsaw. I had to join it without further delay by proceeding immediately to Lublin where a halt as well as a meeting place had been planned.

I spent the whole morning at my office trying to put some order into things and to brief my remaining colleagues on various important matters. The chief manager of my firm Aleksander Leszczynski, with whom I had worked for nine years, had been called up a few days before the outbreak of war. His deputy had left for Denmark a week earlier and that he should now return to Warsaw was, of course, out of the question.

The whole burden of running our big shipping firm, or better still of safeguarding its interests, fell on the shoulders of my senior colleagues and myself. Communicating with our ships at large was not all that easy. The enemy was constantly watching for any opportunity to intercept all our telegraphic messages which would help him in tracing the position of our ships. By a stroke of luck, however, all our larger passenger ships Ms *Batory*, MS *Pilsudski*, Ms *Sobieski* and Ms *Chrobry* were already safe in the free waters of our allies. It should be added that, according to provisions made previously, once Great Britain had declared war on Germany all Polish ships were to come under the orders of the British Admiralty.

My office was in the impressive Palais Kroneberg. The cellars, which had once been filled with wine, had walls about three feet thick. Considered as absolutely bombproof they were to be used as a storage place for all essential documents and files. Making the right choice, however, was not so easy. As I was trying to put some order into my office whilst undecided what to do with a particular file I kept toying with it, acting like a man seen fleeing from his burning house who is clutching of all things a pillow!

After having said goodbye to my friends and colleagues – as if nothing had happened and as if I was just leaving for my annual holiday – I walked to the Ministry for Industry and Trade. It happened to be the highest authority for all matters concerning my firm and the aim of my visit was to notify them of my impending departure from Warsaw. What I saw there was most depressing. The place was a shambles. Among clouds of dust, raised by straw and papers, hundreds of cases filled with files lay scattered on the floors of the once-attractive and spacious rooms and corridors. On the previous night, in common with all ministries and government institutions, instructions had been received to evacuate the offices forthwith. A few employees and porters of the Ministry were wandering about the place like ghosts not paying any attention to visitors. After losing my way I at last stumbled across a Deputy Minister and the head of one of the departments, who, awakening from deep meditation, greeted me in silence. They listened to my few words of farewell and shook my hand but could only utter in reply the solitary words: "Goodbye, Goodbye." Having said this they then resumed their contemplative mood.

The word "evacuation" is a strange one, particularly when it means evacuating the government of a country. It is common practice during wars and clearly cannot be helped. Obviously the average citizen of a capital is perfectly aware of the fact that in case of war one cannot expect the office and building of a ministry to become a fortress, with its staff acting as a garrison to defend it as in a siege up to the last pen and typewriter! Still at the time of war "evacuation" has a very nasty ring indeed. And one cannot suppress a feeling of indignation, bitterness and grief at the evacuation of a government when the capital is being threatened. The government is regarded by the people as a symbol not only of authority but also of guidance. It can be compared to the captain of a ship who is expected to be the last to abandon a sinking vessel.

A great number of refugees, fleeing from the enemy, inundated railways and roads. This affected the reserves of food and fuel so badly needed by the fighting forces. The refugees became an easy target for marauding German aeroplanes. In short, panic now reigned, which is the opposite of what a nation needs in a time of great trial.

Traffic in the city was becoming increasingly difficult. Private cars and municipal buses had been requisitioned for the transport of troops. Electric trams filled up to the brim with people moving slowly in flocks, coming frequently to a halt at the sound of a siren.

After leaving the Ministry I walked in the direction of my house. I crossed the Theatre Square and glancing at the majestic colonnade of the Opera House I was overcome with memories of eleven years spent with my parents in our apartment in that huge building. I reached Saski Square by way of Wierzbowa Street, of which I must have known every inch. Here again I had to bid farewell to the elegant silhouette of the Palais Brühl, the seat of our Ministry for Foreign Affairs, to the Roman statue in bronze of Prince Joseph Poniatowski and at the back of it the Memorial to the Unknown Soldier, particularly dear to my memory, with its huge enamelled effigy of the Order of "Virtuti Militari" on top. At the opposite side of the Square was the Hotel d'Europe. I cast a melancholy glance at the summer terrace of the hotel café amid its well-kept border of scarlet pelargonium. I was re-treading the road of my life, the road of twenty years spent in Warsaw at the time when this city so dear to me started spreading and blossoming.

My house was situated not far from the Belvedere Palais and the Lazienki Park which was a fairly long way from the Saski Square. Too far for a walk and anyway not the right moment for it. I began to wave to passing cars. Just as I was tiring of this fruitless activity a big sports car suddenly pulled up and halted in front of me. It displayed a "Union Jack" on its bonnet! An English friend of mine, now obviously in the service of his government, offered me a lift. I must admit we did not exactly waste our time in a lot of conversation. There was not much to discuss. Deep in my thoughts and in a somewhat sombre mood I continued saying goodbye to the passing streets, to the greenness of squares, and at the end to the attractive shadowy Ujazdowskie Avenue.

The scene of the arrival home, the announcement to the dear ones that in a few hours' time the father will be leaving to join the fighting forces, has been for many centuries the subject of countless paintings, rhymes and songs. A well-known popular Polish verse: "When Johnny went a fighting" came to my mind. This time it was my turn.

I started packing. The same problem cropped up once again. What should I take along with me? For what duration of time should I plan? Should I take into account rainy, cold weather, possibly even winter? My military outfit was inadequate and far from the requirements for modern warfare. It consisted of a summer khaki uniform made from some tropical cloth, a pair of elegant, tight but rather uncomfortable boots, a stiff *rogatywka* (the traditional Polish military headgear), and a belt and a raincoat. To this I added some underwear, two blankets plus a few oddments. All this went easily into a leather suitcase and a hold-all.

Nervousness made me perspire and tears were in my eyes as I rushed downstairs and out into the street. Here I became immersed in an uncanny darkness. Not a single light was to be seen. I had to wait a long time for a tram and use much force to get inside it. Trams, however, as I have mentioned, were the sole means of communication and this one was to take me at a very slow pace across the Vistula river to the Dworzec Wschodni (Eastern Railway Station).

I began thinking more rationally after I had settled down in the tram and composed myself. When nearing the Ujazdowskie Avenue, I realised that to go to war without a proper greatcoat was sheer madness. As it happened Goldberg, a well-established military tailor whom I had known for years, had his workshop in the nearby Nowy Swiat Street. I struggled off my tram in a way which made me think of a cork being pulled from a bottle and soon found myself in a stuffy room full of cigarette smoke and the nauseating smell of cloth pressed by an iron. The tailor, helped by only a few cutters, was toiling and sweating until the late hours.

"Good evening, what can I do for you Mr Lieutenant?" he asked me affably.

"Well, you see, I'm going to war and desperately need a greatcoat. Will you help me? It's of vital importance to me."

"So you're still in town, Mr Lieutenant. Well, let's see what we can do. There are so many coats left and what you can see here are orders not collected yet. Still I can well understand you can't do without one and a warm and solid one too. Look, Ignac, go and fetch those few ones made to measure and we'll see whether they fit our Lieutenant. It's getting a bit late and I fear some won't be collected. Well, this one is for General N. and a bit on the large side. This one would fit better but Major G. might still turn up. But let's have the one ordered by Colonel R. I can now remember having heard some bad news about him at midday. He surely won't ever come now. It's such a tragedy – he was such a brave and good man, with three children too. But for you, Mr Lieutenant, it will fit fine."

It did indeed, as if it was made to measure. Also the coat was long and warm with a fine lining, so we clinched the matter right away.

"You see, Mr Lieutenant," went on my good old Goldberg, "you've been lucky and all I wish is that the coat brings you more luck. However, you can't go to war in such a stiff hat. What you need is a soft cap. There's a hatter just across the road. You run along, Ignac, to this Zalcman and get us the one I've ordered for Captain K. I bet it will fit the Lieutenant."

The size of our two heads, mine and that of Captain K., were almost identical – like two billiard balls. And with its ear-flaps the cap was soft, warm and very comfortable. Later, I often, very often, thought of my dear Goldberg and later still, when the world was resounding with the news of the gory fate of the Warsaw Ghetto, his person became engraved in my memory for ever.

To get to the railway station I had to cross the Vistula river. I travelled by tram over the old Kierbedz Bridge, crowded on that evening with motor cars, horse drawn cars and pedestrians. I gazed down at the dark blue ribbon of the Vistula, now shrunk considerably due to the hot, dry summer.

Suddenly, a few minutes before we were due to reach the station there was a violent explosion which shattered the old tram, breaking some windows and wounding a number of passengers. The 500 kilogram bomb hit the centre of the railway canteen, staffed with uniformed young girls belonging to a para-military women's organization. When I arrived on the spot I saw dozens of killed and wounded people being carried out of the debris of the still collapsing walls. Girls who had survived, helped by some soldiers, were busy carrying on stretchers the mutilated bodies of their colleagues and other luckless victims.

Later, when wandering around the station in search of information about a train, I noticed the same girls smiling affably, as if nothing dreadful had happened, serving hot chocolate and fresh rolls to the milling crowds of soldiers and civilians. Thus I was a witness to what was probably one of the first tragic scenes played by Polish women in the Second World War, women who thanks to their heroism and devotion to their country had contributed to the common cause in the same measure as men.

2. DIRECTION – EAST

The train I was supposed to take was the last train scheduled to leave the capital in an easterly direction and accordingly bore the name: "Warsaw – Lublin – Zdolbunowo, 10 p.m. Express." In fact it left next morning, that is on the 6th September at 3 a.m. It was filled to capacity with people and luggage. It was practically impossible to move inside the coaches. The majority of the passengers consisted of women, children of all ages and elderly men.

Air-raid alarms were frequent and this time were just signalled by the train coming to an abrupt halt in the open. Then, using doors and windows, all those able to jump did so and raced to take cover in the fields, if possible under a tree or a cluster of shrubs. Despite the constant plaintive whimper of children and people wounded by German planes which were machine-gunning any moving object, spraying the entire length of the train with their deadly bullets – despite all the dire conditions in which we were travelling, the general mood among the passengers was surprisingly good. Most people were confident there would be a favourable outcome to the war and were hopeful of finding some calm and comfort at the end of their journey. A sense of humour, the best companion in days of sadness, prevailed in the crowded compartments and corridors, as if all of us travelling on this wretched train were just going on a picnic. Since people occupying the lavatory compartments had the benefit of facilities denied to other passengers: their accommodation was considered the most comfortable on the train!

It was late in the afternoon on the 6th September when due to the destruction by bombs of a section of the railway track our train got stuck in the open and had to remain there for a few hours. Well trained, special railway battalions, working in record time, were busy repairing the line. Bent rails had to be straightened, new rails and sleepers laid and installed. Also many damaged carriages and engines had to be removed. Like children's toys left over after a party they were lying about turned upside down, exhibiting plenty of gaping holes made by fragments of bombs.

Passengers were resting on the stubble where they had formed a picturesque encampment. Tired and exhausted, rejoicing in the calmness in the air — there had been no raids since the morning — they soon fell soundly asleep.

I found among them my cousin Karol Dowgiallo, a Reserve Major in the 1st Regiment of the Krechowiecki Lancers. He had not been called up yet and was on his way to his estate Nowomalin situated near the town of Ostrog bordering on the Polish-Soviet frontier. On learning about my family and their whereabouts he suggested most cordially that they should come and spend the rest of the war at his home with his wife. They would have a roof over their heads and would lack nothing. Since so many people from Poland's western provinces had already descended on them the house might perhaps be a bit overcrowded but still it would be more comfortable and peaceful than Warsaw. He therefore insisted that I should get in touch with my family without further delay so they could proceed immediately to Nowomalin.

This is how dear old Karol imagined things would be. Living so close to the border he, of all people, should have known better. I have to admit, though, that neither he nor I had any inkling as to the true intentions of Poland's eastern neighbour. And so I sent a long telegram from Lublin to Warsaw, but it never reached my family.

About six months later I learned from an eyewitness that when in the small hours of the 17th September Soviet troops invaded Poland, Nowomalin was occupied in a matter of minutes and Karol's wife with all the guests and their children deported to an unknown destination. Karol himself was bundled as he stood into a car and taken to the nearest prison. That was the last thing that has ever been heard of him.

Just a few steps from the bush where I was conversing with Karol a young woman was lying dozing in the furrow of the stubble with her delightful five year old daughter. Up in the skies all over the country the German fighter planes had developed a special technique. It consisted of flying at a very low altitude, no more than 100 metres, in a so called "mowing flight". By doing this they didn't give themselves away by the roar of their engines as the echo would be sufficiently deafened by the earth. Like a hurricane they would appear overhead, rendering any proper anti-aircraft defence impossible. This time it took a few seconds only. Three fighters emerged from behind a nearby wood. The woman screamed with all her might, the little girl jumped up and called out in a childlike voice: "Don't be afraid Mummy, I'll cover you up." She squatted down, spreading out her calico dress with her tiny hands over her mother's head and breast like the petals of a flower. Machine-gun shots sprayed the whole field with bullets, raising straight lines of clouds of dust. The sweet little child slumped into the stubble without uttering a sound. She resembled a plucked flower with its petals tinged with red. Later, her tiny body and her half-conscious mother were put on a wheel-barrow which had been brought from a nearby village and taken to a cemetery for the last rites to be performed.

My journey to Lublin, a city some 110 miles from Warsaw, took forty hours. After I had arrived there I rushed to the Garrison Command but failed to get any news of my unit. Yes, they had seen it passing through Lublin but had no idea in what direction it went. Late at night I was billeted to a room in a flat belonging to a civil servant and his family. The only thing I craved was a bath and a bed.

Early next morning, feeling somewhat refreshed and rested, I went out. The old city, bathed in the morning rays of sunshine, impressed me by her beauty. Although the outstretched hand of the enemy was already grasping at the industrial districts on the outskirts — as one could tell from the rising pall of smoke — the centre of the city with her beautiful churches, the famous walls and gates of the old fortress, her university and many other old relics were as yet untouched.

In the streets were innumerable crowds of people, endless lines of all sorts of vehicles, as well as many military units moving through the city, one was in no doubt that Lublin was on the crossroads of a mass migration flowing from the west to the east or the south.

I mingled with the crowd. First in a coffee house, which was bursting with people and where I had literally to fight for a cup of coffee, later in the streets, gardens, in the Post Office and some shops. Men and women, as well as soldiers, in a state of great agitation were describing their adventures, their fighting with the enemy and of how they had had to leave their homes behind complete with their entire belongings. They were describing in detail their miraculous and narrow escapes. People were discussing where they should next go and arguing about strategical problems, how the war should be fought and so forth. Typical advice to the government and the Military High Command was: "If I only had the power I would teach them a lesson all right, but as you can see, Mister, things have turned out badly. Governments are always in wrong hands. But never mind. I have to hurry up or I'll miss my transport and the rest of my belongings. So goodbye and good luck."

Here and there one could have a glimpse of well-known personalities, government officials, artists, writers and even members of the Diplomatic Corps. If it had not been for the misery and anguish showing on the faces of the majority of them, it would have been possible to mistake some of them who had arrived in comfortable cars, who were well dressed and indulged in leisurely talk, for visitors to a race meeting or an international fair.

I came across a number of friends, even relatives. Among others there was Wanda, my first cousin Kazimierz's wife. He himself was with his unit on the front line in one of the northern sectors. She had left Warsaw with her two boys aged 14 and 16 only to find herself in the chaos of Lublin. Lost and helpless she was, however, full of her usual zest. I ran into all three of them when they were trudging aimlessly through the streets of the city not knowing where to go. I heartily embraced the boys, Janusz and Marek, tall, with curly hair and the look of daredevils about them. They both died heroic deaths five years later in 1944 in September during the bloody fighting of the Warsaw uprising.

Shortly afterwards I saw my cousin Hela Sedzimir with her three young children. She was driving a pair of skinny, scraggy horses dragging a dome-like wagon heavily over-loaded with people and luggage. I made a dash towards her shouting excitedly: "Hela, Good God, where are you going?"

"And you Bron, what are you doing here? I can see you're already in uniform. My God! I had to leave my dear old place. Constant fighting is going on around there. Everything I once owned has been practically wiped out – I couldn't stand it any more and there was always the problem of my children. I'm simply driving ahead. I have friends who live a hundred kilometres from here and so I might perhaps join them. It will be possible to wait there until the storm is over," she said with tears in her eyes.

"And where is Jan?" I asked.

"He's been with his regiment for a week. God permitting, both of you may perhaps meet. If so, try to keep together. Goodbye, Bron." She whipped on the horses and the wagon rattled away.

I did some shopping and bought a few odd things amongst which the most important item was a pair of excellent boots of the type used in skiing. I also bought a pair of puttees. Now I looked more martial. I then performed an operation on my old boots. I cut off the tops which were made of good soft leather and threw away the bottom part. Why I did that I really don't know. I must have had a premonition of things to come for I took them along with me. In fact they were to serve me very well indeed.

I called again on the Garrison Command. It became obvious to me that I was not the only one in search of his unit. In fact there were many more like me and the number was growing constantly. Some of them had either lost their units or owing to the chaotic conditions were prevented from joining them. On that particular day there happened to be in Lublin around a thousand Polish officers of all ranks – from that of Lieutenant to Colonel. The Commander of the Lublin region decreed a strict registration as well as arranging accommodation for them in barracks. His orders, sensible, no doubt were carried out properly. And so, on the evening of the 8th September I found myself lying on straw spread on the floor of a room in a vast school building amongst a mass of other military stragglers. Although all this smacked a bit of improvisation it was reassuring to experience some discipline and to hear the sound of voices crying "Yes, Sir" and "At your service, Sir." The above show, which, in truth, lacked any deeper meaning, lasted for the best part of the night. Eventually, however, all those involved, the ones giving the orders as well as those on the receiving end, lay down on the straw and slept soundly until the next morning. After a breakfast consisting of black coffee and brown rye bread, a new wave of initiative surged among those feeling most eager for action. Attempts to form something like independent units were undertaken. Men were selected according to their age, physical condition and specialization. However, before very long these attempts were proved to be wasted.

In order to annihilate Lublin German planes raided the city in three consecutive waves starting at 10.30 a.m. on the 9th September. Reverberating like silver against the sun the first squadron of bombers pounced on the centre of the city almost simultaneously with the sound of the first alarm sirens. A rain of crushing and incendiary bombs fell and a second and third wave soon followed. This terrible devastating operation took no more than fifteen minutes. The deafening noise of exploding bombs mingled with the ominous rumble of collapsing walls.

If hell has ever descended on earth it is in the shape of a modern bombardment of a city crowded with people, horses and cars with their tanks filled with petrol. Of a city deprived, apart from ordinary trenches, of proper shelters; a city of houses built not in reinforced concrete but old, brittle bricks and timber. To those who had survived the raid the inferno which towered before them was a terrible sight. After having extricated themselves from the fire and debris the wretched victims, stunned by the explosions, were running from the scene, half conscious and screaming wildly. With their dresses in shreds, their hair tousled and covered with a coat of red dust, their faces besmeared with blood, the weird creatures made one think of the human torches at the time of Emperor Nero's games.

I would never have been writing these words if a bomb which had buried itself deeply into a lawn exactly eight steps from the place where I was lying had cared to explode. For some reason, however, it did not.

The city was burning fiercely and hopelessly. There were no means available which would check — even to a small extent — the spreading waves of fire. In a relatively short visible radius two hotels, some churches, scores of shops, coffee houses, offices and blocks of flats were burning like boxes of matches. Where fire failed to reach and where bombs scored no direct hits the strength of the bomb blasts did the job. Windows and their frames were blown in, roofs disfigured and walls suffered huge cracks. Soon after the raid special rescue parties were formed spontaneously and my colleagues and I hastened to join one of them.

Nine months later many other countries, Holland, Belgium, France and Great Britain, experienced the same predicament. Their capitals and cities began to burn and bleed from the hands of Hitler's henchmen. History should remember, however, that it was Poland, poor weak Poland inadequately armed, left to fend for herself, thrown so to speak, to the wolves, with no help at all, which was the first to bear the brunt of the terrible onslaught.

The night before the man sleeping next to me on our bed of straw was a certain builder from Warsaw with an engineering degree by the name of Jozef Laudanski, whom I shall call just Laud. Aged thirty-eight, he was a Reserve Lieutenant in the Sappers. With his round face and pleasant, benign smile he reminded one of a country vicar among his parishioners. An old Reserve Captain, Witold Gorzechowski, a notary in some provincial town, bald as a coot, was snoring on the other side. That he should have known a great deal about people and the world as a whole was in character with his profession, and what he did not know he made up, helped by his vivid imagination. As soon as the dust had settled after the bombardment he started to worry whether the Klub Obywatelski (Citizens Club) had been hit as this was the place where, while sipping coffee on our straw, he had invited Laud and me to a slap-up lunch.

Although time was short, an assembly of officers had been fixed for 4 p.m. and so we set off reconnoitring. Wading over the debris and broken glass we reached the house which up to this morning bore the engaging name of a club. Its whole front had been cut off as if slashed by a razor, chairs and tables, like flies caught in a spider's web, were hanging between floors on some wires and strings. Our cavalry officer, however, did not give up. Sniffing around like a pedigree retriever he squeezed himself through a collapsed gate into the courtyard from where he soon called in his commanding voice,

"Follow me, Gentlemen." Creeping up on all fours along a badly damaged and warped staircase we eventually reached the first floor We found that a part of the kitchen had been miraculously spared. The cauldrons, still warm, were filled with soup, stewed meat and potatoes. The corner of the bar had also survived as well as some tables covered with a layer of dirt and broken glass. With a triumphant air the Captain assumed the role of our host. Not losing any time we treated ourselves to an excellent lunch washed down with a bottle of equally excellent wine. Although now and then our teeth would have to gnash bits of grit still the feast proved to be a remarkable one and like so many other things which happened in those days it stayed clearly in our memories.

The latest military decree to be issued took a new turn. We were told that officers registered originally with the Command of Region No. 1 Warsaw would have to assemble in one place, those from Region No. 2 in some other place and so forth. There were in Poland probably something like ten Regional Commands. Consequently I found myself assigned to group No. 1 which had been given the order to proceed forthwith to the town of Brzesc nad Bugiem (Brest Litovsk) and report to the Garrison Commander of its fortress. This prompted the unavoidable question: "How should it be done?" "You'll have to use your wits," was the answer. "As you well know, military transport is not available at the moment. Those in possession of cars, either private or official, are to raise their hands. Good, let's put down the names. And now let every car-owner pick his own passengers. No arguing, please. Room for all must be found."

Without much ado, Laud, the Cavalry Captain, myself and a few others cornered a car-owner who was standing nearest to us, a dark, elegant man with a monocle which looked as if it had been glued to his eye. He said, in a cool and nonchalant manner, that he could admit no more than three men. His car was on the small side and its capacity very limited − in fact it was a sports car. After some haggling he raised the number of passengers to four. The car, a Czech make called "Aero," was very narrow, long and flat and looked rather like a dachshund. After having obtained a movement order entitling us among other things to an allocation of petrol and after having reduced our luggage by half − we donated what was left to the victims of the air-raid − we squeezed ourselves − and by Jove we needed a shoehorn for that − into our little "dachshund on wheels".

We drove past the ruins and the smouldering cinders of Lublin with bleeding hearts. Dusk was falling and after a hot and sultry day a thick mist was settling down. We were not allowed to use the big head lights and driving on the small ones was not possible. We stopped at some peasant's farm where we were met with great hospitality and allowed to stay until dawn on a fragrant hay-stack in the barn.

After a few hours driving we found ourselves not far from Jablon, the residence of a very good friend of mine. I suggested a short break at his place and assured my companions of an excellent breakfast. My suggestion was met with unanimous approval. On nearing the impressive outbuildings of the estate we could discern the typical smell of milk and manure. After swerving from the uneven surface of the main road into a shaded alley lined with linden trees we proceeded through an open iron gate skirting a lawn with tall spreading silver firs. We stopped in front of the white walls of an old annex overgrown with Virginia creeper. We were greeted by the joyous barking of two sheep dogs, the grizzly Farut of Pyrenean breed and the black Ficko of Hungarian kind. Behind them appeared Gucio with his characteristic shouts and exclamations — my very dear friend Count Augustus Zamoyski!

He was and would for ever remain quite a character. When still only fifteen years old he crossed Europe and America on a bicycle — later to repeat this performance in a racing car. An excellent skier and blusterer of great charm he uncompromisingly ignored all convention. An aristocrat among sculptors — a born artist — he would carve in the hardest granite a woman's body, bringing out all its subtle grace and lithe suppleness. He would be as equally creative in his studio in Jablon as in the studios of Montparnasse, Chelsea, Greenwich Village or Warsaw. He was a born hunter, completely at home in the old forests amongst the game. Here in Jablon ten years ago I had passed through the ceremony of the "hunter's christening." According to an age-old custom the senior hunter at a shoot smeared my forehead with a few drops of the blood from my first wild boar.

The vast rooms of the house were filled with magnificent hunting trophies collected by two generations from various parts of the world. Grzegorz, the old butler whose silver grey hair reminded one of the bark of a birch tree, announced that breakfast was ready. He officiated with the help of the nimble and fresh Frania who was dressed in the bright folk style of the region. Ficko snarled — as he was used to doing — at the sight of the stuffed bear standing at the entrance to the dining room with his paws raised.

Conversation was haphazard, intermittent and lacked direction. Our attention, I must admit, was concentrated mainly on the long table laid with a profusion of all sorts of delicacies: two kinds of fresh rye bread, two kinds of cheese — a creamy one with caraway seeds and another one known as Lithuanian – several kinds of sausages – a fresh and cured one made of wild boar – pickled cucumbers, tomatoes, linden honey, milk, etc.

"Well, Gentlemen, time to get moving. God bless you Sir, and many thanks for your hospitality," mumbled the Captain in his deep voice, wiping his bushy moustache.

I dashed to the terrace for one last moment. Just to cast one more glance at the magnificent park, completely wild, left at the mercy of nature's whims. A wonderful kingdom of pheasants, half-tamed deer and hares. During the last ten years I had spent almost all my free time in it.

Bidding farewell with tears in his eyes and this time without saying a word, our host stood on the threshold of his house. Soon after he was forced to abandon this family home for ever. It was the end of beautiful, lovely Jablon with its hundred-year-old trees. Crushed by the war, ploughed through and through by deep, social changes for the better or worse of posterity – who knows – it went down, taking with it into the rich soil all visions of the past.

We reached Brzesc in the evening after an extremely slow journey. Afraid he would break the springs of his car and hampered by weak tyres our driver firmly ignored our requests that he should get a move on and maintained a speed of about ten miles an hour. We were like potatoes in a bag which when banged persistently against one another seem to sort themselves out, for after a while we all felt better and more comfortable and started to converse with one another. Once in Brzesc we hastened to the old fortress in search of its Commander, expecting to be given our orders. There was no question, however, of getting any information. Muddle reigned everywhere. We spent the night in the filthy apartment of some local merchant who with his family left next morning to seek refuge at some easterly destination.

As we came to know better the owner of the car, he proved to be most resourceful and enterprising, apart from a good companion. Aided by the equally clever Captain all problems of food and accommodation became their responsibility.

Next morning we set off to the fortress once again. This time we succeeded in seeing not the Commander but his A.D.C. and through him, after a great deal of haggling, the Deputy Commander. We asked for specific orders or assignments but to no avail. Meanwhile, the day before a few dozen officers belonging to the same category as our little group of five, that is to the Military Region No. 1, had arrived in Brzesc. Acting on obscure instructions they dispersed to different destinations leading mostly to the south-east. Ten men remained, however, and like us they awaited specific orders.

Nothing happened until the evening, when some motorists and Sappers were summoned before a very pleasant Colonel. I was a Sapper and happened to be one of them. "Under the command of Major S. a reconnoitring party will be leaving the fortress at midnight. It will consist of a few light armoured cars and its aim will be a reconnaissance in depth. You will try to locate the enemy and learn about his position and the main strategic features of the terrain he occupies in the north sector. The Germans are already quite close to Brzesc and the motorized points of their armoured columns are penetrating deep into our lines and cutting them in two. I need four officers to do the job and I request volunteers to come forward." That was his order. Laud, myself and two other men raised their hands.

Midnight had not quite struck as we climbed into the small scout cars. With our Commander's car in front of our little column we set off punctually into the blackness of the night. With much thumping we crossed the bridge on the River Bug which I knew so well from the Sappers' manoeuvres I had participated in from 1927 to 1938. After covering some fifteen miles we halted and waited in silence a long time for the first sign of dawn. We then moved ahead slowly as if stalking a wild boar. This took what seemed an unending time. The eastern horizon was becoming tinged with red when suddenly our Commander gave the order, "Get ready for battle." We deployed our column into a fan-like formation. After the dust raised by the wheels of our vehicles had settled down we saw in the distance, some six hundred yards away, three huge, grey carcasses, rolling in the clouds of their own dust. We could see distinctly that they were German tanks. Such an encounter face to face with the enemy – I have to admit – makes a tremendous impression. A few seconds passed and then there was a crash and a loud bang of a detonator followed by other similar salvoes. We, on our side, fired on the enemy as best we could with our light guns and heavy machine guns. The German armour now began to manoeuvre. There were a few salvoes from the enemy which we reciprocated each time. Our car, positioned second in the line, was hit. A piercing cry and groan reached our ears. After raising enormous clouds of dust the Germans suddenly vanished, and all we could do was fire a series of farewell bullets into their rear. We now realised we had two casualties. A non-commissioned officer had been killed and a Second-Lieutenant wounded in the arm. We also had to tow the damaged scout car. Such was the end of our nocturnal sortie, my first and last encounter with the Germans on Polish soil.

When nearing Brzesc on our way back we watched a fantastic display. It was an air battle. Flying at high altitude over the town and the fortress were two V-formations of German light bombers — some twenty machines in all. The sky was thick with bombs and we could see flames leaping up furiously. The rattle of the fortress's anti-aircraft artillery was exhilarating and the brightness of the sky became increasingly stained by a number of tiny, dark-grey clouds. Suddenly a commotion broke out among the German planes. Two Polish fighters had made their appearance, their pilots showing incredible bravery. After a short while a bomber, soon followed by a second and a third one, could be seen dashing down vertically leaving at their tails a long trail of black smoke. Our joy was such that we embraced each other and wept. Two of our eagles had dispersed the Hun. Another bomber pursued by our fighter was shot down a long distance from the town. In the course of the next few days I was able to watch a few more of such desperate fights in which we were always outnumbered at least ten to one.

Once our group had returned to Brzesc it was ordered to proceed to Dubno in the province of Volhynia by way of Kowel and Luck. We arrived in Luck, capital of the above province, late at night. Hungry like wolves we set off in search of some food. The whole town was blacked out and not a single light was to be seen. After some time an obliging passer-by pointed to a house. We pushed our way into what appeared to be the only restaurant open in town. The place was crowded, and its windows and doors were covered by blankets and curtains. As the local power station had been bombed it was lit only by some miserable candles. The air was unbearably stuffy, but our hunger was strong. We managed somehow to get hold of food and room at the table.

I settled down to eat. Imagine then my astonishment at seeing the man sitting next to me! It was none other than the one-armed, one-eyed General Carton de Viart, VC, a British veteran of many wars including the First World War. Wearing a fantastic uniform with glittering bronze buttons and a Sam Browne belt polished like a mirror he looked most impressive. He acknowledged the few words I said to him in English and thanked me warmly for the glass of tea, and a couple of eggs and bread which I helped procure for him.

The General had settled in Poland after the Russo-Polish war in 1920. He came to live in the province of Polesie, known otherwise as the Pripet Marshes, and he had fallen in love with it. He built himself a shooting lodge amidst ancient woods and bogs and here he reigned serenely in the largest game reserve of Central Europe. In almost complete isolation from the outside world, undisturbed in the quietness and stillness of the forests of Polesie, he hunted elks, bears, wild boars, lynxes, capercaillie, woodcocks and a multitude of water fowl until the day when H.M.'s Government thought it necessary once more to recall him for active service. At the sight of the venerable General I was overcome by a surge of confidence and trust. Poland after all – so I thought – had not been deserted and the Western Powers were still caring for her.

The next day, before reaching Dubno, in order to quench our thirst, to wash the dust from our eyes, as well as stretch our legs, we stopped for a while in front of a well at a little village. Suddenly, as if from nowhere, there appeared a young boy. He was smiling and holding a bucket and a mug. He then proceeded to pump water out of the old well. Next he rushed without a word to a nearby cottage from which he soon emerged carrying a linen towel. After that he brought a jug of fresh milk and a huge slice of rye bread.

Taken aback by the boy's uncommon solicitude and enterprising spirit we asked him if he was from the area and what he was doing in his boy scout shirt, shorts and a wide-brimmed hat which failed to conceal a head of tousled, light golden hair. Smiling with his blue eyes and showing his white teeth he said: "Well, gentlemen, having been on the move for the whole time, either in a car, horse-driven wagon or even on foot, I was feeling terribly tired and sleepy. I've just been driving with a group of soldiers in a truck. They said we would stop here for a while and so I jumped on that hay stack over there and when I awoke they were gone. I asked other soldiers who were passing for a lift but they refused. So now, since you are here, may I perhaps come with you if I may ask this most humbly?" He said all this quickly, intelligently, and with a certain touch of pride, although a slight quiver of his young lips betrayed a trace of nervousness.

"Right, my friend, but where do you want to go? We are on our way to Dubno, would that suit you?" I asked him, clasping him tightly to my side.

"That is exactly where I want to go, Mister Lieutenant. And this is where all our troops are moving too and I want to be with them to fight our enemy."

The verdict was uanimous. In his deep, stentorian voice the Captain said: "Climb up on top, brother, and take a seat if you can find one. Make yourself comfortable and hold on to the wind so that you don't fall off!"

The boy's name was Stas Debicki, he would be fourteen in December and he came from Debica in the Cracow region. His father ran a small stationery shop where he also sold school books. Stas was

attending a local school and as holidays were just over he was about
to go back to his lessons. But, as he told us in his sing-song voice: "In
the meantime came the war. Grown-up people kept saying: 'Let the
Germans try and we shall give them a hiding that will make Hitler
lose his moustache out of sheer fear.' It's apparently a false one, just
stuck on to his face. Isn't that funny, see? Now, it must have been
some four days ago, Mummy and Daddy were packing and kept
shouting at us – me and little Mary. She's still really a child, you
know, only six and won't stop playing with her doll. So I got my boy
scout uniform ready – it looks rather like a military one, doesn't it? –
as well as my rucksack, the one I have here. After that we rushed to
the market place. Daddy ordered me to watch out for the Nowaks'
cart, drawn by two horses, as we were going to travel with them. I
found them near the chemist's shop and we all scrambled on top of
the wagon – there were seven of them and four of us with plenty of
bundles and things. We took the road through Tarnow. There were
plenty of soldiers around as well as thousands of folk from towns and
villages – with horses and on foot. Mummy was sort of crying – our
house had been left with no one to look after it and it would either be
burgled or burnt down. Mary was crying too, but soon fell asleep.
Daddy was discussing the war with Mr Nowak who worked in an
electrical power station. They thought that the Germans would be
stopped in Przemysl on the River San, and that British and French
tanks were pouring into our country through Rumania and Hungary
in their thousands. They also spoke of the 'fifth column' – I then
didn't understand what it meant, but soldiers have now explained it
to me. Ah! those Huns, aren't they real scoundrels!

"Later, I really don't know how it all happened. I'd been telling
Daddy that he should allow me to go on foot for a bit. We were
driving at a snail's pace after all and it would lighten the load for the
horses. What I really wanted, however, was to get on a soldier's
truck. They were also moving ahead very slowly in Indian file. As
they kept halting we more or less stuck together. Sometimes they
happened to be in front of us, sometimes behind, but they never got
really out of sight. Daddy finally gave his permission although
Mummy wouldn't hear of it. So I jumped off and first walked a few
kilometres and later the soldiers agreed to take me with them on the
truck and then I really don't understand what happened. I must have
fallen asleep or something as the dawn was already breaking and it
was rather cold and we were now moving ahead pretty fast. I asked
Lance Sergeant and the Corporal whether they'd seen Mr and Mrs
Nowak's wagon with two horses from Debica and do you know what
they said? That there were many wagons and many people with the

name of Nowak. Funny, isn't it? And then they said that I should get off and surely I would find them as they would not fail to come along before long. I jumped off and found myself on the road. I thought I'd wait for a bit as lots of carts were passing all the time and surely my parents would be here in no time. I also thought of my parents and how very worried and angry they must be with me and this made me feel very sorry. Unfortunately they didn't turn up. I waited and waited but nothing came of it. I thought they might have turned back and gone home. I asked passers-by where I was and they said a long way past Tarnow and not far from Rzeszow. They also said the Germans were no doubt already in Debica. . . . " For a moment, he stopped talking. His light blue eyes glistened and he cast a glance ahead of him, pulled his hat down on his forehead and went on: "I am hoping, however, that I shall run into them somewhere in the eastern part of our country. And, as I was saying, for the last four days I'd been moving forward all the time, either with soldiers or on horse-drawn wagons or on foot until I met you. I would now like so much to be helpful to you and be with you all the time."

After that he inundated us with all sorts of questions. We had some answers ready for him, but often we could not think of one.

We arrived in Dubno, situated some thirty-five miles from the Soviet frontier, on the 13th September. The procedure was always the same: first reporting to the Garrison Command and then becoming billeted. This time we were put in a Greek Catholic monastery, a most attractive old building. As it turned out a great many officers whom we had met in Lublin had also arrived in Dubno. More from other parts of the country were also converging on the town. Meanwhile we succeeded in making for ourselves beds of straw and hay in the huge cool and airy halls and corridors of the monastery. The worthy monks and priests kept us supplied with food from their larders as well as from their vegetable gardens.

Exactly as in Lublin, by the time evening fell the cogs and wheels of the military machine started moving. Our group numbered now some five hundred army officers and we had to undergo another selection according to our age, our rank, physical condition, etc. We were also warned that any wilful absenteeism would be considered desertion and dealt with accordingly. The man who ran the show was a very strict cavalry officer, Colonel B., who informed us officially that acting on orders from General S., who also turned up late at night, he was taking command over the whole of our group of officers.

3. A KNIFE IN OUR BACKS

The formalities at Dubno, as at Lublin, went on until the late hours of the night. This time, however, we had the feeling that something important, something real was afoot – that troops were being concentrated on a large scale in preparation for an important battle. A large influx of all kinds of troops and armour seemed to indicate this.

Part of the force proceeded further in the direction of Lwow where apparently preparations for a decisive defence of the city were in progress. The rest stayed in Dubno.

Next 'morning there was no trace of Colonel B. and General S. Having issued strict orders they had now made themselves scarce. An example not to be imitated.

Eventually Colonel Jakubowski-Shorobohaty introduced himself to us in the capacity of newly nominated Commander of our motley group of officers. An elderly man, rather short, looking very martial and a strict disciplinarian, he was well known among the army officers. The one who busied himself most, however, was the Deputy Commander, Colonel Aleksandrowicz, a shrivelled man, somewhat irritable, but not a bad old stick. General mobilisation had brought him out from a store-house where he had been reposing for many years. And now, dressed in an old faded uniform, he was officiating, issuing orders, swearing like a trooper and at the same time making decisions on administrative, military and tactical problems. He was running all over the place, huffing and puffing from morning till night. We had a name for such old fogies, wearing their old uniforms with the high, tight collars decorated with faded snake-like emblems – we called them "Old grandads from the woods."

Meanwhile, many of my fellow officers had left, and new officers had arrived. Also, our driver who had delivered us here safely in his "dachshund car" let us know that his mission had been accomplished and that his duty now was to surrender his car to the army. Having said this he turned on his heels and, well . . . also "vanished." How and where he went, I don't know, but I do know that near the end of the war he was seen in Paris. I am mentioning this story as many officers, foreseeing a total military collapse of our country, chose to "bolt" abroad. No doubt many were acting with good intentions, aiming to join the new Polish Army that would be formed in the west. I therefore do not blame them totally and today in a way I even approve of their decision. During those days, at the Dubno Garrison however, where our forces were organising themselves and getting ready for some action to come, things looked different. Everyone, including even the "Old Grandads", was doing his best to keep the forces together, to check the spreading wave of disintegration and defeatism. Men were doing this not for their own sake, but for the sake of a common cause and for the sake of defending their country by fighting against the invader. They were working honestly and with all their hearts, and in such decisive moments the disappearance of some officers proved to be most destructive.

Not all officers "vanished". Many were assigned to other detachments short of officers. Among these was our old friend, the Cavalry Captain. He drew himself up, clanged his spurs, flexed his impressive body, saluted and marched off. We shall be seeing him again.

The gap created by outgoing officers was filled by newcomers. Thus our numbers were kept at approximately five hundred. Among these were elderly Reserve Officers — scientists, lawyers, economists and the like. They were joined by professional officers and lecturers at military schools. Young Second-Lieutenants, who had just graduated from military college, also reported for duty. One of them who arrived that day was the Reserve Lieutenant Zygmunt Kwarcinski – a forester aged thirty-five, over six feet tall, of athletic build with dark hair, swarthy complexion and light blue, somewhat feminine eyes. He took the place on the straw vacated by the Captain, near to myself, Laud and young Stas. Zygmunt had studied forestry in Poland and complemented his studies abroad. At the outbreak of war he was manager of some important saw mills in the heart of the huge Bialowieza virgin forest. Emanating from him was the strength of an oak-tree combined with the slenderness of an ash. We made friends straight away. With Laud and Zygmunt we formed the nucleus of a group which events were to forge into an indestructible entity of friendship.

Young Stas was with us. At first we had some difficulty in keeping him with our group of officers. During one of the roll calls I mumbled something about him being my son. I don't know whether I was believed or not, but nevertheless the opposition against him

33

abated and so the little boy-scout was allowed to stay with us, much to his and our satisfaction and amusement.

We left the hospitable monastery on the 14th of September and moved to the barracks of the DAK (Horse Artillery Squadron), located on the outskirts of the town. The whole of the DAK had left for the front a long time ago and was fighting with either the Pomorze or the Poznan Army. Everything was in perfect order in the vacated barracks and the arms stores contained many rifles and much ammunition. We were armed with revolvers and those who were physically stronger and who formed a regular platoon were given rifles, a few light automatics and a complete soldier's outfit. Guards were posted on the gates, a system of permits for leaving the barracks was also introduced, as well as morning and evening roll-calls accompanied by traditional Polish religious songs. We were beginning to resemble a properly-equipped and organised force.

There was a definite improvement in morale in our little compound. Military discipline appeared to be spontaneous and not enforced and respect was shown to our superiors. Besides, there was plenty of work to be done. Apart from normal activities, detachments would be sent out in the daytime and at night to dig trenches, anti-tank pitfalls, fix wiring on barbed wire fences, etc. We patrolled the immediate area and posted sentries on the main roads. They informed passing detachments of the latest troop movements and regulated the constant stream of civilian vehicles which was mainly flowing south. When asked where for God's sake they were going most of the drivers would say to Krzemieniec, Tarnopol, Kolomyja and Zaleszcyzki. It seemed that the whole of Poland had made that picturesque corner of the country a general meeting point.

As far as we knew, liaison with the staff of Supreme Command General Headquarters was practically nil in those days. Wireless communications were paralysed and postal services completely disrupted. As there were no newspapers either, any information received by us came either through the grapevine or from the so-called eyewitnesses. We knew only that the fighting started in September was still going on, that Gdynia and Cracow had fallen and that besieged Warsaw was continuing to fight.

With the last means of communication destroyed we were completely cut off from the rest of the war. We knew only what was going on in our locality. Establishing the depth of German penetration into our country, assessing our plan of defence, weighing up the extent of our defeats and successes – the latter was usually exaggerated – trying to determine the general political situation, and the truth of rumours about our western Allies entering the war – all these were problems of the utmost importance. Lacking any solid information, our imaginations ran riot, and this led to much heated discussion. In fact it all boiled down to a clash of two emotional states of mind. Optimists were fighting against pessimists, faith against despair.

Oh irony! The proverbial Polish autumn reigned supreme in its golden glory over the whole land. From dawn until dusk not a single cloud had appeared in the skies since the 1st September. In fact Goering's pilots could not have had better weather. Hunting down their defenceless victims whenever and wherever they liked they took full advantage of it. They aimed their diabolical bombs, shells and bullets not at military targets only, but at cities, villages and railway junctions. They were also sowing death, fire and terror all along roads jammed with refugees, shooting, as if target practising, at peasant farmers busy with bringing their crops under cover, at shepherds grazing their cattle in faraway fields or in glades hidden in the thickness of woods. Turning off the roads, General Brauchitsch's armoured divisions were able to roam unhindered on the flat, often vast, stretches of dry land which the sun had baked hard as concrete.

The whole population, including the fighting soldiers, was praying fervently for rain, storms and consequently muddy terrain in the hope that these manifestations of nature could halt the Hitlerian onslaught. Our troops would then be able to disperse along the eastern and southern boundaries of Poland and finally concentrate where they could make a last stand against the enemy.

But our hopes never materialized, our prayers were never heard. The whole country was gradually sinking under a shroud of gloom and despondency.

The German planes used to visit us with clockwork precision. Single reconnoitring planes would appear around 6 a.m., almost at the same time as reveille in our barracks, and soon after they would be followed by formations of bombers. Obviously the fifth column was not idle.

The day after we had left the monastery, the old building became a target for an air-attack. So did the Garrison Command situated not far away. The next air-raid would take place regularly between 5 and 6 p.m. On the 16th September our barracks were also attacked. Bombs rained in a short radius over the compound of the DAK's buildings, which fortunately escaped destruction.

In a strange way the people of Dubno and troops stationed there had got used to the bombing. Its accuracy helped people to take shelter in time in special trenches, ditches, etc.

The garrison possessed only a few batteries of ack-ack guns to protect it from the bombers. It was said that a great many planes had been destroyed by them. Maybe it is true, maybe not. I *do* know, however, that since the 1st of September I had many times – fifty, to say the least – watched the sky spotted with black clouds from the guns. I once saw for myself a plane diving down in flames in Warsaw and according to friends another similar case took place in Lublin. A third plane – again I saw it for myself – was brought down in Brzesc. And that was all.

Five hundred German planes were supposed to have been destroyed during the Polish Campaign. If this is true I think most of the credit must go to our heroic pilots, not to the AA gunners.

On the 17th September something different happened. Nearly one hour after the morning raid, that is, at about 7 a.m., a new formation of thirty planes appeared. They were unmistakably flying from the east to the west. This was strange. We had not seen this happen before. Still stranger, not a single bomb fell on Dubno. After firing a few salvoes our ack-ack batteries fell silent.

Zygmunt, Laud and I were standing not far from one of our guns. Puzzled by the unusual display we rushed to our anti-aircraft experts who knew the silhouettes of every aircraft by heart. As we were approaching them we saw that they were greatly agitated. With his usual coolness and characteristic drawl Laud said: "It looks to me as if they are not German planes . . ." "My guess is that they are French or maybe British," said Zygmunt, "and they have come from Rumania. Things will be fine now, my friends, just you see."

The experts were not convinced. They looked anxious: "What sort of planes were they, for Heavens sake, British or French?" they asked.

More of our companions had now joined us around the battery. A general uproar resulted. Finally, put in a spot, the Commanding Officer, a young Lieutenant, announced calmly and distinctly: "Gentlemen, they were neither British nor French, they were Soviet planes (here he stated their exact model). I must admit, I was puzzled myself at first by this strange sight – a German raid coming from the east. As you heard, I fired two salvoes but when they came nearer and I could tell without doubt that they were Russian planes I stopped firing immediately. And now I'm just as puzzled as you are."

Our group became so excited and the hum of conversation was so loud that it made one think of a bee-hive.

"There you are, don't you remember my saying they would end by marching with us, side by side?" one of our men was crying heatedly.

"Well, you might be right but don't get over-excited about it," another man chimed in.

Another still, dancing with joy shouted: "Have you become

completely blind and deaf or something? Did you see a single bomb come down? What does that prove? One thing only – the Soviets are with us. We shall lick those sons of bitches and they will remember it for ever."

"Right," called out a young artilleryman. "But you know an ally isn't born like that, at the drop of a hat. We *are* in the forces, after all, and would our High Command be completely unaware of what was brewing? They would have to know *something* in order to coordinate things. And, at least, our anti-aircraft artillery should have been warned. But there was nothing, a complete blank. We are left to guess whether they are our allies once the planes have appeared overhead. No firing, please. But you can use handkerchiefs to wave them 'welcome'. I only wish I were right."

Still arguing we returned to our barracks flushed and in a state of acute excitement. We buttonholed Colonel Jakubowski and Colonel Aleksandrowicz asking them what they thought of the latest news. Had they heard anything beforehand of some Soviet plane to enter the war? How was the appearance of a formation of thirty Soviet planes in battle array to be explained? Why wasn't our anti-aircraft artillery warned? Why were no leaflets dropped on us by the Soviets? Wouldn't this have been the obvious thing to do?

The two Colonels were trying hard to conceal their own excitement. They were parrying our barrage of questions as best they could. They had so far heard nothing at the Garrison Command of Soviet intentions to join in the fighting. Events, however, were moving at such a fantastic pace that anything seemed possible. Liaison with the Supreme Command had been completely interrupted, severed for several days, and it was to be hoped that the appearance of the Soviet Air Force in our skies would indicate a turn for the better. The Colonels appealed to us to keep calm and to await further orders. Having said this they drove off in a car to the Garrison Command.

Hours went by and the first news started arriving from the Polish-Soviet border. But, as usual in such cases, these stories were no more than hearsay, varying in content according to who told them. Some people were claiming with great enthusiasm that the Soviet troops had crossed the frontier with outstretched, brotherly hands, offering to fight side by side, shoulder to shoulder against the Germans. Others, horror-stricken, were speaking in hushed voices as if afraid of their own words. They were saying the Soviets had invaded Polish soil with the aim of occupying it and keeping it for good.

As before when rumours had flooded in, a violent clash of opinions flared up between the blind optimists on one side and the pessimists on the other who had fallen prey to complete despair. The fight was short lived. As more dismal news came in, the camp of enthusiasts was dwindling fast.

At 3 p.m. Colonel Jakubowski appeared in our barracks and ordered us to assemble forthwith. We ranged ourselves in a quadrangle. Colonel Jakubowski was in the company of General Leon Billewicz whom he introduced to us as the Commanding Officer of the Dubno Garrison. During a few minutes which seemed to us eternity the two senior officers walked in front of our formation of officers, both in animated conversation. Eventually the Colonel stopped, stood to attention, cleared his throat and in a changed, somewhat unsteady voice, made the following announcement: "Gentlemen! In the early hours of this morning, the 17th September strong Soviet forces crossed the whole length of the Soviet-Polish border. No details are available so far. I have, however, received an order which I am conveying to you. The Soviet troops have entered our country in order, we suppose, to fight side by side with us against the German invader. Therefore, in case of an encounter with Soviet units they should by no means be opposed. There are many contradictory rumours circulating already. I beg of you do not believe them. I am, however, allowed to mention one report to you and I trust to God it is a true one. A few instances of fraternisation between the two forces are supposed to have taken place at several frontier points. I also trust that this will prove to be a general occurrence. And now I order everyone to get ready to depart under my command at 5 p.m. As you know only too well there are very few means of transport available. I am, therefore, warning you that you will have to do a great deal of marching, so please make all necessary arrangements for that. You are to keep only what you really need and get rid of the remainder. I appeal to your discipline and good sense."

It was the General's turn now. Very tall with snow-white hair and a bushy moustache and dressed in an immaculate uniform, he looked every inch a military man. Our attention was fixed rigidly on him.

"Gentlemen! Our ultimate aim is the salvation of our homeland and I trust you will attain it. The road in front of you may be long, winding, even slippery; however, your lofty task and its ultimate objective will be your constant guide. I wish you the very best of luck" – he pronounced the above words in his melodic voice. The old veteran of the Polish Army then drew himself up and saluted us.

"Hail, Mister General!" five hundred officers' voices shouted in chorus.

The command "Dismiss!" terminated our short and dramatic assembly.

The words spoken by the two senior officers caused a great stir amongst the assembled company. But soon we were directing our energies to packing our things and dumping anything unnecessary.

The shock we had received brought a strange turning point in the flow of our thoughts. All our heated and passionate discussions suddenly melted away. A nagging vision of unforeseen events took hold of our imaginations. No one felt the need any more to express thoughts of defeatism or optimism.

After reducing my possessions to the smallest possible amount. I brought my leather suitcase as well as the other things which I had rejected to a small wooden house nearby. Zosia, a young and rather pretty teacher at an elementary school, lived there with her mother and brothers and sisters. The enchanting little house lay in the shade of an orchard. It was overgrown with foliage and ivy, and surrounded by flowers and old linden trees. We used to go there with Laud and Zygmunt in the evenings for a nice chat and a feast of fresh milk, bread, jam and luscious fruit.

The women sat under an old tree, busy sewing white and red arm bands for the Civil Guards which were to be formed shortly. Somewhat astonished at seeing me panting with the weight of a heavy suitcase and other things slung across my arm they greeted me with their usual cordiality.

"Are you moving Mister Lieutenant? And where to, if I may ask? To our place perhaps? You'll be welcome, some room for you can be found I'm sure," said the mother with a mixture of worry and solicitude in her voice.

"Many thanks, my dear ladies, but I haven't come to ask that. I have just come to say goodbye to you and to thank you for all your hospitality and all the pleasant evenings spent in your house. Our group will be leaving Dubno in a few moments and what our destination will be, I don't know. I have to leave behind a great many of my belongings, and I thought the best place for them would be in your house. They are yours now — please treat them as such. They'll come in useful, I'm sure, to you and maybe to your children. At the moment I have no use for them myself. But there are just a few trifles, these two photographs in a leather frame, a little diary with some notes — this is all I will ask you to keep for me. You'll find my Warsaw address on my suitcase and in the diary. God willing I shall perhaps call for them soon, who knows." I was blabbering incoherently.

A painful silence fell. Suddenly overcome, her face pale, rolls of ribbon dropping from her lifeless fingers, Zosia whispered in a hardly audible voice: "Oh my God, my dearest Christ! So all of you are leaving, abandoning us. This is how it has to be I suppose and perhaps it is better that it should be . . . . Still we are terribly frightened. No wonder, with all those awesome news bulletins from the east this morning. We are as afraid of the ones from the west as of the other ones. Father is with the forces fighting, our brother has gone to the war some while ago. We've been left on our own with no one to look after us. . . . What shall we do now, what will become of those little children. . . ?" She leant forward, hid her face and wept bitterly.

I clenched my teeth. Oh, let's get this painful scene over as quickly as possible! I couldn't bear it any longer! To be here, in front of those women and children – a man, an officer, powerless, helpless!

"May God be with you," were their last farewell words.

I rushed back to the barracks, feeling much lighter after having shed my load of things but with a heavy heart, heavy as lead. All our men were already assembling in the square, ready to leave. One of my colleagues was just "getting rid" of a bottle of Martell brandy. I downed half a large glass in one gulp.

A company, of some two hundred men marched off first, singing somewhat out of tune:

"How nice it is in a war
When a lancer falls off from a horse."

They were followed by a few motor cars and trucks.

Old Colonel Aleksandrowicz was running around issuing orders and forming into fours the remaining three hundred men, numbering among them many who were either not very strong physically or who held higher ranks.

Despite new voices of protest I was keeping little Stas at my side. Those who were weaker or older clambered up into the ten available trucks. Our luggage went with them. We set off on our journey without further delay. Forming with Laud, Zygmunt and myself a foursome we kept close to the front of the column. We noticed many houses destroyed or burnt down in the streets of Dubno. People, speechless and scared, did not seem to realize what was going on. What they could only understand was that Polish troops were leaving the town on a massive scale and at the same time abandoning them to their fate. Coming from all directions various detachments were heading towards a few main exits and then merging to form what resembled a great snake moving along. After a few hours of forced marching we halted. The night, pitch-black and sultry, was pregnant with storm. A number of peasants' wagons were allotted to us and all who had been marching were ordered to squeeze themselves as best they could into the trucks and wagons. Although somewhat faster than before the overloaded vehicles moved at a very slow pace.

A storm followed by a real downpour – something we had all been praying for the day before and now of no use at all – broke out at midnight. We turned into sponges literally soaked in water. A few trucks broke down and were left behind. Our truck, although howling, moaning and creaking, was still moving on. The next stage was a few hours' halt in Beresteczko.

Rain was pouring down non-stop. The wretched little town, cloaked in pitch darkness, was drowning in a sticky quagmire. With the greatest difficulty we tried to get some sleep. At dawn, before setting off again, we tried to get hold of some food. Stas, the cleverest of us all, had managed to procure us a few eggs, a piece of lard and some milk. The boy was really unsurpassed. After only a few hours sleep he was as alert as a lark. He had washed his hair and combed it and looked thoroughly clean and tidy!

One of our infantry regiments also turned up for a short stop. The untiring Colonel Aleksandrowicz was looking after us like a real father. He requested all of us to report immediately to the Regimental Pay Master who would pay us in equal shares. We all received, regardless of rank, the sum of 500 zloty each which made us feel more prosperous. All well and good, but what was this measure supposed to mean? The liquidation of the Regiment's kitty? On second thoughts this did not bother us unduly. Was it after all not better to have the money distributed among us than let it fall into some unauthorized hands? Stored in a safe those paper bills were worthless, shared out they could be of some use. These were the lines along which our reasoning went and further events proved us to be right.

The next morning we assembled for a roll call. After the command "Count Off" it turned out that during the night our group of 300 men had dwindled to a mere 250. A few of the requisitioned lorries had not arrived and some people had taken advantage of darkness and bolted. During the day our group suffered a further reduction in size. So we set off again. At the various halts about fifty officers were assigned to several depleted units overtaken by us on the road. When reaching Brzezany late at night – a place situated east of the city of Lwow – there were only two hundred men left.

After the storm and the downpour our vehicles were slithering uncontrollaby on the wet, muddy roads. By now our group formed a small part of an enormous military convoy moving southward at a very slow pace. The endless zigzagging, the constant turning off from the main road into secondary roads and also the frequent halts, often for no reason at all, were creating great confusion among us as to our real destination. Contrary to military practice our superiors were far away at the head of the huge column and were failing to communicate with the rear. For a while the opinion prevailed that our target was the city of Lwow, where apparently a large number of enemy troops were concentrated. Since, however, we had by-passed that city a long way before this assumption soon fell flat.

What was really worrying us all the time was the complete lack of news about how far the German troops had penetrated and also the speed at which the Soviet forces were advancing. We knew absolutely nothing. For instance, where their units were at that moment and particularly at what distance from our road, when and where our encounter with them would take place and how it would be.

Despite Colonel Jakubowski's optimistic announcements, we remained painfully ignorant of the real intentions of Soviet forces on Polish soil.

4. DEADLY AMBUSH

Our little Stas was our joy. With his childlike prattle, his curiosity, his exclamations and a constant flow of questions, some sensible, some silly or funny, he would make us forget about sad reality.

"You see, sirs, in my native Debica I was taught geography. As a matter of fact I am very fond of the subject but I find it so hard to remember all those important and interesting places with the help of a map only. And so I have always dreamt of getting to know Poland by going on tours through the country, like the one now – for isn't it a real sightseeing tour?" We were just passing in front of the magnificent, historic Podhorce Castle, situated in beautiful hilly countryside. We became immersed in thoughts about that land during long bygone ages.

Stas was jumping from one subject to another like a grasshopper. "Is it true that there are a few mountains in the world named after our national hero, Kosciuszko as well as a few islands? And in America there are supposed to be even a few towns? Our school mistress Miss Laura taught us this. She also told us that in America people used to live in houses as tall as the Giewont.* Is that possible? And on top of this she told us other things also about America. She knew what she was talking about as her aunt lives there. Namely that young boys like me drive big cars. I think I could drive too."

"Don't talk nonsense, my friend, you couldn't tell a car-spring from a horn," our driver teased him good-humouredly whilst fiddling with something in the engine during a short halt. "You'd better get us a bucket of water from the pond over there. Our samovar is boiling like mad." Stas, dispirited but on the other hand pleased because he'd been given something to do, was back in no time carrying a bucket full of muddy water.

After having passed Zloczow and some time later Pomorzany it became obvious to us that we were not heading towards Lwow. We arrived at Brzezany after nightfall, in pitch darkness. The narrow little streets of the town were absolutely jammed with all sorts of

* Mountain in the Tatra range – Trs.

vehicles and with troops and civilians. With difficulty we managed to get through to the market square where Colonel Jakubowski ordered an hour's halt. As always in such cases we rushed in search of food and water, the latter particularly, for a wash. The woollen puttees which I had bought in Lublin were burning my legs like hell and I chucked them out. I drew up on my calves the light soft tops which I had cut off from the boots left behind at Lublin. The combination of ski-ing boots and ordinary tops proved to be a most practical one.

Three of our trucks proved to be completely unfit for further driving and had to be left behind. About thirty of us therefore had to squeeze into the remaining seven vehicles, which were also on the point of breaking down. Getting disentangled from the maze of traffic and people in Brzezany called for the greatest possible effort and took a long time too. But eventually we succeeded in reaching the wide road which, as we soon made out, led eastwards. Somewhat taken aback by our Commander's navigation, we were even more astonished when we realized that our small convoy of only seven vehicles was moving ahead on its own without any armaments other than revolvers and without any military cover either at the front or at the rear. On the outskirts of the town we were stopped by the Military Police assisted by ordinary police. A conversation ensued which, since our car happened to be second in line from the front, Laud, Zygmunt and I could follow distinctly.

"Mister Colonel," the Senior Sergeant was saying as he flashed his electric torch over the Commander's open map, "we wouldn't advise you to go to the village of Potutory on this road on such a dark night without any proper military cover. The local constable, who knows the region inside out, has just informed me that Soviet patrols have apparently been observed nearing Brzezany and there are various rumours as to their behaviour. I would suggest you wait until the morning."

"Thank you for your information, Sergeant. We shall manage all right. Drive on," ordered the Colonel to his chauffeur.

The engines roared, the gears uttered their characteristic howls and we started off into the pitch black night. Thick mist was rising from the vast marshes which lay to the right of the road. Moving at a snail's pace we advanced some seven or eight kilometres. Many of us were dozing. Some anaemic lights flickered in the distance. "This must be the village of Potutory mentioned by the gendarmerie," we thought.

The road in this particular sector ran downhill towards the village and was bordered on both sides by high banks. Suddenly, as we were descending, the sound of gunfire came from the darkness. Three

44

machine guns were spewing bursts of bullets at us. The blinding glow of the muzzles seemed to be just a step away. It was not possible, however, to assess the exact distance. Shots of single guns magnified the strength of the fire. The planning of the ambush had been masterly. The target was easy – a column of big trucks stretching along a road downwards in the direction of the aggressors. But neither was it possible to assess their strength and undertake rational defensive action, particularly when revolvers would have to confront machine guns. The enemy was also firing a great number of incendiary shells which flashed and hissed like fireworks and easily penetrated the inflammable trucks which soon went up in flames. The crackling, spluttering fire was fed additionally by petrol which had spilled from the bullet-ridden fuel tanks. The scene of the massacre could not have been better illuminated. The enemy could see as if on a plate whom and where to aim at.

The ambush was so sudden that the truck drivers had failed to brake in time and had therefore bumped into one another. The horror-stricken moans of the first victims could already be heard around us. Often clumsily and without the necessary speed we jumped from the high lorries to the ground. Greatcoats, blankets and other inflammable possessions burned behind us.

After the first shots the strong and alert Zygmunt had thrown overboard his half-asleep, half-conscious companions. Stas had emitted a groan – I first thought he had been asleep and had just woken up. With all the strength I could muster I lifted him in my arms and, helped by a push given by Zygmunt, we both dropped down, landing on the hard surface of the road and rolling on further into a ditch. Lying there flat I was still clutching Stas. My hands were wet with blood, but I suddenly became aware it was not my blood. Oh Christ! Stas was wounded, he was moaning and whispering something. Overcome with despair I called for Zygmunt, for Laud, but no one could hear me. My voice got drowned in the roar of shots and the crackling sound of burning lorries. I tried to crawl uphill by way of a ditch. Stas's body was limp and totally inert. I looked into his little face and in the brightness of the fire could see it was calm and white. Still breathing, he opened his blue eyes. A ghost of a smile flickered on his tiny lips which were oozing a trickle of blood. I pressed my head against his lips. All he could whisper in an almost inaudible way was: "It hurts, Mummy, it hurts. . . ." And that was all . . . his end.

This is how – with his heart shot through – our little Stas Nowicki died. A young boy-scout from Debica.

The massacre went on. The dead – whose uniforms were already starting to smoulder – were lying all over the place, around the trucks, in the ditches. Some men, seriously wounded and unable to move, remained on the platforms. Those who tried to come to their rescue became victims themselves of either bullets or flames. Every now and then one could see a raised hand or frantic head of a victim burning alive but still fighting for a last spark of life. All this was an unspeakably ghastly, horrifying sight.

Dragging Stas's body I continued to crawl along the ditch. I at least reached a spot sheltered from the blazing light. A human log rolled down suddenly into the ditch and almost into my arms. "Zygmunt, Good God, are you alive?" I yelled recognizing him instantly.

"Not only alive, but unhurt, just a few scratches. I wanted to see what was going on up there. I thought that those swine would try to encircle us from the other side. They don't seem to have done, but they are shooting up there like the devil, almost as much as down here. Too bad. Those sons of a bitch murdered a lot of our boys. But how are you and Stas, are you all right?"

On seeing him and hearing the voice of this dear friend of mine I heaved a sigh of relief. Then I dragged him towards me, closer to Stas's body.

"Look, look my friend. They killed him, they murdered him."

Zygmunt suppressed a roar. Without saying a word he knelt down, took off his cap, kissed the pale, cool forehead of the boy and made the sign of the cross on it.

Meanwhile there was a general hubbub. Voices were calling out to retreat at once up the road leading to Brzezany. The fire was now thinning gradually. Flames from the burning cars, fed probably by a new flow of petrol, were shooting up intermittently. Lighting up the horizon they gave away the survivors, who then became ideal new targets for the machine guns. Zygmunt and I, however, were slowly retreating from the scene of the carnage. We could now see in front of us a number of silhouettes of people up the road. We put Stas's body down in a cluster of high grass near the trunk of an old weeping willow. After that we helped to lift the wounded. While we were carrying a man with severe stomach and arm wounds, two other men, hobbling along slowly with shots in their legs, were leaning heavily on our free arms.

My head was spinning and I felt weak. While I was aware that I had not been wounded, a painful sensation of numbness crept all over my body – probably a result of light concussion. Bullet holes and burn marks showed on my greatcoat. We dragged ourselves to the top of the hill and, seeking cover behind a thick stump of a tree, sat down for a while. The sound of gunfire receded. What next, we thought, how shall we ever get the wounded and ourselves to Brzezany some seven kilometres away? What shall we do with the bodies of the dead? Four trucks were completely burned out and three out of order. News went round however that our Colonel had sent a few young strong men to Brzezany to report about the events and to ask for medical help.

Meanwhile the few doctors who happened to be in our column were frantically busy dressing the wounds of the worst cases in the most primitive conditions. No proper medical outfit was available of course. For bandages, the doctors had to rip up shirts which had been offered to them.

Our retreat had started. Bullets were still whistling but we were already beyond their range. The two Colonels, besmeared with blood – whether their own or someone else's it was hard to tell – were counting the procession of trudging survivors. Losses were enormous; at least 30 killed and 50 wounded. After we had covered the first kilometre a few groups of men carrying the severe cases, either on their shoulders or on coats used as stretchers, dropped out of the column. Stepping aside they laid down the bleeding loads on the grass and just waited for mercy. Several men thus died on that "via dolorosa" before medical aid could reach them.

Shuffling along with the greatest difficulty and halting every few minutes to change hands we were looking back all the time and listening for signs of the enemy pursuing us. We thought they would try to outflank us from the left and the right and thus finish off those still left alive. They chose not to chase us, however. No doubt they preferred to make surprise attacks.

I cannot recall how long the ordeal of our retreat lasted. We were perhaps a kilometre from the outskirts of the town when we were passed by a column of ambulances. A few halted. Helped only by the light of torches it took us a long time to load the badly injured. The men with lighter wounds had to walk a short distance to a dressing station which had been organised hastily at the entry to the town. We came across our good, brave Laud with a light wound on his forearm. He was bearing the pain without complaint. It was wonderful that all three of us were together once more.

At the dressing station, situated next to a well, we witnessed shattering scenes. Blood covered the bodies of the wounded but surgeons and stretcher bearers were performing wonders with their nimble hands. Removing the dirt and blood they expertly dressed the wounds. Soon patients emerged with white turbans, slings and dressings which would later show from beneath the split sleeves and trouser legs of their uniforms.

Colonel Jakubowski ordered all those of us who were unhurt or with light wounds to assemble in the building of the Garrison Command at 6 a.m. The severely wounded were to be transported to the hospital. Not many wished to be among them. No wonder, for to remain alone and wounded at the rear of our unit had few attractions.

Zygmunt and I poured a bucket of cold water over each other's heads. Despite the late hour some brave woman asked a number of us to her nearby house. We sat down at a table lit by a paraffin lamp and tea with some food was served. Colonel Jakubowski and the old man, Colonel Aleksandrowicz, turned up too. Unable to understand why Jakubowski had taken the decision which had led to such disastrous results and still dazed by the horrible murder of our companions carried out by a so far unseen and unidentified enemy, we did not enter into any discussion with him. After half an hour of stifling silence spent at the house of our good and hospitable hostess a messenger suddenly appeared. The Colonel was to report immediately at the Garrison Command. He looked round at our gloomy faces enquiringly and asked who would be willing to accompany him. Zygmunt nudged my elbow and we both stood up. The Colonel asked our names and reminded the rest of the group about next morning's assembly at 6 a.m. We managed to whisper to Laud, who lay dozing with his arm in a sling, that he should not oversleep and should attend the parade without fail.

The car waiting outside took us to our destination. The time was 3 a.m. and the day the 19th September. On reaching the huge building I soon found myself in a vast dark hall, badly lit by a few small paraffin lamps and candles stuck into bottles. The flickering lights lit up the faces of some twenty senior officers seated at a long table and about a hundred junior officers standing around. The unshaven and pale grey faces of our superiors revealed their utter exhaustion. They were all in command of various units stationed that night in Brzezany. I recognised among them a few well-known faces: the lean and pale one of General Aleksander Kowalewski, obviously the senior of the group: General Leon Billewicz, the white-haired veteran of Dubno; Colonel Edward Saski; Lieutenant-Colonel Feliks Kopec of the 22nd Infantry regiment; Lieutenant Jozef Grodecki, a Sapper. Major Sobieslaw Zaleski, looking like a bulldog, was snarling all the time and Major Walenty Miller, a young Artillery man, would now and then cut in with his somewhat acrid and witty remarks.

As reports had come in from various quarters, the story of the bloody Potutory ambush was already known to them. The account of the incident presented by Colonel Jakubowski was more like evidence given by the defence in a court of law. After his short report he had to face a series of scathing questions and remarks: Why did he separate himself from the main forces at Brzezany last night and proceed on his own, without any assistance, at the head of a small and unarmed group of officers? Why did he not follow the advice of the gendarmerie which obviously had some reason in warning him? The Colonel was defending himself as best he could without convincing anybody and without succeeding in justifying his decision. After that came our turn. Zygmunt and I gave a detailed account of the bloody massacre which we had had the misfortune to witness.

After some heated argument the incompetence of Colonel Jakubowski was forgotten as discussion focused on a problem immeasurably graver than the Potutory massacre — namely, the prospect of crushing defeat.

Suddenly it seemed that a belief held sincerely by all ranks was being exposed for the illusion it was. The belief was that the entry into Poland of the Red Army would prove to be a bold, magnificent gesture, that the brotherly Slavonic hand was ready to take up arms against the German invaders. That on the battlefields memories of differences and quarrels would eventually fade. That misunderstandings due to differences in political structure of the two countries would also recede into oblivion and a common language would be found to unite the two nations. And finally that any secret agreement with the aim of a collaboration between the Soviets and the Nazis would prove to be impossible. And still . . . .

Now it was clear that interlocking their predatory claws the satanic forces had thrust them into the body of Poland to tear it to pieces.

A young officer made his appearance. He had arrived a few moments ago from Potutory where he had been sent at the head of a strong unit to reconnoitre on the site of the ambush. He reported to General Kowalewski. He was speaking in a strong distinct voice and what he said fell on the audience like the sound of a whip.

"Sir, on the strength of a detailed inspection carried out at Potutory, I am bringing to your notice respectfully what follows: Last night at about 9 p.m. a detachment of Soviet troops arrived in the village. It numbered about two hundred men armed with machine guns and ordinary rifles. The inhabitants were ordered at gun point not to leave their houses. Heavy posts were put along the main roads and crossroads. Facing the road to Brzezany the main force took up its position in a semi-circle. What happened next and the ambush's final result is well known. I can only say that what I saw of the battleground — if a battle it was — was not a pretty sight. In fact it was shattering. Four of our trucks were still smouldering and the remaining three I have managed to get towed here. With the help of our stretcher-bearers who had arrived on the spot before me I loaded the bodies of the 32 killed and the 8 wounded whom I found to be alive. Everything seemed to be calm in the village although the people betrayed signs of having been terrorized. The enemy had retreated eastwards well before midnight, that is after having carried out its mission." The young officer pronounced the last words slowly, stressing every syllable.

And so this is how our first encounter with the Red Army came about. The brief but telling report outlined accurately one incident only, one that had occurred in the small sector of Brzezany and its environment. It pointed, however, to a picture of similar events, grisly and catastrophic, which, in all probability, had taken place along the whole of the Soviet-Polish border.

The dismal conclave went on. The question of how and by which road our forces — amounting in Brzezany to some ten thousand men — could be pulled out from the closing trap was discussed in stormy fashion. A barrage of questions and answers were fired. Was there any liaison with the General Staff of the High Command? No, there was none. The President of the Republic, members of the Government and the Commander-in-Chief of the Army had crossed the frontier to Rumania on the 17th September. Other names of well-known personalities were thrown into the discussion. Where are the Generals: Sosnkowski and Sikorski? No answer. Where does the present German-Polish front line run now? No answer either. Maps were unfolded and people became absorbed in studying terrain and roads.

The time was now 4 a.m. The assembly was for 6 a.m.

Unable to bear the stifling atmosphere I was falling asleep. Dragging Zygmunt along with me, we moved surreptitiously to another room. We were soon fast asleep, stretched out on two tables, like dead bodies.

A great hullabaloo woke us up before 6 a.m. Numb and half-conscious we tried to put our thoughts together. We realised that we now possessed nothing at all. Literally all our belongings had perished in the burning trucks. Fortunately in the garrison canteen we were lucky to get hold of some soap, toothbrushes, towels, socks, cigarettes and other trifles. We took enough for Laud also. We then packed all these valuables into an ordinary bag. After a hasty breakfast consisting of a mug of coffee, bread and a piece of dry sausage, we made a dash to the assembly place. Some survivors of the last night were already there, among them – as a number of white bandages and slings indicated – those with lighter wounds. Since, apart from the losses sustained, about twenty-five officers had been assigned to depleted battalions and companies our group during the night had dwindled to one hundred men once more. Four dilapidated trucks were produced like rabbits out of a hat and allocated to us. They each had to carry twenty-five men.

It was a beautiful, sunny day. An enormous procession of all kinds of armed forces was moving along. The earth was groaning under the weight of guns belonging to a heavy artillery regiment, stationed normally in Praga, one of Warsaw's districts. Rumbling along were pontoon and bridge battalions of Sappers; field guns and horse artillery rolling. Marching in the heavy dust raised by all this were long, snake-like columns of infantry, overtaken now and then by some single squadrons of cavalry, moving at a trot.

The procession was not just a military one. Throughout the column there were long queues of various civilian vehicles. Some of them were private cars, of all sizes, filled with women, children and luggage. Then there were taxi cabs, which in their brightly painted yet dilapidated condition looked pathetic against the military drabness. Even more so the big, colourful municipal buses, coming – as indicated by their painted emblems – from cities so well known to all of us: Warsaw, Poznan, Katowice, Gdynia. One could sense that all these abandoned women and children, separated from their menfolk, had been drawn by instinct to the armed forces, clinging to them for protection. Caught up in the procession they did not care where they would eventually land and whether fate would prove to be merciful to them. In those days of great sorrow and worry "Let's stick together" seemed to be the general motto.

Despite the severe reprimand he had received at the meeting with his superiors, Colonel Jakubowski remained in command of our depleted group. This time, however, he was not travelling in a truck but in a car with other commanding officers in the vanguard of the column. We were proceeding extremely slowly in a south-westerly direction towards the town of Rohatyn. From this fact we assumed that our superiors were trying to get to the Rumanian or Hungarian frontier through a corridor which appeared to be free of foreign troops. However, no official announcement to this effect had yet been made. Higher ranks did not confide in junior officers as far as such plans were concerned.

Still, all those capable of thinking rationally did not fail to grasp

what the treacherous activities of the Red Army now meant for them
and Poland.

5. EYE TO EYE WITH THE ENEMY

We sensed why the officers in command of our huge column thought it unnecessary to share their plans with us. It had become clear to everyone that our only aim now was to leave the country still armed.

More than that — since an endeavour to escape from captivity is every soldier's duty — it will also be clear that our march would not be considered an act of cowardice or desertion. The vision of captivity in the hands of German or Soviet forces was now looming large in our thoughts. But at the same time we harboured the hope that at some later stage of the war, on some far off battleground, we would be granted the right of retribution and the chance to fulfil the mission which history had thrown upon us.

This is more or less how the reasoning went among our little group on the truck. We were still ignorant as to the width of the supposedly free corridor we were following between the German and what should be now called the Soviet front. Rumours gleaned along the road seemed, however, to indicate that the impetus of the German offensive had slowed down for the time being. Also significant was a complete lack of any activity in the air for the last two days. Except for some single reconnaissance planes no major German formation of aircraft had appeared in the sky. We assumed from these two bits of information that the German and Soviet armies had agreed to divide Poland between them, therefore confining their operations to their own distinctly defined zones.

We were arguing intently about ways of reaching the nearest frontiers. The Rumanian one, closest to the radius of Soviet invasion, seemed to be the least feasible. There remained, however, the frontier with Hungary. A year ago it had been a frontier with Czechoslovakia as the province of Karpathian Ruthenia had then formed part of that country and had only become incorporated into Hungary after the Munich agreement. It could be reached through a few well protected mountain passes: those of Sianki, Lawoczna, Wyszkow-Hust. Our thoughts and our only hope were therefore directed to that area.

Our group was moving slowly about 500 metres behind the

vanguard of the column. Frequent and uncertain halts were ordered at forks in the road or junctions. They were followed by councils of war, the study of maps, and questioning of the local population. This lack of direction and decision at the front was immediately apparent right down the line, as though an electric current was running from the front to the rear.

Once, in a hilly place, at a road junction, the whole of our column was directed along a narrow and precipitous road which after approximately a kilometre proved to be the wrong one. It is easy to imagine the ensuing mess and complication. We literally had to lift the heavy lorries with our bare hands so that they faced the way we had come. Achieving this about-turn of the whole column took up at least two hours of our precious time.

We passed the locality of Zurawno at about 4 p.m., moving ahead under armed cover in case there was a diversion or an ambush. It looked now as if we would be heading from here towards the town of Stryj, an important road junction, situated at a distance of sixty kilometres from the Hungarian frontier. An unforeseen tangle, however, caused an impossible confusion. The huge column was to be split in two parts. One of them began to uncoil itself, as it seemed, in the direction of Stryj, the other one, to which I belonged, spread out along a dusty road and later secondary field roads, southwards — presumably towards the town of Kalusz. The reason for this manoeuvre, we guessed, arose from the problem of deciding whether Stryj was occupied by the Germans or not. Our Commanders must have been divided on this matter, hence the splitting of our column.

Had we chosen the road leading to Stryj how very different would have been the fate of my friends and I and all those thousands of men among whom we found ourselves! Stryj was after all not in German hands; it was still unoccupied by foreign troops.*

About 6 p.m., when crawling up a sandy hill in a wooded area, the column suddenly screeched to a halt at a fork in the road. This time our group happened to be very close to the front of the column. And this time too, like so many times before, we sensed a lack of decision amongst our commanding officers. What next, which of the two roads to choose? The obvious choice, our instinct told us, would be the one to the right, that is, leading to the west.

The evening was still. Some peasants were beckoned by our Commanders and rushed to their vehicles. Information was obviously

---

* Since the German-Russian demarcation line — agreed on a temporary basis on the 17t. September, 1939 and later fixed for good on the 28th September — left a wide corridor on the side of Soviet Russia, during the September Campaign many localities situated in that area never fell into German hands.

being sought, matters discussed. To our great amazement, after some ten minutes, the vanguard of our column started moving ahead slowly, dragging the rest of the column to the left. We were all seized by a nervous tension. Voices of harsh criticism concerning the wisdom of our Commanders were raised and even some swearing could be heard. In our little group we spoke in whispers and in short broken sentences.

Zygmunt, Laud and I continued to be inseparable. Poor Laud's arm was still aching. Reserve Lieutenant, Marian Piskorski, a railway engineer with the Franco-Polish line linking Katowice and Gdynia, was sitting next to us. He was a steady, quiet chap, wise as an owl. Clasping my arm Zygmunt said: "Never mind, chin up! Look at that wonderful, bright sunset. It means fine weather for tomorrow. You'll see, this very night we shall arrive at the Hungarian frontier. Budapest is a magnificent city on the shores of the blue Danube — and you can take my word for it. Our envoy there, Leon Orlowski, a splendid chap, will get us out in no time and we'll then make a bolt to France."

The time was 7 p.m. The road was bending slightly downhill towards a vast valley at the bottom of which spread a small hamlet — Dolna Kaluska. As if anticipating retirement for an early night it was wrapping itself in a shroud of light evening mist. There was a wide stretch of swampy pastures to the right of the road and on the left side from the peasants' cottages and farmyards rose the smoke and the smell of burning peat. The yawn-like lowing of cattle seemed to signal that it was time for rest. In front of us a large wooden bridge spanned the river and on the opposite side one could see more cottages forming a large patch of whiteness. They were leaning against a rather steep rise overgrown with trees and brushwood. This bucolic picture, as if painted in pastel colours, became deeply ingrained in my memory.

The cars carrying our Commanders as well as a few trucks had already rumbled over the bridge. They accelerated to climb steeply and then swerve sharply round a tight corner, disappearing one after another in clouds of dust behind a curtain of thick green foliage.

It was then that a violent burst of bullets spluttered from the opposite bank. Trailing behind the vanguard of our column the first vehicles halted abruptly just before the bridgehead as if rooted to the spot. Right behind them were four trucks carrying our group of officers. The fire was gaining in intensity with every second. From the top of the hill right across the road and from a distance of not more than 150 metres two machine guns were clattering and firing like mad. The line of fire, formed now in the shape of a semi-circle, was spreading like a lit fuse. On the flanks more machine guns were coming into action.

From the first moment, as at Potutory, incendiary bullets were hissing through the air. Artillery shells fell too. The first of them were exploding right near the bridge, the next ones, aimed higher, were directed all along our column. Cars hit by incendiary bullets were now burning furiously. Hay and corn stacks had caught fire and high columns of dense smoke rose above them. The same happened to peasants' cottages and other buildings close to the road.

The ambush had happened so suddenly and at such a fast pace that despite our previous experience and the still relatively bright daylight it seemed almost impossible to get an exact idea of what was going on. The same questions cropped up once more: what is the enemy's strength? Are we in a position to put up an effective resistance, always bearing in mind that a column of motley troops, exhausted by a long march, a few kilometres in length and containing a number of civilian vehicles is of no military value at all? Did all that mean that we would now have to surrender?

We tumbled out of our trucks and on to the road or ditches as quickly as we could, at the same time rolling down huge tanks filled with petrol. Trying to save the rest of our belongings was, of course, out of the question. Fire was already devouring all the vehicles which happened to be near the bridge. The smoke was choking us and biting into our eyes. Bodies were hanging from the cars or still writhing in their last convulsions in the dust of the road. The agonizing moans of the wounded resounded over the "battlefield".

After a while single rifle shots from our side could be heard and a machine gun started rattling somewhere at the far end of our flank. During short intervals in the shooting, which occurred now and then, distinct shouts from the enemy's side would reach us. They were deafened, however, by the powerful drone of engines and the screeching of the tank caterpillars. It was clear to us by now that we were confronted by Soviet armour. Here and there on our side voices were raised "No shooting . . . that's the order."

I took shelter with my friends in a ditch partly protected by a little bridge linking the road and the field. We had to lie as flat as possible, keeping close together. A machine gun positioned right in front of us was firing briskly, aimed in our direction. Emitting a short whistle, bullets plonked into the wooden structure of the bridge and the turf around us. Sand was pouring into our eyes as well as behind our collars.

During another short pause in the exchange of fire our attention became focused on a strange apparition. A thin, tall man with greying hair, bushy eyebrows and an aquiline nose appeared suddenly as if from nowhere on the edge of the adjoining field. We had first noticed this strange person during the last days of our journey. Dressed in a bright civilian overcoat and with a wide-brimmed hat on his long head, he would sit silent like a big grey bird sunk deeply in his thoughts, perched high on one of the trucks over a mass of bits and pieces. He was addressed as "Captain". Obviously this must have been his rank and being a Reserve officer he probably hadn't had time to obtain a uniform.

He advanced a few steps into the open, halted, and pointing his gun at the enemy called in a loud voice: "Follow me, Gentlemen. Spread out to the right and to the left in extended order." His commanding and authoritative voice energized those closest to him. They began to crawl obediently and then leapt up to form the ordered formation. None of them possessed a rifle and only a few officers had revolvers.

All this happened when the fire from the opposite side became very intense again.

The chivalrous gesture of the "Grey Gentleman" could not fail to conjure up the vision of a Longinus,* of Somosierra,† or of Don Quixote, of legend merged with history. And yet the picture I was witnessing was real. Such acts of folly and heroism form the material from which legends and fairy tales are made. Later on, when fading away in space and time, the hero dons a visor instead of a hat, puts on armour in lieu of an overcoat, takes up a Crusader's sword and leaps onto a charger instead of a prosaic truck. Though deprived of logic and common sense a heroic feat has the strength, distinctness and durability of physical elements.

Still leading his meagre and fast-dwindling band of men the "Grey Knight" was rushing towards the bank of the river. As he was about to wade through this obstacle and storm the walls of the fortress he suddenly fell on his face, hit by a bullet. But he did not die. After many weeks I came across him once again. Emaciated, haggard and, as always, silent he was hobbling about with great difficulty within the compound of a prison camp.

While we observed the "Grey Knight's" heroism our little ditch was filling up with more people. First came Laud, groaning occasionally from wounds he had received, his head almost squeezed into a small aperture under the bridge. I was next to him with my

* Well-known character in Sienkiewicz's "Trilogy" – Trs.
† Narrow mountain pass – scene of the famous gallant charge of the Polish cavalry in the Peninsular War – Trs.

head between his legs. Zygmunt was at my side and then came Marian Piskorski and Bogdan Janowski, a jolly farmer from the region of Wilno.

Between bursts of gunfire there was dead silence, interrupted only by an ominous murmur of engines and shouting from the opposite side of the river. During these periods, gnawing fear was creeping into our bones. This sensation was far worse than ordinary fear, the so called "butterflies in the stomach" which one experiences when shots are fired and bullets whistle and when you are well aware of the simple truth that you will either be hit or not. No, this was different. Some dark monstrous spectre seemed to advance gradually, and rhythmically, crushing one by its sheer mass and weight. As in a dream when a person pursued by nightmares suddenly feels his legs turn to lead, there was no escape from this monster.

Right behind us the piercing cry of a woman could be heard. Janowski, the first to see what had happened, shouted: "Oh my God, that's the pretty wife of the Major whom we saw on the road today." Indeed, she had been driving with her husband and her young daughter in a little Fiat car. Because of its size the tiny vehicle was hidden among the big trucks and was therefore protected from bullets. But it was not immune to the flames of the fiercely burning fires along the road. The mother was the first to jump out of the car which had caught fire, but after a few steps fell dead, hit by a burst from a machine gun. The agonizing sobs of the child would vibrate later in our ears for a very long time.

There was a spell of silence again. Suddenly, quite close to us, a powerful voice called out in the accent of a Russian peasant: "Perestan strelat, zdavaysya, vy okruzheny. A to wsyoch perebyom." (Stop firing — you are encircled. Give yourselves up or else we'll finish off everybody.)

For the first time we could hear the Russian language. And so the remaining shreds of illusion had gone for good. At that very moment the document recording the history of the last two days, written in the blood of Polish officers and other victims, had been signed and witnessed by the few words of a Soviet soldier. And down came the red seal of the hammer and sickle.

What I am going to say now might sound banal. I am convinced, however, that not only alone in the ditch, but many others who had taken cover alongside me and elsewhere were toying with similar thoughts to my own, like when fingering beads on a string of a rosary. In my right hand I was holding a brand new gun, though somewhat blocked with grit and sand. I had used it once only — a little while ago to check how it worked. Work it did and quite well too. I could still feel its recoil after it had discharged.

I was well aware of what lay in store for me in the future. What would come immediately I did not know, the picture seemed muddled and dark. Various scenes from bygone days, often faded, were flashing onto my mind. Moscow in 1917, the October Revolution. I am seventeen. I am here with all my family as refugees from Poland which we left in 1914 when it was threatened by the German offensive. In the spring I pass my final exams at a Russian school and in the autumn I enlist at Moscow University. The first courses start. I have many good friends among the Russians. The deceitful and fallacious Kierenski period passes and then the October Revolution explodes into life. I recall fighting in the streets, revolutionary banners, dead bodies, wounded people. Every night we could watch from our apartment on the fifth floor the luminous arc of artillery shells spanning Arfat and the Strastnaja Ploszczad on one side and the Theatre Square, the Metropole Hotel and the Kremlin on the other. My younger brother, fourteen years old, is on duty as a porter. It is a dark and ominous night. He has been posted in the porch with a huge gun in his little hand as a symbol of authority. A ricocheted bullet has broken the window pane and landed inert on the bed where I sleep. Now, twenty-two years later, I am faced with the same bullets, coming out of the same barrels, but this time no longer ricochets — whistling and glittering, gay as fireworks, but livelier and more shiny, particulary as night is now falling swiftly.

And so there I was toying with my gun, pressing it against my temple or would it not be better in my mouth? No, with my mouth wide open it looks so stupid. Damn it, no! Dash it all, this would be too easy. At that moment I felt suddenly as if somebody had wanted to snatch my cap from my head. Zygmunt yelled behind my back: "For God's sake hide your head or you'll lose it. Are you all right?"

"Yes, I think I'm all right. Only that slight, burning sensation."

"Didn't I say to you, keep your head between Laud's legs. Now turn on your back and let's have a look. That's better. Does it hurt? No — so it's nothing really, just a trifle. Let's hope nothing worse happens."

Something sticky was oozing down my nose. With his usual resourcefulness, my good, old friend Zygmunt wetted a handkerchief from a waterbottle, drew himself nearer to reach my head, removed my cap, parted my hair, wiped it and leaving the handkerchief on my head, pulled my cap deep down over my ears.

"It's nothing, Bron, just a pin scratch. You lie here quietly. . . . I bet a nice longish walk awaits us all so we'll be leaving soon," he said, smiling.

During a quiet period following some hopeless shooting which had lasted for about three-quarters of an hour, a young Lieutenant of our Airforce, carrying a stick with a white scarf fastened on top, appeared suddenly on the road. He was up on the bridge in no time. A complete silence had fallen. Walking towards him from the other side was a larger group of men. It all took just a few minutes but to us it seemed like eternity. After a while the Lieutenant returned alone and then he and a Lieutenant-Colonel walked slowly back again, step-in-step, into the lion's den to discuss the capitulation of the Polish Army. Only the day before yesterday the Soviet enemy was regarded as the brotherly Slav. Today he had shed his mask, revealing a face of hate out to finish off dying Poland.

Single shots were still being fired from distant flanks as our men started to raise their heads and emerge from their hiding places. A general uproar and tumult ensued. Doctors with their first-aid kits were rushing to bring help to the wounded.

With bayonets fixed, a screaming and yelling gang of Soviet *boytzy** (ordinary soldiers) were already running towards us from the opposite side of the river. They were shouting to us to lay down arms and move on across the bridge. At the same time, appearing from the right and left flanks, masses of Red Army soldiers were forcing their way up to the road. We were encircled indeed. As it turned out later almost the whole of our long column had become trapped between strong pincers with no possible means of escape.

All this happened on the Tuesday, 19th September at 8 p.m.

---

* "Boyetz" warrior or fighter. Also used to denote a soldier in this book – Trs.

6. IN SOVIET CAPTIVITY

Smouldering cars and burning tyres were giving off a terrible choking smoke and stench. The *boytzy* were dragging us up to the road whilst yelling, swearing and shouting obscenities. We were ordered to dump our arms. Soon rifles and guns, almost all of them with their locks removed at the last moment, thrown aside as far as possible or stepped into the ground, were being heaped on a big pile. I myself managed to push my revolver deep into a molehill somewhere near the ditch.

Zygmunt was at my side, supporting me firmly by the arm in a grip of steel. Laud on the other side was doing likewise. The noise was growing stronger and stronger. Using force against us the *boytzy* were pounding the bodies of those not in step with their butt-ends. Some of our men wanted to remain on the battlefield to bury the dead and take care of the seriously wounded. There was no question of that. The Soviets were simply jeering at us! Some Soviet *komandir** of an undisclosed rank cried sneeringly: "The dead and wounded are to stay. Off you go beyond the bridge the rest of you."

"The dead and the wounded"— as if they were one and the same thing! This sounded ominous. Not wishing, obviously, to come under the latter category and be left behind Laud concealed the white bandage and sling under his overcoat. I, for my part, was wiping away the trickle of blood on my face. We were certainly not taking any chances.

Once past the bridge whole gangs of the *boytzy* went to work searching us in a most brutal fashion. Completely overpowered, we were turned into rubber balls and flung from one pair of greedy hands to another. The soldiers were supposed to look for hidden arms and ammunition – in fact they seized the occasion to loot us. Wedding and signet rings were torn from our fingers. Also watches, at the sight of which their eyes were set ablaze with greed. They were also after our leather belts, map-holders and bags. In some cases our men were even robbed of their greatcoats. A number of the more

* Commanding officer irrespective of rank held–Trs.

61

zealous *boytzy* went so far in their ignominy as to tear off our epaulets and the eagles on our caps. A few victims were trying desperately to resist, shouting: "This is an utter disgrace, this is illegal." A rain of blows would send them to the ground in no time. Personal documents and money bills, extracted from wallets, were floating in the air. What the first, second or third *boytzy* missed the tenth would pluck out.

After undergoing this humiliating experience the three of us met up again. We did not want to get lost in the darkness. Trying to check his fury Zygmunt was hissing: "Steady, steady! Just keep together. This is all that matters at the moment."

Our first encounter, eye to eye, with Red Army soldiers gave us all food for thought. Despite the falling darkness we were able to see the faces of these men, most of whom were still very young. They showed a strange terror, which was further expressed by their senseless shouting and the way in which they searched us, brutally prodding our bodies as though our uniforms concealed bombs. It was not a common fear. Its reason was hidden deeper. What we could see was the result of a hatred artificially implanted in them from childhood by the authorities, a hatred which eventually became a dominant factor in their thoughts and imaginations. They were presumably expecting to come eye to eye with cannibals. For twenty-two years the authorities had been cramming into their heads the idea that anybody living outside their country was automatically an enemy of the people, of the Soviets, a bandit and a *krowopijca*, that is, a man who feeds on the blood of the exploited masses of working class people or peasants. We Poles were described as *pany* (masters), *pomyeshchyki* (landowners), *oficery* (officers), symbols to the Soviets of what is the worst and cruellest in mankind. No wonder the young Soviet soldiers showed terror on their stupid faces. Taught those few "foreign" words like parrots they made frequent use of them, enriched with traditional Russian swear words.

As though looking at pictures in a textbook of ethnology I saw in these soldiers a comprehensive display of the various nationalities that make up the Soviet Union. Ranging from the upturned "potato" noses of the blue eyed "Malorusy" (inhabitants of the southern regions) to the slanting eyes and yellow complexion of the Chinese-looking Uzbeks, they were, nevertheless, united in smelling strongly of a mixture of sweat, Russian leather and *makhorka*, an inferior kind of tobacco.

The hand on the clock of history was ticking rhythmic seconds. And how very few seconds are needed to overpower a few thousand regular troops and transform them into a mass of people deprived of their dignity and rendered helpless. On top of everything we had been thwarted in trying to achieve our ultimate aim, that of opposing the German onslaught either on the blood-stained battlefields of our homeland, or, should they be overrun by the enemy, by continuing to fight outside our country, in some other theatre of war. For our intention was to carry on at the side of our allies. But nothing was to come of it. Acting hand in hand with our western enemy, our eastern neighbour was completing the odious task.

Scattered over our eastern provinces, from the frontiers of Lithuania and Latvia in the north down to the borders of Rumania and Hungary in the south, our troops were being crushed mercilessly by the Soviet war machine.

Right from the start we were divided into separate groups of officers, non-commissioned officers and privates. Columns – five men abreast – were then formed. Attempts by our captors to have us counted were also made but in this they failed. Finally, we were marched off to a nearby highway and for about one kilometre we had to walk along a line of heavy Soviet tanks, their exhausts belching flames, heat radiating from the engines and suffocating fumes of badly refined petrol filling the air. It started to drizzle when night fell and the weather grew cold and wet.

At one point the vanguard of the column swerved from the highway into a vast, freshly ploughed field. It soon became filled with prisoners and the Soviet guards started yelling: "Vsye lozhys. Molchat!" (All lie down and keep silent!)

There was nothing we could do but lie down flat on sticky, muddy ground. My head was bursting with pain. Laud was groaning. The stillness and darkness were nerve racking. Some of our men, however, fell asleep as if nothing was the matter. After a long hour, during which our thoughts became increasingly gloomy, we sensed a certain commotion and some men tried to stand up. New angry Russian voices rose once more: "Lozhys, govoriat vam" (Lie down, we are saying it again) after which another voice shouted: "Attention, attention, all of you. Listen to the voice of the *komandir*."

A loud and sonorous voice in Russian reached us. The man stated his rank and functions – that of a Colonel, if I remember correctly. "From now on, all of you here are prisoners of war of the powerful Red Army. I presume you know how you are to behave and what would be the consequences of disobedience and of an attempted escape. I therefore order an absolute and total obedience to every soldier in this convoy, who henceforth will be your superiors. And now attention. Should any of you possess any sharp instruments, such as penknives, ordinary knives, razors, etc., you are ordered to hand them over to your escorts right away or else, I remind you, things will look bad for you if you don't do as you're told." On finishing his speech he added some unintelligible sentences.

That was what the *boytzy* were waiting for. Whilst we were prostrate in the mud they pounced on our bodies like vultures, pilfering our pockets again and snatching the prohibited articles from us.

After we had lain a few more hours on the wet ground we were interrupted again by loud shouts: "Sobeyraysya! Stanovis! Nu davay, davay, pozhywyey." (Get ready, stand up. Come on, come on, hurry up.)

We had some difficulty in regaining control of our stiff, aching limbs. At the front of our column, which was five men wide, were the officers, then behind them the non-commissioned officers, followed by privates. A thick line of Soviet troops escorted us with bayonets fixed. The *komandirs* of undisclosed ranks — they held no rifles but guns only — were bustling all over the place, shouting and brandishing their revolvers.

We reached the highway once more, turned right and for some time again we passed tank after tank, radiating heat and emitting foul odours. Eventually we reached a road-junction after a few kilometres of quick marching. It became obvious that the youngish *komandirs* did not know in which direction to go. As we were not far from the vanguard of our column we could overhear their conversation. Some of our men offered to indicate the right road if only they could be told our destination. This was answered by short barks "My znayem, nye vashe dyelo, molchat!" (We know all right, it's not your business. . . . Silence!)

We thus wandered about in circles hopelessly until dawn. We would often turn from the highway into field roads, carefully avoiding any of the small, scattered hamlets. On several occasions the *boytzy* would rush to some detached cottage and hammer at the window-panes to ask the frightened peasants the right direction. Dawn was breaking when we reached the same place we had left six hours before. All Soviet troops and tanks had gone. They were obviously busy penetrating deeper into Poland. The departed tanks had left oily patches of lubricant and road-metal torn from the road by their caterpillars, as well as wide flat lanes of crushed grass and stubble in the fields alongside the road.

A halt was ordered and we were allowed to leave the hard surface of the road and scatter along the ditches. We all collapsed exhausted and in a matter of seconds were fast alseep . . . . The halt did not last long, however. It was called off after ten minutes. Half-conscious, driven like cattle, we continued to trudge along. Either by chance or design one of our men at the vanguard of the column managed to obtain the name of our immediate destination. It was Bursztyn – a small country town.

Daylight had come and it looked like a fine, hot day. On seeing us the few peasants we met on the road were absolutely stupefied. We asked them how far it was to Bursztyn. As it turned out, their answers were highly inaccurate. Instead of the 10 or so kilometres they indicated, we had in fact another 25 kilometres in front of us.

During our wanderings preceding the night of the 19th September many officers and privates had left the column, to be replaced by new faces. In this situation very few men managed to form any sort of friendship, the sort based on common experiences and the awareness of being linked by fate. I had the fortune, as I have said, to make friends with a little group of fellow officers. In those days, however, the majority of our men, either travelling by car or marching, were primarily preoccupied with themselves, their own thoughts, worries, experiences, even their own belongings. Finding some room on a truck seemed to be of more importance to such people than finding a spare seat for a companion slogging along on foot. All in all the real sense of comradeship, the determination to help each other, was, unfortunately, a rare phenomenon in those days.

This egoism was dispelled suddenly and quite spontaneously on that memorable evening of the 19th September. From the moment when the *boytzy* began arranging us in fives, everyone started to look into the eyes of the man next to him, to seize him by the arm and wish to make friends with him. All had the feeling of being linked by some invisible bond and it became clear to everybody that, by marching inseparably in step to some unknown destination and by holding each other firmly by the arm, the burden of events would be easier to bear. Against the looming spectre of some great, all-encompassing misery the old adage "A friend in need is a friend indeed" became very real.

Although the night proved to be pitch dark and we had difficulty in making out the features of our closest neighbours we nevertheless sensed that links of friendship and a spirit of sincere companionship had been born.

At dawn the slowly emerging human snake was beginning to acquire a proper size as well as a proper shape. We passed several fairly large villages on our long march. Their inhabitants, huddled up to the front of the cottages, were gazing at the procession in a state of stupor, not yet realising what was going on. Some threw chunks of bread or sour apples to us, despite warnings from our escorts that such action was prohibited. We on our side cried for water. Carrying a bucket of water a smart nimble young lad got through the line of the convoy into our midst. Like desperate people in a desert we drank avidly from the palms of our hands.

Every few hours our escorts allowed us to halt for ten minutes. As any contact with the local population was strictly forbidden our stops were made out in the countryside. Once we managed to wash our tired and aching feet in a wayside pond, all silted up and muddy. We had had nothing to eat for thirty hours. Hunger – as it is generally known – has its own curve of intensity. You suffer from it most after just a few hours when the body realises it has been cheated out of its normal intake of food. After that comes a period of numb insensibility which, strangely enough, will often last for quite a long time.

We reached Bursztyn in the late afternoon. On entering the little town, in order to prevent any exchange of words with the local population, we were hurried on with shouts. We squeezed ourselves into a narrow courtyard, fenced off by a tall, wooden palisade, covered by a thick net of barbed wire – our first barbed wire! At the back was a large school building where we found a few hundred Polish officers cooped up. They had been taken prisoner a few hours before our arrival. Officers only were allowed to join them from our party – privates were taken somewhere else.

We came across friends and acquaintances. The stories we had to tell each other did not differ much. Their basis was always the same – it was sorrow, apathy and humiliation.

After many hours of waiting a field kitchen was at last produced by Soviet soldiers who started dispensing oatmeal, bread and boiling water – the legendary Russian *kipyatok*. Some of our companions were in possession of cubes of compressed, sweetened coffee which after being dissolved in boiling water produces an excellent beverage. The great problem was we had no crockery. However, the kind-hearted population of the town came to our rescue. Children, women, men – no matter whether Gentiles or Jews – threw mugs, bowls, spoons over the fence. In return we gratefully gave them what remained of our money. Seen from a distance this must have looked like a scene in a zoo at feeding time! There was however a marked difference. Our benefactors on the other side of the fence instead of having fun were wiping tears from their faces. And together with the priceless utensils were passed hopeless and heartbreaking questions. But the chances of finding a satisfying answer were, like in a lottery, one to a million: "Haven't you seen somewhere my man, my father, my son, my brother . . . ?" they would ask. Our conversations did not last long. The *boytzy* were brutally pushing away those who dared to come too close to the prohibited wires.

A well with clear, fresh water – what a blessing this was! We washed ourselves. As no medical outfit was available our doctors dressed the wounds and sore feet of those in need as best they could. With his agile fingers a young doctor deftly cut a patch of hair from my head and applied a clean, fresh dressing. This as well as the oatmeal and coffee made me feel a bit more comfortable.

There was an appalling lack of space and air inside the crowded building. With Zygmunt and Laud we pushed into a room which had been used for musical and theatrical performances. On a platform serving as a stage we discovered with the greatest difficulty a place where we could lie down. Backstage we found some very odd props which this time we used for real, practical purposes – that is, as cushions on which to rest our heads. The walls of the room were still decorated gaily with Polish red and white national flags.

Owing to a stroke of good luck some of our companions who had preceded us to the school building succeeded in saving part of their belongings. The majority had nothing at all except what they were wearing. Zygmunt, Laud and myself were in the latter category of paupers. Lieutenant Olgierd Szpakowski, on the other hand, a young electrical technician, who as we discovered during the night, proved to be our closest neighbour, belonged to the category of particularly "affluent" people. He owned, of all things, a suitcase containing underwear, soap, razor blades, tobacco and also a rug and a magnificent sheepskin which when spread out wide would cover up four people. I was to benefit from its warmth for a long time after as well as from other priceless things which good old Olgierd generously shared with us.

At dusk we went early to sleep. The place seemed at first to be seething and buzzing with voices like in a beehive. Some men were speaking with great excitement, others with effort as though they would rather have been asleep. Now and then dirty jokes would be heard followed by bursts of laughter. Soon, however, the exhausted men began backing away gradually from the scene of conversation and, lulled by the receding hubbub of voices, sank into heavy sleep. Finally silence fell, interrupted only by loud snoring.

Around 5 a.m. – the day was the 21st September – we were woken up by a high-pitched, drawling voice calling in Russian: "Vstava-aay! Dava—aay, sobyeraysya s vyeshchami" (Get up, come on, get ready with your things.)

Good Lord, what's that, where are we? It was damn difficult to shake off one's dreams suddenly and get back into the rut of reality.

67

This was, after all, only the beginning of our new pattern of existence and we hadn't got used to it yet.

More *boytzy* appeared on the scene. They were shouting and pushing. Insistently we asked some of them where they were taking us. One of them, probably bolder than the others, when driven into a corner answered phlegmatically: "Nu, povidimomu zagruzim was na gruzoviki. A kuda svyezut, etovo nie znayu." (We shall be putting you on trucks. Where you'll be driven, that I don't know.)

For breakfast we were given a Russian national dish – a soup called *shchi* consisting of boiled cabbage and beetroot plus a quarter of a loaf of brown bread on top. After that we marched off past the gate and past our first prison wires. We reached a picturesque little market square nearby where a number of trucks – twenty-five in all – were lined up ready for us. They were American Fords, copied from the original but made in the USSR. The soldiers loaded twenty of us onto one of them and then three *boytzy*, armed with rifles and guns, jumped up after us. We were squeezed in like sardines. According to my rough calculation there must have been some five hundred men in the convoy.

We set off. We went eastwards along bumpy field roads, as if on a cross-country drive. The idea was obviously to avoid main highways and keep us away from larger agglomerations of people. Consequently we were doing some incredible turns as well as diversions through meadows and fields. Our trucks were bouncing over hundreds of pot-holes, their bodies vibrating, as though they were threshing machines. Whilst crawling intermittently through sand and marshes now and then one of the trucks would get bogged down up to its axles and then all the strength of the twenty men aboard was needed to get the vehicle out.

Many of us knew the region well and were explaining in a whisper our supposed position. After having made a wide detour we passed in the distance the town of Podhajce. Our experts kept affirming that we were heading towards Czortkow or Kopyczynce. Whether true or not, the road we were on was leading unmistakably to the east.

It was well past midday and we must have covered some seventy kilometres when we came to an abrupt halt in an open space. Our *boytzy* jumped out of the cars and spread out to form lines along the two sides of the trucks. Soon they were shouting in chorus: "Nu davay, vylizay, rozgruzhayvya s vyeshchami!" (Come on, get out, with your things!)

We did not like that. The addition "s vyeshchami" (with your things) could mean only one thing, that there was to be a change in our means of transport. The Commanders of the convoy gathered some distance from us in the fields and we could watch them discussing intently among themselves and eventually issuing orders to the truck drivers. The latter started the engines and after fifteen minutes or so reversed their vehicles and drove off in an elongated column of empty trucks in the direction from which they had just come. It was obvious that they had gone to fetch a new party of prisoners. As for us, it became clear that we would have to continue on foot. But where to? To the Soviet frontier presumably. We made a quick mental calculation. The distance, as the crow flies, from this place to the frontier must amount to some seventy kilometres.

The *boytzy* had by now started to shout as usual, urging us to line up. And so began another hard, tiring slog towards — there was no more doubt about it — the east. Inside the large column groups of men, linked by new bonds of friendship, had formed small, closely-knit units which continued to stick tightly together.

With every kilometre the possessions we were carrying became more burdensome. I was experiencing a curious feeling. The further we progressed in our march the less I regretted things I had lost or left behind. Anyway, I wouldn't have been able to carry them any longer. My dear old greatcoat was gaining in weight all the time and pressing on my shoulders. I had been prepared several times to sing the valedictory aria from Puccini's "La Bohème" to the faithful friend I was carrying! True to our team spirit, we were carrying collectively the belongings of the few "rich" people, such as Olgierd Szpakowski. He really was showing remarkable tenacity. Pale from exertion he would not let go of his suitcase in case he lost any of his valuables. We, however, helped him by turns as best we could.

The longer our march lasted the more its speed diminished. We were now, at the most, doing four kilometres per hour including short halts lasting a few minutes each. The column was visibly thinning and lengthening. As the evening wore on the older and weaker began to lag behind and eventually fell off by the wayside. A few *boytzy* stayed with them. We did not know how many failed to follow us as it was not possible to count them. But we worried a lot about their fate. Fortunately some of them caught up with us in the early hours of the morning, having travelled on requisitioned, horse-drawn peasants' wagons. Whether all of them — who knows?

At midnight our Commanders ordered a halt. Despite the acute hunger and cold which were tormenting us, we huddled up to one another and fell asleep on the wet grass. Some single shots, loud and frightening, woke us up suddenly. "What is the matter?" we asked each other. Someone, as if speaking whilst asleep, said: "Obviously some daredevil has tried to bolt, but has not found it very easy. You won't get far with a bullet in your posterior."

After three hours they made us spring to our feet with their characteristic prolonged shouts to which we were becoming increasingly accustomed: "Nu davay, stanovis, pozhyviey" (Come on, get up, hurry up.) Half asleep and soaked to the skin with dew we staggered on again through the darkness. And this is how we began the 22nd September – trundling along to some unknown destination.

There was no question of any food. Later, around dawn, a single truck caught up with us and halted in front of the column. While we stopped the *boytzy* made a beeline towards it. Food had arrived but it was not for us. As we watched them gobbling up hot oatmeal, bread and tea our guts were turning inside out . . . .

The Commanders of the convoy continued to prohibit any contact with the local population. Despite all their endeavours we could not help, presumably for geographical reasons, marching through some picturesque villages or hamlets. Situated further to the east, they must have fallen prey to the first wave of Soviet forces starting on the 17th September. Therefore the population must have been well aware of who we were and where we were being taken. These good, kind-hearted people said goodbye to us in a spontaneous and moving way. Although forbidden to do so and despite all the shoutings and brutal blows from rifle butts, whole groups of women and children were running behind us. They even succeeded in passing us bread, fruit and mugs filled with milk or water. Tearing from their necks little holy crosses and medals they pushed them into our hands. They also removed coloured scarves and shawls from their heads and shoulders. Pieces of soap and linen towels were thrown at us – all these riches sent by God! And on top of all this, with tears in their eyes and words of prayer and comfort, they bade us farewell. "May the Virgin Mary protect you . . . " rang in our ears movingly for a long time.

Amidst such unforgettable scenes we proceeded in our march to the east. We skirted the town of Kopyczynce from the north side before noon and then took the highway leading directly to the Soviet frontier. Later, early in the evening of the 22nd, we at last reached Husiatyn on the River Zbrucz – the frontier post of the Polish Republic.

We passed the railway station situated on the outskirts of that little town. On the left hand side of the road, past the station building, the embankment of the railway track still ran ahead for a short distance, as if trying to span the deep ravine of the river and the higher side that lay opposite without losing momentum. But it turned and ended abruptly. A long time ago, before the First World War, when the frontiers of the neighbouring countries were less separated, this railway line used to connect the rich land of the Ukraine with Southern Poland and with Central Europe.

Soon we were descending the highway leading down to the valley of the River Zbrucz. And then, before reaching the first human dwellings, we turned to the right into a vast field of stubble. A huge mass of troops could be seen in the distance. They consisted mainly of privates. They had been driven here in their thousands from all parts of Poland's eastern provinces as if for a last, dismal, roll call within the frontiers of their country. All of them were completely worn out and hungry.

We were looking round, asking each other questions and enquiring about companions in arms, relatives, acquaintances. Bustling amongst the huge crowd were young boys from Husiatyn who in spite of being chased away constantly by Soviet guards were busy selling us bread, apples and cigarettes. The speed and dexterity shown by those children in running to and fro to get all the most valuable articles was a stupendous athletic performance. It was, of course, done for the sake of making some money but also out of a sincere, urgent wish to bring help to Polish soldiers in dire need. We were, no doubt, witnessing the last manifestation of "free trade" on Polish soil, something we did not realise at that moment. Today we know only too well how individual, creative thought was strangled, how any private initiative stifled and how gradually but systematically the character of Poland was buried by the uniformity of Soviet life. The population, stunned and paralysed by the Soviet invasion, was rewarded by a "just" redistribution of property along the lines of the Soviet "paradise".

I had been asleep for an hour at the most when the guards started to urge us once more to line up. To avoid getting lost we stuck together in our-well-organised groups. I was munching slowly a piece of bread and an apple not so much to ease the cramp in my stomach as to kill the hunger I felt. Our guards proceeded to put us into formations according to the established order. First came officers, followed by non-commissioned officers and lastly by privates. Once again they started counting us most clumsily, taking a long time over it. Finally we re-formed into a column.

Dusk was falling. We passed in front of the railway embankment where it ended. On its steep slope, against a carpet of turf, we saw a mosaic of a huge White Eagle made of whitewash and red bricks. In silence and anguish we spontaneously saluted it, our hearts aching. After by-passing it we still turned our heads back to cast a last glance at the vanishing symbol of our homeland.

Our procession acquired the solemn and joyless character of a funeral. Scared people from the last hamlet near the Polish frontier were emerging from their ruined houses, victims of a hopeless, heroic attempt at resisting the invaders from the east. Here and there without saying a word they were bidding us farewell by waving to us timidly. Meanwhile we were descending to the River Zbrucz. Only debris remained of what used to be the bridge over it. Looking for a ford or a foot-bridge our column halted in front of the ruins.

A narrow shaky foot-bridge was found. It was now pitch dark and we crossed the river slowly in Indian file. Eventually we set foot for the first time on Soviet soil.

Not the tiniest light could be seen around us – we were entering a world of complete darkness. All this took place on the 22nd September at 9 p.m. The road went up steeply from the shores of the Zbrucz. On both its sides, silhouetted against the darkness, were the outlines of some strange, soulless little houses. Feeling more at home now our guards intensified their wild roarings and shouts. After we had crossed the foot-bridge we were once more lined up into fives. Marching along the road in this formation we came to a vast plain. Our eyes had become used to the darkness, but we saw no trees along the road or dwellings of any kind – only that strange eerie desert. This was the 30-35 kilometre-wide protective "Cordon sanitaire" running along the whole of the border with Poland. Over many years the Soviet authorities had been eliminating all traces of human life from the area.

7. TO THE EAST IN STAGES

There is no way of getting to know the Soviet Union in its state of total isolation from the West, an isolation which has been engineered deliberately by the authorities who fear even the slightest contamination from poisonous foreign infiltration. In the vicious circle of internal oppression this huge country is stewing in its own juice of ideological as well as physical hatred for everything which happens to belong to the outside world.

Such were the thoughts which we, on the threshold of our expedition into the interior of Soviet Russia, were sharing with our closest companions. Closing our discussion Olgierd Szpakowski had remarked, chuckling in his high-pitched voice, that observing through the key-hole of a prison cell the body of some colossal beast one can see only a fraction of its trunk. The question is whether what we see corresponds to what we think it is. But, of course, to pass a thousand-strong army through a key-hole is impossible. So in some strange and significant way, whether they wanted it or not, the Soviet frontier guards had, for the first time since the Communists took power, allowed a large number of foreigners to cross the border into their country. One could only guess what the effect might be on the Soviet people.

We were proceeding in the same order as when we had started our march three days ago. Zygmunt, Laud, Olgierd, Bogdan Janowski and I were forming a line of five. Laud was limping – he had a sore foot. Carrying his boot over his shoulder he had shod his ailing leg in some old woman's felt slipper. Sharp, uneven pebbles on the road were punishing everyone's feet, whether they were sound or sore. Showing much resilience and fortitude Zygmunt was marching at my side. We also continued to help Olgierd to carry his belongings. But with every kilometre this was becoming more and more difficult. The same could be seen in other ranks too – men were sharing the weight of suitcases, bags, rucksacks. However despite a strong urge to salvage all these priceless things, ditches along the road were becoming increasingly littered with abandoned belongings. Our earthly possessions were fast diminishing.

We noticed a flickering light in the distance. Was it perhaps a railway station? There was, after all, a rumour of our impending entrainment. We asked our guards whether this was true and what the light meant. All in vain. They either brushed our questions aside or muttered "nye znayu" (I don't know) or "nye vashe dyelo." (It's not your business.) We marched past many more of those lights without seeing a trace of a train. Olgierd remarked that the lights must have been special effects just put up in our honour.

A halt was ordered at about 4 a.m., a time when exhausted and hungry people suffer most from the cold. We were allowed to step down into the ditches but not a step further. Like dogs before they come to rest we turned round and round, trying to get comfortable. But after a while we all fell asleep on ground which was wet with dew. These are moments when one becomes indifferent to everything. One only wants to curl up and sleep. There were some single shots — perhaps just to frighten people off, perhaps not. Zygmunt started swearing in his sleep: "To hell with it, silence . . . we don't want to be disturbed!"

We slept as though nothing in the world would budge us. After the halt had been announced we all thought they would allow us to rest until the morning or for a few hours at least. We also thought we would get some food — forty-eight hours had elapsed since we had had something to eat. All this proved to be a pipe dream.

We were woken again by the *boytzy's* shouts and cries passed on from man to man all along the huge column: "Vstava-aaay, sobyeraysya!"

Our halt had lasted for thirty minutes only.

We went on marching. The gnawing feeling of sleepiness which affected our bodies and bones with a kind of crushing sensation did not recede for a moment. It is worse than hunger, you cannot forget about it for a moment. Your shoulders no longer support your head, your legs, as though attached to a different person, move forward uncontrollably like automatons. The dark silhouettes of those marching in front of us conveyed the impression of men who were completely drunk. Every few moments we had to rescue some lonely man seen to stagger to the side of the road, who but for the help of a few stronger companions would have soon found himself in the ditch!

The fate of those who out of sheer exhaustion were getting visibly weak was far worse. More and more frequently voices could be heard crying: "I can no longer carry on! Let whatever happens happen!"

We tried to continue carrying them but this was impossible. Ranks would break up, one man would tread on another's feet and the speed of the march would slacken. Our appeals to the guards that they should take care of the poor wretches and provide some kind of transport were always countered with laconic and stupid wickedness.

An elderly and rather stout Major got entangled in our ranks. Dropping back from the front of the column he eventually landed with us. He could hardly stand on his legs and we had to grasp him under his arms and hold him up. A short and stocky *boyetz* who for some time had been marching at our side saw this. Coming closer to us in a voice thick with rage he spat out: "Hey, you blithering old fool you're just feigning eh . . . ? You don't want to carry on? I'll make you run and teach you a lesson, fuck your mother." Having said this he struck the Major a strong blow on the shoulders using his rifle-butt. The old man reeled and would have fallen but for Zygmunt and Bogdan who caught him and carried him in their arms. We marched like this for another few minutes but to continue any longer was out of the question.

"Many thanks, my dear friends," said the Major. "You had better leave me here. I'll have to join the others who have fallen off. It may be that we shall, after all, get some help and be given a lift. Who knows? We might perhaps even meet again. I was a veterinary surgeon in Warsaw and my name is Maksymilian Labedz. If the time should come please remember me." He said the last words in a tired whisper. And who would not have heard of Labedz – the most popular vet in Warsaw? Perhaps the reason why he was generally known and liked was because he loved animals and took care of them. He stepped out of the column and sank into the ditch. We went on marching.

In further episodes of our story we shall come across many of those who fell by the wayside during this terrible march. For, the rule of shooting dead on the spot those unable to march in step with the column was fortunately not yet practised on columns of Polish prisoners of war being driven into the interior of the Soviet Union. It is a well-known fact, however, that particularly during the hasty evacuation of Soviet prisons in occupied Polish lands due to the German advance in 1941, Soviet guards would shoot indiscriminately at anybody not strong enough to keep up.

When day broke we were able to see what an enormous number of Polish officers and soldiers there were in the column. Owing to the hilly undulating character of the province of Podolia those marching in the vanguard of the column were in a position to get a good view of the whole of this huge human snake. It stretched for at least three kilometres. We were able to count about 1,200 officers and 12,000 privates.

We were being allowed to halt for a very brief time – only just long enough to tend to our aching feet. With a linen towel pushed at me by a good woman in one of the Polish villages I made – following a Soviet practice – the so called *onuce* and used them for wrapping up my feet. For what was left of my socks were only miserable shreds.

There was no question of a meal, not even the tiniest slice of bread. Several times we managed to approach some wells situated near crumbling derelict peasants' cottages, once forming part of a hamlet. The pits were old and all overgrown with weeds and full of vermin. But we drank the stinking, repulsive water.

The pace of our march was constantly slowing. Towards the evening the column had stretched to such a length that its end was out of sight. We heard rumours, emanating from the vanguard, that our destination was near – that is, the railway station where we were supposed to entrain.

Hunger had by now reached a stage when one no longer feels it. Now and then some of us would crack a joke and enumerate with a great deal of solemnity long lists of the most exquisite dishes full of all kinds of culinary refinements and accompanied by an appropriate list of best wines. The subject of food, normally relished even by those who are replete, let alone by the hungry ones, never left us and provided much fun.

Midnight was closing in. I felt cold and weak and had to lean more and more heavily on Zygmunt's arm. He tried to comfort and cheer me up by telling me jokes. We halted on the crest of a hill and saw in front of us down below a great many flickering lights. People were saying the place was Jarmolince, a little town with a railway station situated some seventy kilometres from the Polish frontier. So we had covered the distance in twenty-seven hours on empty stomachs and without a proper rest. Not a bad record at all.

The Commanders of the convoy were running about gesticulating wildly and obviously discussing what to do. Without asking permission we lay down as we stood. I tried for a little while to fight the all encompassing weakness which was taking hold of me but soon fell into a deep asleep. I have no recollection of what happened next.

I woke up shivering with cold. I was lying on straw. I could smell its odour and it cracked as I moved. It was almost dawn outside. I felt for my cap, the dressing on my head, my greatcoat. Everything was covered with hoar-frost. I raised my aching head with difficulty and saw Zygmunt and Laud asleep near me. I was feeling too weak to get up and look around to see where I was. And so after digging deeper into the straw I fell asleep again. When I woke up and started regaining consciousness it was broad daylight. Zygmunt was standing over me, laughing heartily and in order to get some warmth was thrashing his arms vigorously. He then bent down and did the same to me!

"How do you feel, dear Bron?" he asked. "You just fainted away at the last stop before Jarmolince. But as you can see we've made it after all — we've reached our destination."

"Zygmunt, for God's sake tell me how it all happened. I don't remember a thing. From the moment I fell asleep at the top of the hill it was just a complete blank. What I *can* remember, however, are all those lights and somebody mentioning the name of the place — Jarmolince."

"Well, you suddenly became weak and passed out — as simple as that. We stayed there for some fifteen minutes and then set off downhill through a hamlet adjoining the town. Bogdan and I had to carry you all the way — something like two kilometres — and we just tucked you into the straw. But never mind, your body is as light as a young girl's so we managed it all right," he went on gaily. "Isn't that so?" he asked Bogdan who was just struggling out from the straw.

"I feel terribly ashamed that I should have let you down just before our final goal. Please accept my humblest apologies and warmest thanks," I said, getting up slowly from my lair and stretching my stiff, aching limbs. I then looked round.

We were in a vast farmyard surrounded by small outbuildings as well as by a wire fence. In the centre was a big red brick building, quite attractive and probably a country house many years ago. It now housed a school, as a large notice board indicated. The whole place was crowded with our officers who were moving about trying to warm themselves up. Some were trying to light a fire.

"Look here, Bron," said Zygmunt "there are plenty of our people inside the school building. They were driven down here a few hours before we arrived. They are still sleeping like logs. Let's go in and have a look at them."

The sight which presented itself to us was uncanny. All the rooms and corridors were packed to capacity with intertwined bodies. The stench was nauseating, but still I was glad to get some warmth. One could see from their uniforms that all the men were officers. As Zygmunt pushed his way farther in to reconnoitre I sat down on a few inches of muddy floor between somebody's legs and gazed with compassion at this picture of human misery. Soon I was again overcome by an urge to sleep. This time it was not to last for long, however. The mass of human bodies began to move, stretching and unwinding their tangled limbs. Men were getting up to greet friends, relatives and even brothers whom they had never expected to meet again. The air was filled with exclamations and loud greetings. To recognize a face, however, was not at all easy — all the men looked hairy, unshaven with fairly long beards and revoltingly scruffy. The greater part of them were Reserve Officers. Among all the filth, overcrowding and general weariness they were still sticking to their civilian code of behaviour and manner of speech. Apart from being incongruous, all these forms of civility and good manners seemed to be a little out of place.

"Really, I am terribly sorry Sir. Will you please excuse me but we are a bit squeezed in here, aren't we?" a man was saying to another one treading on his legs.

"Never mind, never mind," replied the other man as he tucked his legs in.

Suddenly the ant hill became the scene of a commotion hard to describe. Food was coming. Grub had actually arrived! In fact several field-kitchens had just thundered into the farmyard. We lined up obediently in long queues for a meal — the first for three days — consisting of *kasha* (oat gruel) and bread. There was a shortage of utensils and several men had to use the same spoon and eat out of the same bowl. With the advent of daylight and with our hunger partly satisfied the general mood improved and one could even sense a resurgence of the spirit of enterprise. We were soon washing ourselves, cleaning our dirty uniforms, tidying up the farmyard. I shaved with Olgierd's safety razor, using also his soap and towel. Others were busy getting out the rest of the potatoes from a dug-up patch of field situated within the wire. Burrowing like moles with bare hands and little sticks they were turning the earth upside down to find the miserable little bulbs. Later, these were baked in the fires which had been lit with a great deal of difficulty. Making a fire was forbidden by our guards but we dismissed their orders with jokes although more than one fire made with a few bricks was smashed by the hefty kick of a boot.

The day was dragging on and nothing startling had happened. In the evening we were each given a ladle of hot water with cabbage — in other words the soup called *shchi*. Our mood was deteriorating for it was getting cold. We started busying ourselves with trying to secure a proper site for the night. Nothing doing however. There was not a spare square foot of room left in the whole of the school building so all that remained was the farmyard with its trampled straw. Dear Olgierd lent me a bit of his sheepskin. Up to midnight I somehow managed to hold out but having been frozen to the bone I went by myself inside the building in search of luck. I wandered about for a long time until, whilst crouching in pitch darkness, I found in a corridor full of mud, the semblance of somewhere to rest on someone's legs. In the warmth and stench of it I slept for a few hours more.

The next day differed little from the previous one. Our *kasha* arrived once again in the morning. We even composed a little ditty in its honour which we hummed in chorus. We also discussed intently the general situation, that is, what had happened to our country and the future of our forces which had succeeded in crossing the frontier and had taken refuge in a neutral country But first and foremost we were concerned with what the future had in store for us. It was now, at the very beginning of our captivity, that the first attempts were made in a rational, analytical way, to assess our position. As it happened, there were amongst us not only high ranking officers but also lawyers with a knowledge of international law, so various points of view could be taken into account in our discussions. Later on, this "brains trust", became an important source of knowledge, particularly regarding legal matters, and it also gave us mental stimulus. The majority of its members believed consistently that prompt and effective intervention by our Western Allies was vital in determining the fate of Polish prisoners of war in the USSR.

Many of the *boytzy* whose faces we had got to know during our long march had been superseded. Amongst the new personnel, there was a new sort of soldier. This was the so-called "politruk".* A *politruk* was recognisable by his cap, which had a red rim.

It was some time before we realised the full implications of this change. We had been passed that day from the hands of the Red Army into those of the NKVD, the all-powerful police and military organization, responsible to the Commissar for the Interior and holding in their iron grip the whole of life in the Soviet Union.

The *politruks*, as we came to know them in those days, behaved in a way entirely different from that of the *boytzy* and even of the army *komandirs*. Because of the instructions they had received from their superiors and also because of their strict training, the *boytzy* kept their mouths sealed and despite all our assiduous attempts – smiles, jokes, good cigarettes – were not to be humoured nor was it possible to get out of them any semblance of human reaction. *Politruks*, on the other hand, were a very different proposition. I am speaking of the *politruks* with a "diploma" who knew their job well. They had under their command a mass of ordinary NKVD *boytzy* who, like their colleagues, the "Red Army *boytzy*" were deaf and mute. I have never tried to fathom the mystery of the *politruks'* ranks, their badges and marks of distinction and seniority. Some of them sported

* Abbreviation of "politicheskij rukowodityel" meaning "political instructor".

on the collars of their uniforms red enamelled squares, others had no special insignia at all. In no way did this indicate that they were intelligent or stupid – both kinds were represented among them.

And so at Jarmolince we got into the grip of the *politruks* and they were to stay with us until the bitter end. Their task was to come to know us, to understand us, to make out who and what we were, to provoke us into confidences, to eavesdrop, to irritate and to stir us up by spreading all kinds of rumours, bad and good, to try to weigh up our moods, and finally to systematically fill our minds with Soviet propaganda. All this was done with a smile, by the promise of a small favour or by projecting pictures of some rosy future. But here I am running ahead with the thread of my reminiscences!

On that first day as well as in the days to come, these Russians whose ranks, grades or aims were completely unknown to us were extremely well received by the great majority. The reason was simple – they were not dumb like the *boytzy*, but were willing to talk to us.

We Poles, who tend to be a little gullible, reacted enthusiastically to this, and some of us were carried away by a propensity for garrulousness, others approached the *politruks* consumed by a concern for survival and anxiety about the future. With others it was sheer curiosity unsatisfied for a whole week. The "red capped" men became quite popular among us, and whole groups would form round them deeply engrossed in discussion. Our younger officers, temperamental and quick witted, given to talking and thirsting for news, were, in most cases, unable to speak Russian. They were trying to communicate with the *politruks* in a broken language which often resulted in the conversation going completely awry. Zygmunt, Laud and I moved from one group to another (the three of us knew Russian perfectly) and listened from a distance to the incongruous exchange of words and sentences. Here and there, some senior Polish officer could be heard making conversation in fluent Russian and keeping it up to a decent standard but on the whole the quality of what was being said, of questions asked and answers given was very poor. In our condition of hunger, want and anxiety it was strange that some should wish to know such things as: Will our belongings, rugs, underwear, watches and wedding rings be returned to us? Shall we be given knives for cutting bread, toothbrushes, soap, razors? Will there be any shops where we will be able to buy the above things? Shall we be getting our officers' pay? Will it be possible for us to correspond with our families? Will there be any books for us to read, stationery for writing letters, etc? For some time, until they saw through to the reality, many continued to ask such questions, and they were invariably met with brief prepared answers, spoken in a monotonous voice. The answers were usually in the affirmative, sometimes evasive, seldom in the negative. This is how they went usually:

"Da, da, u nas vsyo yest, u nas vsyevo mnogo." (Yes there is plenty of everything in our country.)

"Da, konyechno, eto budyet," etc (Of course it will be like that. We shall return all your things, and there will be soap too. Tomorrow, the day after tomorrow.)

"Nothing to worry about. We shall make you feel safe."

"We don't know where you will be taken. Nor when. No doubt you will be entrained and of course you will be fed properly. Trains in our country are wonderful and restaurants plentiful everywhere. There's plenty of everything in our country."

This last parrot-like refrain – "There's plenty of everything in our country" – so characteristic in its mendacity and which kept recurring, would haunt us for a long time. Even today it still rings in my ears.

Many of the *politruks* were clever men and fluent debaters but everything they said about the Soviet regime was based on expressions and sentences that they had learned by heart during their training. It therefore happened that some of our more excitable speakers, arguing from the weaker position of a prisoner, physically and morally subdued, not sufficiently versed in their social system and inadequately familiar with the Russian language, would lose on points to a seasoned *politruk* who knew by heart the theory of communism, including its critique of capitalism.

In the evening we were officially told that we would be loaded on a train a few hours later. On learning that we were definitely going to be taken into the centre of Soviet Russia a shiver went down our spines.

Friends started flocking together. We were overtaken by a new surge of friendship and a mutual desire to help each other. More and more people seemed to drift into small groups. The average size was about ten men each.

My two old friends from Warsaw – the brothers George and Joe Machlejd* – our families had been friends for years – joined the group I happened to belong to. Our meeting took place in the darkness and stench of the school building. Looking very much alike, they both wore the same uniforms and blue berets they had worn in the Anti-Aircraft Artillery. Both of them had been made prisoners of

* When referring to the brothers Machlejd the author uses English Christian names. This was probably due to the Scottish extraction of their family. As many Scots had done in the bygone ages a Macloud had settled in Poland and the surname changed eventually into Machlejd – *Trs.*

81

war when they were about to cross the Hungarian frontier. They had been driven forcefully on foot, hungry and humiliated. Their morale, however, was remarkably high and we talked for nearly half a day. Feliks Daszynski, tall and thin, looking like Don Basilio, became one of us too. A globetrotter, a polyglot, a sportsman, he was the son of Ignacy Daszynski – a well-known socialist – and a former speaker of the Seym.* Another who joined us was Andrzej Prosinski, a distinguished lawyer from Warsaw, a man of great charm and impeccable manners, looking elegant despite his week-old beard and tattered uniform.

The more farseeing occupants of the school building were behaving like tramps, rummaging in the square and inside the building and collecting all they could lay their hands on: pieces of wood and iron sheets, fragments of wire, nails, even pieces of broken glass, since they thought anything would come in useful later on.

In those last hours preceding our departure we were aware that a nucleus of Polish authority was forming amongst the prisoners. This was regarded as a necessary development because it meant that a channel of communication could then be established, linking the Soviet authorities and the Poles. The real importance of this development, however, was to come to light in the next phase of our life in the Soviet Union.

Dusk was falling when we were told to line up. Soon the whole square was filled with orderly rows of officers. After a roll call it appeared that there were 1,500 officers, from the rank of Colonel to that of Second Lieutenant.

Major Sobieslaw Zaleski appeared in front of us amongst a large group of Soviet *komandirs*. He had been known to me since the dismal war council held in Brzezany. He was a tall man, strongly built with the face of a bulldog, but with an engaging smile. He addressed us in his stentorian voice:

"The Soviet authorities decreed that we should choose from among ourselves a Polish Commander of the camp. Since no one came forward I offered my services to the Soviet authorities. The matter is most important and urgent. We have to form a constant liaison between the community of prisoners and the Soviet authorities. I know the Russian language well and I shall, when the necessity arises, explain to you their measures. I shall also take into my hands all matters of an administrative day-to-day nature. Since all of you will have to become subordinate to my instructions and since I am not the senior officer here – in fact I can see here many

---

* The Polish Parliament.

higher ranks than mine — all I am asking you is to give your agreement and consider me from now on as your superior."

Voices calling "agreed, agreed" rose from the first rows where Colonels, Lieutenant-Colonels and Majors had congregated. Obviously, no one had any desire to fill the position. After a few words exchanged with the Soviet *komandirs* Major Zaleski addressed us once again: "What I can tell you now is that we shall be leaving very soon .... Our destination is unknown and don't take the trouble of trying to solve the mystery, particularly don't ask any questions from your escorts. Such are the regulations concerning the transport of prisoners. We shall be travelling in goods carriages which are waiting here in Jarmolince. There are two types of box-cars — the smaller one which will take 48 men and the larger one which will take 80 men. Please stick to what I've said."

He then asked a few officers who could speak fluent Russian to come forward and help him in his job. After having selected his aides Major Zaleski finally said to us: "Gentlemen, I have taken upon me a great responsibility and a task which is far from being easy. What I am asking of you you already know and what I shall expect from everybody is to cooperate with me in a spirit of comradeship. Since I and my aides have assumed the duty of liaison officers between you and the Soviet authorities I strongly request you to refrain from trying to get directly in touch with them, regardless of their rank and functions. From now on I am going to be your intermediary. On top of that I strongly request that everybody, without exception, should curb their tongues and stop gossip-mongering. It does no good, Gentlemen, and it only points to our weakness. It has a destructive effect on our morale too and in view of the difficult days we are facing, to keep our morale is of paramount importance. And finally I promise you that any specific communication I receive from the Soviet authorities I shall pass on to you immediately."

These were bold as well as meaningful words. There could be no doubt that many *komandirs* and most certainly the *politruks* — although they tried to conceal it — knew Polish. But such was the character of Major Zaleski.

The *politruks* were now busy moving between our ranks. They were obviously no longer relying on the *boytzy* to take the roll calls as this time they were counting us themselves. Others were taking down our names and ranks, but they soon had to stop as it had become very dark by now. A few continued to push their way through our ranks flashing their electric torches in our faces.

8. OUR FIRST CONTACTS WITH SOVIET REALITY

Owing to a strange quirk of fortune two married couples reached Jarmolince as well as several dogs, among them a beautiful Doberman, who was inseparable from his master and would follow him step by step. Although I did hear about the presence of two women among us, I never actually saw them neither during the march nor in the crowded square. Both, dressed in uniforms and greatcoats, were masquerading as men. During the roll call they hid in the darkness and thickness of our ranks. However, nothing came of their attempts to follow their husbands. They were picked out by the Soviet guards and brought by force in front of the assembled men. On seeing this scene we subconsciously flexed our muscles as if wanting to save the women. But sobbing bitterly, they were dragged away and locked up in the school building. A similar fate befell the Doberman dog. Under the threat of having his dog shot on the spot his owner took him and shut him in some shed. As we marched out of the gate of our transit camp the poor animal was heard howling desperately in a pitiful way.

When describing Jarmolince in his immortal trilogy would Henryk Sienkiewicz* have ever expected that in *Anno Domini* 1939 the very same place would play such a part in the dismal story of Polish troops in Soviet bondage!

According to the well tried Soviet system of avoiding at all costs any populated areas we were taken once more along some roundabout paths, even across open fields. At about midnight we arrived at a railway track running along a high bank. There was no trace of any railway station, railway building or any loading platform. Above us, lined up along the track, an enormous black mass of men cast its shade. We communicated with them by shouting. They were all our men — non-commissioned officers and privates — who after our last long march had probably become separated from us. But we had to move on along the railway track for

* Famous Polish novelist, author, among others, of *Quo Vadis*, for which he won the Nobel Prize – *Trs*.

84

another kilometre or so, where we were lined up facing the rails.

After a while we heard a thudding, rumbling noise and soon a long train of huge, empty box-cars appeared. Their weird profiles paraded a long time in front of us until they eventually grinded to a halt with a loud screech.

An enormous box-car of four axles, one for eighty men, came to a halt right in front of us. But when we looked inside it seemed to us hardly possibly that it could hold so many "passengers." We had been told that box-cars, used in the Soviet Union for transporting troops, had a built-in system of two or more tiers of wooden plank beds. However, there was no trace of those "amenities" in this box-car – just a filthy floor covered with a layer of stinking animal excrement. Our churlish guards were shouting in their usual way: "Nu davay, vlezay, zagruzhaysya, poskoryey." (Come on, get inside and make it quick.)

Climbing on each other's shoulders we began boarding the train. Those who had managed to clamber inside first were trying to sweep away the stinking filth. In the complete darkness the box-car gave the impression of a dungeon. But it soon began to fill up. Despite all attempts at observing consideration and care we could not help treading on the legs of those who had already laid down. Swear words mingled with jokes and laughter. We were not allowed to strike a match or to smoke a cigarette. People were still scrambling in and it seemed that the walls would soon start bursting. But the *boytzy* did not stop shouting for a moment: "Vlezay, zagruzhaysya, poplotnyey." (Get inside, get loaded, make it tight, be quick.)

Once in we were ordered to choose from our number a "carriage representative." We felt like a pack of dogs in a pen and no one seemed to be in a hurry to hold such an "honour." On the other hand we were well aware of the fact that it was essential to have a representative for such things like establishing our number, our food rations and for many other necessities too. After a prolonged discussion and much haggling, bordering often on the comical side, a young road-building contractor from Bydgoszcz, Lieutenant Jan Steffen was acclaimed by a majority as our "leader." Whether he liked it or not the brave chap had to accept the mandate although, to the great delight of all, he did not speak a word of Russian.

With its frail anaemic light a candle which a *boyetz* gave us disclosed a scene of utter desolation and depths of human misery and degradation. After a while the heavy doors slid to a close and the locks bolted leaving on one side a gap about ten centimetres wide, no doubt to allow people to carry out their natural functions.

Everyone became very drowsy. We settled down on the floor or, to be more correct, we turned into a mass of stiff bodies. Our heads had the advantage of being propped up against the panels of the box-car walls, but other parts of our bodies, particularly our legs, had to stretch to the opposite sides and would at the best come up to the behinds of those lying in front of us.

"I say, sir, you in front of me this is going a bit far. What the devil do you think you are doing with your legs pushing into my armpits? Pull them up, I don't like being tickled!" was the standard conversation exchanged between us. There were a great number of strapping fellows with long legs who would have gladly had them shortened for the duration of this particular journey!

In order to establish our numbers Steffen counted laboriously for a long time. He started from right to left and after a while in the opposite order, from left to right. A suggestion was put forward that he should count all the legs in the middle of the box-car and divide their number by two. A risky proposition, however, in case the total would prove to be an odd figure. After a great deal of trouble he attained the impressive figure of exactly 88! So they did squeeze us all in after all, right up to the top of our huge rolling box!

The train pulled out around 3 a.m. The date was the 26th September. A complete silence fell in our carriage, even the most talkative refrained from speaking. Hardly anyone could sleep. No wonder – how could one rest and go to sleep in this dark, stinking coffin which thundered monotonously over the rails? Nagging thoughts kept coming to mind – what happens next, where are we being taken, for how many will there be a way back?

I kept imagining what had happened in the nineteenth century when our forefathers suffered the terrible ordeal of deportation to the Siberian mines and penal camps. Immortalized in poetry and prose by Polish literary geniuses, recorded in painting and music, their example inspired later generations. Siberia was the price those men had to pay for taking up, in the Polish insurrections of 1831 and 1863, the fight against the Tsars of Russia. They paid the price for their boldness in defending the rights of the Polish people and in defending the Polish language, both prohibited. Socialist youth suffered in the same way at the turn of the twentieth century for any revolutionary acts directed against Tsarist oppression. Siberia thus became an ominous word and a symbol of Polish martyrdom over a span of 125 years.

After twenty years of freedom in Poland it was now difficult indeed to visualise a journey more dismal and more wrapped up in mystery. A journey leading towards some unknown destination, and the passengers regarded not as individuals but as a mass, a common commodity. For what reason should the Poles bear such a punishment? And by what right? Was it perhaps because they had dared, inadequately armed, to put up a resistance against Hitler? Or were we being penalised by the Soviets for having fought for our rights against the Tsarist regime for 125 years?

Oh, Lord, have mercy on me. Let me see through this most harrowing riddle! In my raving, tired mind appeared three large sign-posts pointing to three distant destinations — that of north, south and east. Sticking out from them in various directions were smaller arrows and one of them would have to be our journey's end. But which one?

What I did already realise was that our convoy was just one of many which were taking the overpowered Polish Army from Poland to the USSR. There must have been hundreds of such convoys either being taken west by the Germans or east by the Soviets.

Our train halted for the first time in the early morning. The *boytzy* started unbolting the doors on one side of the box-cars. Our unshaven and filthy faces, our stained and crushed uniforms and greatcoats looking as if they had been torn out of a dog's throat, were revealed in the bright daylight. We were allowed to leave our box-cars, and we jumped off as fast as we could to enjoy a breath of fresh air. We found ourselves amongst a maze of railway tracks and goods trains. One of the trains contained Soviet troops and the flat wagons were loaded with field guns, ammunition trailers and light armour. Hundreds of bewildered faces gaped at us from the open doors of box-cars similar to our own. We asked the Soviets where they were going. They answered reluctantly and shyly: "Govoryat w Polshu. A tepyer to ush nye Polsha, a zapadnaya Ukraina, da zapadnaya Byelorusya. A vy to shto? Polyaki, Pany?" (They say to Poland. But now it's no longer Poland but Western Ukraine or Western Byelorussia. And who are you? Poles, "Panys"?)

Completely stunned I felt as if somebody had hit me on the head. New geographical terms, new ethnographic concepts! Some huge, historical upheaval was taking place in Europe of which we were informed by a *boyetz* on his way to Poland.

Walking away was strongly forbidden. We were allowed however to go up to the water pump. We stripped down to the waist and washed, splashing water like little children. We filled all utensils in our possession with water — the excellent Polish mess-tins and water bottles, known as bananas on account of their shape, as well as mugs and often strange pots which had fallen into our hands during our journey as Soviet prisoners.

Near the engine of the train I bumped into an old friend of mine from Gdynia, Captain Jan Blichiewicz. How on earth did he manage to reach this God-forsaken place? This man, weighing at least 18 stone and well into his sixties, had been forced to march on an empty stomach. He was shaving his rounded face and washing most meticulously in hot but filthy water which he had scooped out of a pipe on the engine! I followed his example, using the shaving accessories which he kindly put at my disposal.

We drew our ration of bread which was a quarter of a loaf each. With much difficulty I dissolved in cold water the last few remaining cubes of processed coffee that I had in my pocket. I had to be content with this for my breakfast.

The cry "Zagruzhaysya" (Get loaded) resounded suddenly along the whole length of our train. Doors were bolted and we found ourselves again in an almost complete darkness. Only a thin shaft of light penetrated the narrow urinating aperture between the wet and stinking boards of our box-car. This was also used as our observation point but could only be manned by a few people who in loud voices were describing to us what they saw. We listened avidly.

Enormous undulating stretches of arable land were tinged with the gold of stubble and here and there were covered with big patches of uncollected wheat. The golden uniformity of the fields would be interrupted in many places by vivid black stripes of freshly ploughed up soil. Hardly any buildings were to be seen nor, for that matter, people working in the fields. Very rarely a slow-moving tractor or a single truck hopping along a field track would appear. A few herds of scraggy, lean cattle completed this strangely dormant, autumnal picture of the Ukrainian countryside. And yet this was supposed to be agriculturally the richest province of the Soviet Union. We assumed that owing to the centralization and mechanization of agriculture in the USSR according to the system of large *kolkhozes* and *sovkhozes*, the work in the fields would not be so apparent to passengers on a train.

Still, many of our farmers, peering with great curiosity at the Ukrainian cornfields, through the crack of the box-car, could not fail to notice with their alert and expert eyes the substantial deficiencies in the tilling of the soil. There were huge bald spots caused by careless, untidy sowing, and considerable amounts of good soil had been wasted due to extravagant and faulty ploughing. The vast stretches of uncultivated, fallow land were also hard to explain as they seemed to be unfit even for pasture. And finally there was the sight of corn which had not been brought in on time and which in view of the already strong ground frost must have become overgrown and rotted. These were the first and obvious manifestations of a society where people had been deprived of their possessions.

Without any apparent reason the train would halt from time to time either in the open or in a maze of railway tracks but never in front of a railway station. We were all suffering increasingly from hunger and thirst. On top of that because of the sunny weather our box would get unbearably hot and stuffy. Some men were squatting, others standing in order to stretch their aching limbs. To overcome the feeling of apathy which was gradually getting the better of us we were talking in small groups keeping our voices down. I was leaning my aching back against Zygmunt's raised knee, only to curl up after a while and lay my head on his lap. This magnificent man proved to be a tower of strength and my real support. He was relating most interesting things about the virgin forest of Bialowieza and its bison, about the art of forestry and about his studies abroad. His beautiful, melodious voice had a caressing and soothing effect on us and we were cheered up by his delightfully robust sense of humour and laughter. Laud, on the other hand, was in bad shape. We were trying to draw him into our conversation but he would not say a word. Lying motionless on his back he had his eyes glued to the ceiling of the box-car. We were even more worried about George Machlejd. He was in the grip of a fierce fever and despite all the rags and overcoats we had heaped on him he was shaking like a leaf. He was raving and groaning incessantly. Not possessing any medicaments we were absolutely helpless. How utterly depressing it was to think that on these very boards, still stinking of excrement, lying unconscious, in a state of high fever, was a young thirty-eight year old member of the Seym, elected only a year ago by the people of Warsaw: a doctor of philosophy, a distinguished historian and amateur geographer.

Many of our companions remembered the area we were passing from the time dating before the Russian Revolution. We were listening avidly to their tales and to their descriptions of various localities. There was much arguing as to their respective names, distances and the direction towards which we were presumed to be heading. We were soon clear on the last point – we were heading for the city of Kiev.

We first glimpsed the attractive silhouette of that city in the early hours of the evening. The sight of the many churches which had survived the anti-religious campaign, their domes glittering in the last rays of the sun, left us in no doubt that this was the capital of the Ukraine. A wave of great excitement overtook us and our box-car turned into a real bee-hive. All this, however, did not last long. The train had no intention whatsoever of stopping at the railway station. Using various side tracks from which nothing could be seen it was

ploughing ahead until somewhere a long way past the city, after a few moments of hesitation, it came to an abrupt halt. A high bank, completely concealing any view, rose in front of us and close to the box-car ran a fence of barbed wire. A long spell of suspense and silence followed. Nothing happened for a long while. At last, however, bolts were loosened up and doors half opened. The head of a *boyetz* appeared in the opening. We also caught sight of a long thin, bayonet. The *boyetz* looked inside and shouted: "Ey, vy tam, komyendant. Skolko u vas ludyey v vagonye?" (Hey, you Commander! How many men do you have in your box-car?)

Our Commander, Steffen, mumbled the figure of eighty-eight in his own peculiar language of which the *boyetz* did not understand a word. We explained in Russian in chorus and fired at him a string of questions.

"Pozhaluy dadut vam poobiedat." (It's likely you'll be getting a meal.) The *boyetz* emitted these few words after some reflection. The news was met with a general outburst of enthusiasm and the bemused *boyetz* was overcome with compliments and cheers. It was not a joke, we really meant it. We Poles are outgoing kind-hearted people. Ever since our first contact with Soviet soldiers we had been trying without success to elicit a gesture of humanity from them. Now it had come it brought out in us a response of sincere friendliness, affability, even gratitude.

Our *boyetz* slid the other half of the door open and made us unload and form in pairs. One orderly and those who were sick – as it happened, there were few of them – were to stay put. It was decided we would bring them food in our own utensils.

Moving at a snail's pace we had to queue up for three long hours before, thoroughly frozen, we reached the lit-up windows of the canteen. What misery and humiliation we had to go through by waiting such a long time for a piece of bread and a bowl of soup.

Railway canteens have existed for a number of years in most of the more important railway stations of the Soviet Union. In view of the general lack of restaurants in the USSR as well as a very limited number of dining cars operating on a few main lines and catering for privileged passengers only, they obviously became a necessity. Since travelling in the Soviet Union is a mass phenomenon the aim of these canteens is also to feed large numbers of people. Mass transport in that country is a normal everyday occurrence. This is because of several factors, such as, for example, the forcible movement of population to remote places like Kazakstan or Eastern Siberia. Also, there is a constant shuttle service taking an enormous number of workers from one place to another according to local needs. And there is a constant migration of prisoners transported to forced labour camps over distances of thousands of kilometres and the movement of troops and recruits.

The Polish prisoners from our convoy were taken to the sort of canteen I have described. It was well after midnight when my group, starved, numb and almost frozen to death, arrived at the longed-for destination. The main hall contained long files of benches and tables on which huge jars filled with soup were steaming most enticingly. Enamelled bowls and spoons could be seen and also portions of bread for every person. Knives and forks are things rarely used in the Soviet Union and still more rarely seen. Spoons, on the other hand, are a universal eating utensil.

We sat near to each other so that as many men as possible could squeeze in at the tables. We started with the tasty soup called *shchi*, laced with milk. The new environment with its electric light, its warmth, tables, benches — and of course food — contrasted so strongly with the black box-car that we simply could not believe it. Those of us particularly sensitive and prone to optimism had already mounted a galloping steed of fantasy and were devising various rosy visions of days to come.

We were served quickly, mainly by young, plain, bosomy girls. Despite our deplorable appearance, our innate Polish gallantry was aroused by the sight of them. We talked to them in Russian all the time saying things such as "thank you very much, yes, this is very nice indeed, how nice to be able to sit here" and the like. Sometimes our conversation would provoke a ghost of a smile. Less often, although uttered with visible fear, even a word with some human undertone was spoken. There was no question, however, of a lengthy conversation. The *politruks*, who during our journey on the train seemed to have vanished, once more made an appearance and were doing the rounds of the hall. In such favourable conditions they would not, of course, miss the opportunity to talk to us and to drag us into making confidences. And there could have been no easier starting point than to ask a starving man whether he enjoyed food which had been offered to him. Of course the man liked it, in fact liked it very much. So the ball of conversation was sent rolling in the right direction. And this was exactly what they were aiming at.

A portion of goulash with millet gruel and a mug of tea with sugar as a dessert were our next courses. After this "feast" we were overcome with a kind of drowsiness. Some of us were now talking of settling down in an easy chair, some would have preferred a sofa, others were dying for a Havana cigar. After being deep frozen for so long our bodies now became warm, our muscles and nerves started to relax and we sat back and surveyed the scene sleepily. All this led us to believe, for a brief moment, that we had gone back to normal conditions. The spell was soon broken when we realized that we had to get up and return to reality. More of our men were waiting outside in long queues and in bitter cold for their turn to be let in. Joe Machlejd took along with him some food for his sick brother. In order to retain the warmth gained in the canteen and to get some sleep until next morning we covered the distance back to our lairs in the stinking box-cars at a brisk walk.

For the next forty-eight hours we continued our eastward journey, but this time on a bread and water diet only. The train was shuffling along, halting frequently. We were allowed, from time to time, to get off and relieve ourselves. We would then see an unusual sight. Wherever the train stopped, no matter whether in an open field or in a railway junction, masses of human excrement could be seen everywhere – between the rails on the sand, on the sleepers, in the ditches, even in the fields. Why was this? The answer is simple. Most people in the Soviet Union travel *en masse* but not on normal passenger trains which possess the usual toilet facilities. They are transported in box-cars exactly like ours, with no toilets available. So what are the poor wretches supposed to do? Consequently we too paid our tribute to Mother Earth. I would have given much for the chance of photographing such a scene – people in action in a squatting position.

We passed the town of Poltava on the afternoon of 28th September. From then on it was pretty certain we were going to Kharkov. Sure enough, we arrived there on the same night. And here, at the strange hour of 3 a.m. exactly, we were woken by prolonged shouts. Dinner was ready for us! And we were to get up without further delay! We rose in record time as if some fire had broken out and were faced with the same procedure as before. The canteen was similar to that of Kiev. This time, however, we were less impressed. All we had was a bowl of *shchi* with a scrap of meat and some bread. We saw nothing of the huge city of Kharkov.

Our train halted about midday on some side track. Doors were slid open and we were allowed to get off. The name "Kupyansk" could be seen on a middle-sized station building. It meant nothing to us, however. As usual we made a dash to the water pump. Word went round that *kipyatok* was available. Several times before where our box-cars had stopped there had been a little brick building with a boiler inside and a tap outside from which one could draw boiling water – the famous Russian *kipyatok*.

From time immemorial, since Rurik's* epoch probably, *kipyatok* like bread has been part of the Russian way of life. Neither is there any shortage of it in today's Soviet Union. With a few tea leaves added it is drunk in the day time and during the night, indoors and outdoors, in the freezing cold and in scorching heat. We also developed a liking for this boiling water. "When in Rome do as the Romans do" as the saying goes.

At Kupyansk our train stopped for some reason by a vast group of civilians. Standing on both sides of the line, they were presumably waiting for another train. Why we were allowed to stop no one knows. Was it the engine driver who halted the engine in the wrong place or the dozing *komandirs*, overlooking the fact that the unavoidable consequence of our leaving the box-cars for a while would be that Polish prisoners would come into contact with a large number of ordinary Russian people, albeit in a remote part of the Ukraine? Whatever the reason, however, both these people and ourselves were equally surprised by this unscheduled stop. Not a minute had elapsed when all along the file of box-cars our khaki uniforms were seen mingling with the grey jackets and working blouses of men and women. Not knowing why a mass of foreign soldiers had suddenly descended on them here, in the centre of the Ukraine, they approached us at first with shyness and distrust, but a burning curiosity soon got the upper hand.

Speaking in fluent Russian my two friends and I struck up a conversation with a group of people. Some of them were stocky men in the prime of life rather sure of themselves – clad in dark *roubashki* (shirts) and boots with tops in the shape of a harmonica. There were also some women covered with shawls in such a way that one could have imagined they were ashamed of themselves, an old man with long grey hair leaning on a stick, a few gaping youngsters and an old woman, her face furrowed by wrinkles, wrapped up in an old worn-out black shawl. Although they were scowling whilst looking at us we could sense they were devouring us with their eyes. The youngsters touched our uniforms. Attracting everybody's attention, the excellent quality of Zygmunt's boots and my clipped leather tops stole the show. One of the men, visibly fascinated by the latter, touched and caressed them shaking his head in admiration: "Kozha to ush ochen khorosza, skolko to khochesh za nich?" (Your leather is no doubt very good quality. How much do you want for them?) he asked, ready to clinch a deal on the spot. I answered that

*Semi-legendary ruler of one of the oldest principalities in ancient Russia. Of Norman stock he settled there in the ninth century and became the founder of a dynasty which eventually ruled over a united Russia. – Trs.

unfortunately I had nothing else to put on and was in no position to sell them. Paying hardly any attention to what we were saying he went on ogling my tops intently. Our conversation would get stuck for words from time to time. We were speaking Russian, their language was closer to Ukrainian.

They obviously wanted to know where we came from. We told them from Warsaw. "But where is Warsaw?" asked one of the women. The grey haired old man forestalled our answer: "Da izvyestno v Polshe! Vot dura ty etakaya!" (In Poland you silly goose, everyone knows that.) Another women added a comment: "Eto gorod v panskoy Polshe. A vy to shto, vsye voyennyje oficery?" (It's a city in the country of the Polish "pany's." And all of you, what are you — army officers?) Her words could not fail to disclose a touch of malice, but common curiosity prevailed.

We explained to them our status as prisoners of war and how, without the slightest intention on our side of going to war against the Soviet Union, we were surreptitiously attacked and disarmed by the Red Army while we were engaged in a gruelling war against Hitler. They shook their heads, looking over their shoulders with fear in their eyes.

They were well aware that all men under sentence, no matter whether common prisoners or prisoners of war, were the same as lepers — contaminated beings who shouldn't be touched. Displays of curiosity, let alone compassion, might be regretted later.

We asked a few more perfunctory questions, such as: "What about food, will it be possible after we have reached our destination to buy this and that?" . . . There was silence. They stood, scratching their heads. A fight must have been going on inside them, a fight between instilled mendacity and a sense of honesty. At last, without much conviction, a man answered one of our questions: "Da pozhaluy rozryeshat vam kupit jedu i vyeshchi" (Yes, maybe they will allow you to buy some food and other things.) Laughing, a not unattractive young women added with some pathos: "U nas vsyo yest, u nas vsyevo mnogo," (There's plenty of everything in our country) which brought a ghost of a smile to the faces of the others. It seemed that this parrot phrase, which we had heard when we first came into contact with the Soviets, was being repeated all over the country, including the Ukraine.

At the sight of the *boyetzy* and at the sound of their "rozaydis" the crowd, who so far had not seemed unduly worried about them, started to disperse slowly. But when the NKVD came into sight their behaviour was very different. Travelling separately and in comfort in the only coach on the train, the *politruks* and other *komandirs* had just realised the results of their deplorable negligence. On seeing their red caps the crowd broke up hastily. In a state of panic, they ran about shouting and scolding so as to put an end as quickly as possible to the scandalous show of fraternisation.

For a while the old woman remained at my side. I asked her how she was keeping, how life was treating her. Tears showed in her eyes: "Badly, my son, very badly. Everything is so different now and life is so hard, there is nothing but a great deal of misery all around. But you 'golubushka' (my little pigeon) you must run along to your carriage as otherwise they might beat you up. And God only knows where they will take you! Here, take this, it's not much use for me and to you it may come in useful. May God be with you!" With her bony, shaking fingers she pushed a few coins into my hand. I accepted the gift. I took the alms offered to me by a poor, old women out of goodness and compassion, from the depths of her heart. "Blagodariu, spasibo vam bolshoye" (I'm most thankful, thank you so much), I whispered deeply moved. This is why I remember the railway station of Kupyansk so well.

They made short work of us and order was soon restored. When the heavy bolts were pushed across we became overcome by darkness in our airless, stuffy box-cars as if night had suddenly fallen. Before our train pulled out we watched through the cracks in the boards the people who had remained on the platform. They were standing motionless, staring blankly at the huge red car in which "Polyaki" – the Poles – were being taken to some unknown destination in the depths of their country. And who knows, perhaps some of them were thinking at that moment of their fathers, their brothers or sons who, in box-cars like ours had been taken as far as the Siberian hard labour camps, perhaps for a temporary stretch or perhaps for ever. All this for offences defined in such a simple way that either you are an enemy of the people of an enemy of the workers' revolution.

Thinking back to our short contact with the Soviet people we discussed what had happened and repeated what we had been told. I turned in the palm of my hand the five coins I had been given. They amounted to eighty kopeks. "Look at what I was given by the good old soul," I said. "Eighty kopeks – a genuine alms offered by one beggar to another beggar! I am deeply moved."

Laud, who had gone back to his usual position of lying on the floor and staring at the ceiling, said after a while as if waking from a sleep: "I told you the ordinary people are not what you thought. For twenty years the authorities have tried to eradicate from their bodies all human reactions, to stultify their brains and immunize their hearts to the misery of their fellow creatures. But there are still left in them some feelings of goodwill, kindheartedness and understanding of the unhappiness of others. It was not only the old people who showed compassion, their feelings formed and were given substance before the State tried to rid them of such emotional 'irregularities'. Their pity was shared, though to a lesser degree I must admit, by the younger people too. Led by their instinct and possibly a pinch of curiosity, they realised the nature of our tragedy — the tragedy of a mass of powerless, foreign troops driven here from a country far away.

"And although we come from different countries and speak different languages and wear military uniforms, I didn't have the feeling that those people were looking upon us as their enemies. Nor did they regard their own *boytzy* and *komandirs,* who were pushing us around so much, as great heroes. Quite the contrary. It was only after they'd caught sight of the red caps of the NKVD that I sensed in their eyes a flash of fear and hate — just as though they were confronting a real enemy. It's a strange country here and odd things will happen . . . " he added with a sigh.

Zygmunt drew up his long legs, leaned his head against his knees and, looking into Laud's face, said, in his calm, persuasive voice: "This is all very fine, my dear Laud — you are an incorrigible old poet. But even if these people were sincere in their friendliness towards us — although I have strong reservations about this myself — you must not forget, damn it, that we didn't come on a visit here and it won't be they who will be receiving us with true Slavic hospitality and wiping our tears away, either here or wherever our engine should care to take us. Don't forget that we are in the clutches of the NKVD and they are a very different kettle of fish. This 'prestigious' organisation exists for the purpose of maintaining the Communist system and to punish severely those who endanger it. Now you should ask yourself the following question, my dear Laud: Why have we found ourselves in their power? The answer is simple. It is because from the point of view of our national, our religious as well as our class convictions we are thought to be a risk. This would apply if we were still in Poland, under Soviet control. Whether there or in the Soviet Union, we are all seen as a threat to the established order. This is what all of us must bear in mind.

"And there is one more thing I want to tell you," Zygmunt continued, getting more and more excited. "When climbing into our box-car I saw Major Zaleski. As he is the best informed of us all I asked him whether it was true that we were now in the hands of the NKVD and not of the Red Army? Whereupon he roared in his usual way: 'Yes, it is true indeed! Our protectors are now the NKVD.' I replied: 'Why is this so, Sir? Why the devil should we be in the hands of a police organisation and not, according to the custom of war, in the hands of the Red Army?' The Major said in his flippant way: 'Why? You'd better ask Uncle Joe! I can see you've got fright, cold feet . . . eh? Never mind, you'll get used to it. And one more thing. In the future I strongly recommend that you refrain from scenes like the one a while ago with the local population or you'll pay a high price. Remember my warning, and tell your companions.' "

Zygmunt presented Major Zaleski's words in a loud, clear voice addressed to all of us in the box-car. They were received in silence and no comments were made.

We passed a station at a place called Valuyski. Darkness was falling and it became very cold. Like sheep, we pressed against each other to keep warm. I would wake up every quarter of an hour or so with pain in my hips, loins and shoulders and particularly with a strange burning pain in the lobe of my ear, which was pressed against some bundle hard as stone. No wonder I was yearning for a soft pillow. The wound in my head was healing gradually but the hard scab stuck to my hair and tore at it mercilessly. Felo Daszynski was talking incessantly of some oil in Venezuela or Columbia. George Machlejd would now and then add a few remarks. Although still very weak he was beginning to feel better.

9. CAMP STAROBYELSK

At about seven o'clock in the morning of 30th September, our train ground to a sudden halt, causing the long string of box-cars to jar against each other. Many minutes later, the guards slid open the heavy rusty doors. It was a clear cold day and our teeth were chattering. In the sunlight we looked repulsive – dirty, unshaven, unkempt.

Our box-car had stopped almost opposite a station building bearing the sign "Starobyelsk". There was no trace of any civilians, except for a few railroad workers who paid not the slightest attention to us. Close by were two or three warehouses and the familiar mushroom-shaped water tank mounted on a pole – THE *vodokachka*. Further off there was a melancholy landscape – sandy, hilly terrain with occasional clumps of withered grass, huts arranged helter-skelter, and trees, by now bare of leaves, veiled in the morning mist and white with a heavy frost.

As usual, we dashed for water to wash ourselves and to drink. There was a cauldron with boiling water. So we started off the day with a drink of our *kipyatok*, just as if we were taking the cure at some spa back in Poland. Then we walked up and down the platform. An hour flew by, and then we saw several horse-drawn field kitchens arrive. In the twinkling of an eye we had queued up on the station platform. We stood in line patiently for a long time, as we had done before. The experience we were gaining was to stand us in good stead. When we got to the cauldrons, we were handed a bowl and a spoon each, which we were allowed to keep. The bowl was filled with hot oatmeal (*kasha*) and we were also given half a loaf of black bread.

After another two hours we heard the drawn out cries: "Davay, sobiraysya s vyeshchami!" (Come along with your things!)

We had already learned that there were two basic ways of summoning us that were similar and yet diametrically opposite in meaning. One was "Davay, sobiraysya" and implied an ordinary roll call. The other, "Davay, sobiraysya s vyeshchami" was fraught with far-reaching implications, for the addition of the words "with your things" indicated that we were to be transferred immediately to another place.

Everybody made a break for the box-cars to sort out their scattered belongings from the miserable mess and to make up bundles, knapsacks or suitcases. The place suddenly took on the aspect of a madhouse. The "s vyeshchami" version of the command was a matter of indifference to me, for I had been carrying all my worldly goods on my person and therefore had no need to enter that loathsome car for a last look around.

Major Zaleski and his aides urged us to fall into line quickly and to maintain order and discipline. This time we ranged ourselves four abreast. The roll call indicated that more than 2,500 people had arrived on our train. While we were falling in, the empty box-cars rattled away and a new serpentine train rolled into the station. Jammed into box-cars like ours, its passengers waved to us through the cracks in the as yet unopened doors and called out words of greeting in Polish. They were compatriots. A fresh transport of prisoners had arrived.

That would suggest that we had reached our destination. Could this really be journey's end? Would we ride any further? Was this the start of a new, perhaps permanent, phase of our enslavement? Excited and consumed by curiosity we showered our guards and *politruks* with questions. Where are they taking us? Will we have far to go? What sort of a place is this Starobyelsk? The guards maintained a dead silence. The *politruks,* strangely for them, were not very communicative either. "Nu nye byezpokoytyes, vskorye sami uriditye!" (Don't worry, you'll soon find out for yourselves.)

"Ma-a-a-rch!" the command rang out in front and its obedient echo travelled down to the far end of the column.

We moved forward along the wide impassable road, criss-crossed by treacherous ruts, and entered the town proper, or rather a typical village, sprawling lazily over the barren sands. A well beaten path ran parallel to the poor-looking huts and rickety fences. On this path the inhabitants of Starobyelsk gathered slowly and fearfully to watch our strange procession. The younger children and the adolescents, boldly lined up in front. Behind them the women, young and old, stood in knots. Their colourless faces, all of them alike, mirrored their surprise and curiosity.

Occasionally we caught awed whispers: "Smotri, smotri, vyedut Polyakov!" (Look, look they're leading Poles.) Sometimes a boy's high-pitched insolent voice cries: "Polyaki! Pa-nih!" The latter word, spat out by these young lips, perverted in meaning by Soviet propaganda, was painful to hear.

But elsewhere in the row of interested faces we came upon an old mother who betrayed her compassion in a barely perceptible but unmistakable swaying of the head. We saw the face of a girl brightened by the trace of what may have been a friendly smile. Ever hungry for signs of human emotions, ready to pay in gold for the copper coins of kindness, we smiled and conveyed our greetings by a wave of the hand. But nobody dared to wave back at us.

The deeper we moved into town, the thicker was the crowd of spectators. The guards acted like sheep dogs, running up and down along our columns and chasing away the intrepid souls who came too close to our flock. But their zeal was unnecessary for the population was well trained and knew that talking to those under convoy was forbidden.

No doubt, the most sensational thing about us in this sad sleepy town was our external appearance. The natives stared with unconcealed curiosity at our different faces, at the unfamiliar cut of our uniforms, at our four-cornered caps and our off-duty caps with silver eagles, at the silver stars on our epaulets! Those epaulets, symbols of class enmity, objects of hatred and mockery trampled in the mad fury of revolution . . . . They looked us over, they whispered amongst themselves, they wondered, but they did not mock. They pointed at those epaulets, at the high boots in good condition that some of us still had, at the knapsacks, at the occasional leather suitcases, at the colourful steamer rugs (for some possessed these) and the blankets. And though it was not pleasant to be the target of hundreds of pointing fingers, we did try to understand that the motive was not ill-will but simple human curiosity. The populace of Starobyelsk had never witnessed a spectacle like this march of thousands of human beings, whom, for the first time since the half-forgotten days of the Revolution, Soviet Russia was forcibly assimilating from beyond its own airtight borders. Though they were guarded by bayonets, these newcomers from distant Poland seemed neither terrible nor formidable . . . .

The vanguard of the column made a few turns. In the centre of the street there suddenly came into a view a narrow hump of useless pavement consisting of field stones. Apparently we were near the centre of town. The wooden buildings were now interspersed with old one- or two-storey brick structures. They housed the remnants of pitiful stores selling junk, but they were generously draped with red paper bunting and displayed the faded portraits of heroics of the revolution.

We could not help feeling pity at the sight of all this misery and melancholy.

Though we were prodded on, we proceeded slowly, for we were weakened by hunger and fatigue. We made another turn and found ourselves on a side road, which, judging from the fewer number of buildings, lead to the town limits. This street, or rather road of sand and clay, was called Kirov Street. After his murder in 1934 at the hands of anti-regime fanatics, the Kremlin perpetuated the name of this outstanding Communist Party leader in thousands of towns, villages, collective farms, factories and streets. I don't think I am wrong in stating that the "use" of Kirov's name in the Soviet Union ranks third, directly after Lenin and Stalin.

In the distance, on the left side of the road, a high long wall glistened white. Silhouetted against the sky behind the wall were the rooftops of a number of buildings dominated by the bulbous outline of a dark blue church cupola. As we approached the wall, we saw that it was reinforced on the outside by a high barbed wire abatis and dotted with many wooden mushroom-shaped towers inside which we saw machine guns and huge searchlights.

The column's vanguard came to a halt, wavered and then started to disappear inside a gate in the wall opposite the church. It took a long time to enter the gate because our guards again counted us slowly and laboriously.

From outside the gate I took a good look at the building on the other side of the wall. It was a big ungainly edifice, several stories in height, though there were no windows in the upper part. Placed asymmetrically on its summit was a copper cupola covered with a green patina, its sharp point adorned by a cross, still bearing the trace of gilding, with the diagonal Orthodox line cutting through below it. The cross did not reach upward in a proud vertical line. Corroded at its base by the rust of time, it hung crooked and inert. Symbolising sadness and oblivion it somehow extended a sorrowful welcome to the Polish soldiers.

Soon the creaky gate of Camp Starobyelsk was swung in place behind us.

In the next few hours, the prisoners who had come in our wake also poured into the camp. Nor was this all. During the next twenty-four hours, the camp population was further augmented by yet more prisoners, this time chiefly enlisted men. The population of the camp soon numbered about 10,000 people.

To visualize this mass of humanity requires a vivid imagination. It is not enough to conjure up a picture of a football stadium or of a huge cinema in which every spectator has his appointed place in a comfortable chair where he will spend a few hours in agreeable circumstances. The reader has to try and imagine an area of eight and a half acres surrounded by a thick wall six feet high, crowded with the most varied conglomeration of buildings — churches, cottages, stables, barns, sheds and storehouses, in a state of utter ruin, with or without roofs, having only beaten earth covered by dried manure or rotted boards for a floor, with rats and mice cavorting all over the place, with bedbug- and flea-infested double-decker bunks, and as far as the major part of the compound is concerned, with *no* shelter save the sky above and Mother Earth below. Within this area 10,000 people must somehow manage to live.

Starobyelsk — a country town situated in a barren area of the eastern Ukraine, within the radius of the industrial Don Basin, on the Valuyki-Voroshilovgrad railroad line, on the Aydar River, which is a tributary of the Donyets River, which is in turn a tributary of the Don. As the crow flies, it is 250 kilometres north of Taganrog. That was the information given us by George Machlejd, our infallible geographer, who carried in his head a detailed facsimile of the globe. Having shaken off his fever, he had regained his old spirit and had put his memory apparatus back into its original fine shape. And he certainly had a perfect command over that apparatus. Later on, when world developments drove us to seek geographical facts, George would give us precise information, without us having to consult maps, which none of us had anyway since they were strictly forbidden. Even if a clipping of a small war map published in the Soviet press happened to be found in some prisoner's pocket during inspection, it was confiscated forthwith and the hapless culprit was condemned to hunger and cold in solitary confinement.

Unfortunately, however, George's aptitudes did not stand him in good stead as far as the history of our camp terrain was concerned! It was a long time before we arrived at a relatively accurate history of our prison, the "Starobyelski Monastyr". But we managed it, with the aid of our sixth sense, our suppositions, our excavations and brief interviews with the occasional civilian workers who appeared in the camp. All our attempts to lift the curtain of secrecy from the Monastery's history by interrogating the *politruks* were completely futile. These are topics that fail to arouse the conversational instinct in the guardians of Soviet ideology.

Until the outbreak of the revolution of 1917, the Monastery housed the Orthodox clerical seminary which produced Orthodox priests. We were able to speculate about the scope and level of the knowledge which the graduates of this ecclesiastical forge disseminated throughout the Russian world by, twenty-two years later, living the kind of life they lived in the same primitive conditions. During the Revolution, the place had served as the site for a large-scale massacre, traces of which were still visible in many spots. All we had to do was a little digging to come upon heaps of human skulls and bones. It was rumoured that after the churchmen had been murdered, many other executions had taken place inside these mysterious walls. In several parts of the east wall the bricks bore the unmistakable bullet-chipped contours of the head and chest of unfortunate victims, who had been stood against the wall of their open execution chamber and had given up the ghost to God on this consecrated ground. Whenever we passed this grim sight, and we passed it often, we could not control a shudder of horror.

After the revolutionary period, the Soviet authorities transformed the Monastery grounds into either a prison or military barracks, to judge by the numerous bunks and the brick two-storey building which was relatively new and barrack-type, having been erected probably in the 1920s. All the remaining buildings dated from the dim past.

Our first impression when the gate was bolted behind us was that after a long chase, we had finally been trapped like mice. At the very outset, as we passed through the gate, the throng of *komandirs* and *politruks* assembled on the stone steps leading to the monumental church gave us orders in a sharper, more commanding voice than hitherto, brandishing their revolvers as they regulated traffic. They directed officers to the left, to the northern part of the camp, and enlisted men and NCOs straight ahead and to the right.

Zygmunt, Laud, the brothers George and Joe Machlejd, Felo Daszynski, Olgierd Szpakowski and I formed a group of seven. We bivouacked on grass that had not yet been trampled. Nearby, Andrew Prosinski, Bogdan Janowski and Marian Piskorski encamped in their own congenial group.

It felt good to stretch out on the ground instead of on the black boards of the box-car, to stare at the clear sky that looked the same the world over, to forget, if only for a moment, one's misery and worries and to know that one was surrounded by loyal friends. And though the human anthill around us hummed and swarmed we lay there a long time, shutting away reality. Our affluent Olgierd had managed to lug his precious belongings all the way from Poland with our aid. He now offered us his last few good cigarettes and spread out his soft sheepskin in which I nestled like a lover to his mistress's bosom.

The hours went by. Dusk fell and brought a penetrating cold with it. In pairs we went on an inspection tour. We peered into a few buildings and sheds but we were out of luck. Every corner, every board of the bunks was already occupied by bodies and rubbish. Surely, we would be better off outdoors. That's what we thought. But when day died away, when we began to feel the hunger gnawing inside us, when the frost started to clot the damp earth, we dragged ourselves up from our sties and went in search of shelter.

Zygmunt and I wandered a long time in the pitch darkness, which was illuminated occasionally by the blinding glare of a searchlight. Stumbling over the piles of human bodies that seemed to be lying everywhere, we finally squeezed into the black maw of a big building. It was the old church with the broken cross on the top. We bedded down on the rotting floor in the huge hall which resounded up to its very dome with the humming of lowered voices and the breathing of a thousand people in uneasy sleep.

The building in which we had slept had, years ago, been a kind of supplementary hall used for religious occasions. Daily services were held in it as well as courses in religion and classes in choral singing. Adjacent to this main hall were the living quarters of the friars. The main church would be used for "molebni" (religious services) on Sundays and feastdays only, conducted with all the pomp of the Greek-Orthodox faith.

All this I learned secretly, at some later date, from an old *govnovoz* (shit carrier) who would, from time to time, turn up in the camp with a long, cucumber shaped barrel, drawn by a thin, shaggy horse and used for removing our excrement from the latrine. My conversations with this brave old man, whose face was completely covered by a long matted beard, used to take place in conditions of strict secrecy. That is, when with the help of a bucket fixed to a long pole he was toiling heavily, drawing out from the deep ditch of the latrine the revoltingly stinking liquid; I, seated on a beam like a crow perched on a pole, would pretend to perform my natural functions, while in reality bombarding him with questions. It was impossible to talk in public as it would have cost the *dyadya** a heavy penalty.

He could well remember the old times when on feast days the gates of the monastery were left wide open and huge crowds of worshippers would fill up the church. The singing was beautiful and everything seemed so colourful and splendid. Once Laud offered the old man a tiny metal cross which he was probably given at some church fair. The *dyadya* was overwhelmed: "Krestika to ja ush davno nie vidal. U nas tyepyer ikh nyetu." (Haven't seen a cross for a long time. None are to be had now.) He would thank us with tears in his kind, deeply-set eyes for the slice of bread or pinch of *makhorka†* which we

*Old man – Trs.   † Cheap, inferior kind of tobacco – Trs.

104

would offer him on his visits. His condition, one of a permanent, hopeless misery, was even worse than ours. "Spasibo vam, barin," (Thank you, Sir) he would say using the old term applied by a servant when addressing his master, "dobryje vy, milostivyje liudi." (You are good, kind people.)

Our building was known at the time as "building number five". It sounded slightly more vivid in the Russian − "blok nomyer pyat". We, however, named it "the Circus". This was because of the many tiers of bunks in the buildings. These were extremely hard to reach, calling for the agility of a monkey.

The main hall, which was once the nave of the church and was now black with old age and filth, had been fitted for many years with a weird structure of bunks which reached seven tiers high into the cupola. All the bunks differed in manufacture. Some consisted of loose boards, others of logs and only a few were held together by nails. The whole structure was liable to collapse at any moment. To enable people to move up and down the lower levels were connected by steep, rickety stairs, the higher bunks by small ladders and finally at the top of the flimsy structure there were iron or wooden clamps driven into the main supporting timber. The lower parts were constantly shrouded in darkness, made even darker by the clouds of particles of dirt which fell from the top. Access to the upper bunks was more difficult and even dangerous, but they were considered to be the better ones. This was because of the small amount of light and fresh air which would seep through the holes in a row of small hatches running around the cupola.

Zygmunt and I went out into the fresh air with a feeling of great relief. The roofs and the trees had been whitened by a thick layer of hoar-frost. The first aim of our morning walk was to get hold of some water. Of the three deep artesian wells that we had found in the camp one had refused to work so the remaining two had to satisfy the needs of all ten thousand inmates. Although the winches groaned mournfully and the unsteady iron rocked with the weight of the water, on the whole the wells worked satisfactorily. Pumping never seemed to stop. Water of a milky whiteness and a strong sulphuric smell flowed down into a long, wooden trough in which a dozen or so men could wash at a time.

After a long search we found the rest of our group. To avoid getting lost again we fixed an old poplar tree as our future meeting point. Soon the first field-kitchens appeared. Major Zaleski was quickly improvising a team to help with the distribution of food. There were many candidates for this job. It took half a day of cooking to make the tough *kasha* fit for consumption. Dispensing it as well as bread lasted until the evening. After the kettles had been washed water was boiled and the *kipyatok* became our first evening "meal".

Meanwhile the Soviet camp authorities got down to work. This consisted in the first place of finding enough room for all prisoners in the dozen or more so-called blocks. It was an impossible task. At the most only half the prisoners could be housed. And to complicate matters further the Soviet authorities insisted categorically that privates should be separated from officers. And then the officers had to be separated and grouped according to rank.

Eventually the camp was divided into two spheres by this invisible demarcation line. Soon we were dropping into the quarters of our "Johnnies" for a chat and they revisited us in great numbers. According to a cursory count there were about 2,500 officers and 7,500 privates in the camp. Probably never before in any army have such friendly relations existed between officers and soldiers as those observed in the first weeks of our mutual misery. Such relationships helped to obliterate social differences.

Officers, on the whole, were far worse off than the soldiers as regards material possessions. In many cases the latter had been fully equipped and were wearing the full military outfit when captured by the Soviets. Unlike us officers they were not robbed of all their possessions. Whether this was because, like the *boytzy*, they were simple soldiers, or because there were more of them, is a mystery. The fact remains, however, that many of them were dressed in fine uniforms, wore excellent boots and possessed knapsacks, haversacks, water bottles, dinner pails, a few changes of underwear and often two rugs. On top of that some lucky men had woollen socks, woollen scarves and gloves, soap, cigarettes and other riches!

No wonder that with such a wealth of goods the soldiers became busily engaged in commercial transactions. Most of the officers still had some money — Polish "zlotys" of course. But prices were stiff and tended to go up. However, the main motive which induced soldiers to dispose of their possessions was the belief in the rumour then circulating that they would soon be allowed to go home — *domoy*. When questioned on that subject the *politruks* would nod assent: "Da, da, ryadovyje i unteroficery pozhaluy vskorye poyedut domoy" (Well yes, privates and non-commissioned officers will maybe go home soon.) Our dear boys, believing what they heard, would often give away their things for nothing! "Here, take this, it's good wool. Winter is round the corner and winters in Russia are severe. It will no doubt come in more useful to you than to us. We shall manage all right at home," they used to say, with words which came straight from the heart.

I was once with such a hospitable group of privates in a shed patched up with boards, tree branches and leaves. They were telling stories of their adventures during the hopeless fight against the Germans. Their simple but colourful words brought the narrative vividly to life. A young handsome Corporal with golden hair was describing with much gusto the first clash with the Germans in the border zone near the town of Ostrow: "If only we had possessed more anti-armour guns we would have made a hash of them. But what could we do — there were two guns to a company only! And those Huns' tanks were swarming wherever you cared to look. We were forced to fall back and suffered great losses. I was then wounded and taken to a hospital, moved later to another and finally I landed in Tarnopol. I was by then almost all right and thinking only of returning to the front when those bolsheviks attacked us . . . well, what happened next we all know. But there are now rumours we'll soon go home. Whether this is true God only knows . . . . "

I was listening to his story as if in a trance. Suddenly I felt my arms grasped by a pair of strong arms: "It's me Sir, Kazik of Jablon! Do you recognize me? My God, this is marvellous!" I couldn't believe my eyes. It was indeed Kazik of Jablon, the gamekeeper responsible for breeding pheasants. Both very moved, we told each other about our own experiences and later indulged in various reminiscences. I had known him for ten years — from the time when promoted from coachman's assistant he became an independent gamekeeper. He had lived with his young wife and two children in a delightful little house of red brick which stood in the old park along with his beloved pheasants. That he should have seen me was due to pure chance — he just happened to look inside the shed. Otherwise we could have never come across each other in that human anthill. On hearing of my miserable condition he immediately supplied me with clothes. So after only a few hours I was already in possession of a change of clean linen, a few pieces of cloth used for wrapping round one's feet to serve as a substitute for socks (the so-called *onuce*), a few handkerchiefs and a cake of soap. Kazik also helped me to wash in icy cold water my shirt and underwear which by now had become revoltingly black. In the next few days he brought off another extraordinary feat — he appeared with a warm blanket and a pair of first-class woollen gloves. The fact that I managed to save my hands I owed to my dear Kazik.

I spent that very night with my soldier companions in their leaky lean-to. Dried cattle dung served as our bedding, but I preferred this to the bottom bunks of the Circus.

The next morning the NKVD went ahead with the segregation of the officers and accommodating them in the prescribed barracks or "blocks". My group was put in Block 8. This was a little wooden house standing on half-metre high posts. It contained a few tiny rooms and one long larger room. The only entrance was over a crumbling balcony and through a short corridor without a door. We were put in the larger room. The *politruks* and the *vachtyors*, a new category of "guardian angels" who were soldiers of the NKVD performing the necessary duties inside the camp, applied themselves energetically to pushing and squeezing us into our new accommodation. The size of the room was $3\frac{1}{2}$ by 12 metres and I remember those figures well as our bodies were used as measures.

The room was $2\frac{1}{2}$ metres high. Infested with bugs and lice the lines of three-tier bunks were built so tightly together that only with the greatest difficulty could two men squeeze through the passage between two rows. Some men were not allowed bunks. Being the least privileged, they were forced to occupy the floor under the bottom bunks. To get there these hapless people had to lie flat and pull themselves over a constant layer of greasy mud. They used to affirm that because its cooler air was supposed to be healthier they preferred the filthy black bottom to the stench in the upper regions. But this they probably said in order to boost their and other's morale.

Our group certainly didn't subscribe to that theory. Securing the unanimous agreement of the rest of the men all seven of us clambered up to the top tier. This had its good and its bad points. It had the advantage that there was nothing between the bunk and the ceiling, a space amounting to 75 centimetres. In this space one could assume a half-seated position. This was impossible to achieve on the lower bunks. On the other hand a most unpleasant aspect was the stench that rose to the ceiling. Also, we had to climb to reach our bunks and in doing so our muddy boots would drop clay on the people lying in the lower bunks. This sometimes caused much anger and irritation.

During the first five weeks 168 officers from the rank of Colonel to that of Second Lieutenant were billeted in this room. Each person was allowed a width of only 37 centimetres. Since the length of each bunk was $1\frac{1}{2}$ metres the legs of even the shortest men were forced to hang down. One would get the most vivid picture of this unbelievable misery at night in the light of one anaemic electric bulb. In the daytime half the occupants of the room were either working or somewhere within the enclosure of the camp, but at night all had to be in their bunks. Nearly two hundred filthy bodies clad in revolting underwear, devoured by masses of bugs and lice, were forced to sleep so closely against each other that it was impossible to turn away from the stink of one's neighbour's breath. A few hundred naked, cadaverous, stinking legs sticking out from the four layers of bunks and men; stacks of clothes and boots, strewn helter-skelter across the floor and taking up the rest of free space – this was the nightmarish scene night after frozen night at Camp Starobyelsk.

All prisoners in the camp, irrespective of their age and rank lived in similar conditions, at times even worse. About twenty tents were later pitched for the privates to sleep in and they found this form of shelter fairly tolerable.

Physical suffering was at its worst in the first few weeks of our captivity. Hunger and disease were rampant. Nevertheless, the great majority of our men bore their burden of adversity with pride and dignity. They were to be helped by a set of beliefs – that Hitler would be overcome, that their conditions would improve, that the Allies would come to Poland's aid, that there was justice in history, that Providence would take care of us . . . .

Later, the dry rot of uncertainty and doubt was to spread slowly and steadily until the pillars of our beliefs came crashing down one after the other.

10.   A DELEGATE FROM MOSCOW

Gradually we began to tell the *politruks* and *komandirs* apart, for some of them had been watching over us since Jarmolince. But we didn't know their names as it was they who asked us our names and rank during conversation with us and not the other way around. Besides, the matter of remembering our names was of secondary importance. None of our so-called Soviet "protectors" or "hosts" were able to master the sound of Polish names. But they had perfected their visual memories and eventually became quite expert in recognizing us.

From our very first day at Starobyelsk, it had become clear to us that one figure who on casual observation looked no different from our other guardians exercised supreme authority.

In his early forties, with strong semitic features, clean-shaven, ruddy and red-haired, he would stroll about the camp without visible aim, in an insignia-less brown leather jacket. Only his cap with the red band denoted his membership of the NKVD. He generally took his walks alone. In the course of them he would accost the prisoners, and with a faintly mocking smile, engage them in conversation. Intelligent, clever and self-controlled, he used a friendly tone that was sometimes jesting and sometimes betrayed a note of superiority. Showered with a variety of questions, he skilfully parried the more embarrassing ones with a meaningless sentence containing a nebulous promise, selecting only the easy ones for a detailed reply.

That was still the time when we accepted almost all the explanations and assurances of our camp guardians at their face value. It was a kind of defence mechanism on our part to maintain our morale under the burden of our worries. Many moons were to pass before we learned how to distinguish better between truth and falsehood. However, we never did arrive at the stage where we might be able to tell with complete certainty whether we were or were not being told the truth.

The measure of this little man's authority was the fact that at the sight of him *politruks* and *komandirs* of one rank or another stood to attention, looking into his narrowed eyes with humility and obedience.

For this unimpressive looking fellow in brown leather jacket and red cap was Kirshin, the camp's political commissar.

The night of October 4th seemed longer than usual. Leaden clouds screened off the dawn. Instead of the prickly frost, which would have offered a refreshing relief from the stench of our quarters, a cold autumn rain was falling. The clay earth of the camp had turned into a slimy, slippery pool.

Zygmunt and Felo Daszynski were the first to jump from their bunks and pulled me and the others in our group of seven out by the feet. Our teeth chattering, we ventured into the dark courtyard. With desperate courage we pulled off our shirts. Dressed only in our underpants, we stood in a row under the streams of soft rainwater flowing from the roof down the leaky drainpipes, and squealing like a bunch of young girls, we started to scrub one another. It was not an opportunity to be missed, for in spite of the raw cold, the rainwater seemed warmer than the icy and malodorous well water. Using the beautifully lathering piece of soap tht Kazik had given me, I finally washed off the repulsive scab from my head! After this therapeutic ablution, we threw ourselves into laundering all our personal linen in the rain sent from Heaven. Soon, the interior of our barrack was permeated with the new stench of drying underwear, *onuce* and a collection of rags. That morning we had to wait longer than usual for our oatmeal, because our chefs had trouble getting a fire started with the wet wood.

Now these deviations in our routine caused by the capricious change in the weather were soon effaced by the sensational arrival in the camp of someone who Olgierd declared was a "highly placed person!" His importance dimmed even the omnipotence of commissar Kirshin, who, looking for all the world like a small dog surrounded by a flock of smaller pups, accompanied the visitor on an inspection tour of the camp. The funniest thing was that our caller, whom we unanimously imagined to be a Kremlin representative or at least a delegate of the top command of the famous Lubyanka prison, in Moscow, in no way differed from his entourage. Quite the contrary, he looked like an ordinary mortal, somewhat like an overseer of a small estate. He was wearing a civilian overcoat of heavy tobacco-coloured cloth, trimmed with leather, and a sports cap to match. His long trousers were tucked into huge galoshes. Of medium height, on the heavy side, with a round well-fed face, this singular "civilian" trod on the clay mire as if it were a parquet floor, looking in here, peering in there on his tour of the prisoner of war camp . . . .

Major Zaleski's liaison officer hurried up to us as we were standing under the eaves and said: "The Major warns you against being too talkative with that man. If you must talk with him, be careful what you say. He's a big shot from Moscow. And remember that Kirshin is taking everything in. Pass on this information!" He hurried away to other groups huddled under the eaves.

Before we could press through to get a close look at this mysterious potentate, he had already retreated into the cow shed out of the rain and away from the advancing throng of the curious. It was there that our group and others came upon him and surrounded him.

A volley of questions was let loose at him. George Machlejd called us all to order and asked for one question at a time. When the hubbub had subsided, he himself addressed a courteous query to the visitor: "Please tell us whether the Soviet authorities regard us Polish Army soldiers as war prisoners, and if they do, whether we shall enjoy the rights to which we are entitled under international law."

From beneath the tobacco-coloured jacket and cap issued a ready reply delivered in a melodious tenor voice, a reply as laconic as those we had heard so often from the man's trained *politruk* subordinates: "Da, da, (Yes, yes) since you were a Polish officer, you are now a Soviet prisoner of war. Da, da – and you will enjoy the rights due you . . . . Don't worry . . . . "

"In that case, will we get our pay?" someone else asked, to which the "civilian" replied without hesitation: "Da, da, you will get 50 per cent of the pay you had up to now," and he calmly went on to answer another question: "Da, da, of course, you will be able to assign part of that money to your families . . . ."

One of the most burning issues was the right to correspond with one's family. "Da, da, you will certainly be permitted to write letters. When? Well, soon, soon. Yes, yes, we shall provide you with writing paper, pencils, pens and so forth . . .

"You'll get other items too, yes. There will be a special shop here soon that will sell many useful articles . . .

"You'll have movies, a radio, newspapers and books . . . ."

We felt stunned by this wealth of promises being showered upon us. And then Felo Daszynski suddenly fired a question at random – a question he had made up on the spur of the moment. He phrased it in Polish for he did not know a word of Russian. Zygmunt translated it: "Is it true that the United States, through its ambassador in Moscow, is to take over the interests of the Polish Embassy and extend its protection over Polish prisoners of war in the USSR? In connection with that, can we draw up a mass petition to the American Ambassador asking that we be freed immediately and be allowed to fight the Germans again? Will the camp authorities back us in this?"

The delegate from Moscow played for time. He stared intently at Felo for a long while, measuring him slowly from head to foot. He took a few steps toward Felo, then stiffened as if preparing to spring. With ill-concealed rage, he flung a question in Felo's face: "And where did you get such news?"

He stopped suddenly, regained control over himself, relaxed, drew back to his original place and continued in a level voice: "Hm, hm, I don't know, perhaps . . . ." He remembered the second part of the question and seized upon it eagerly: "Of course you may write your petition. The camp authorities will do everything to help you. You may be sure it will reach the proper authorities . . . . "

Thus came to an end our talk with the "highly placed person" whose name or position we never came to know, for he never again appeared in our camp. With his retinue he proceeded deeper into the prisoner of war jungle to spread the good tidings.

A few hours passed. The rain did not stop. We were lying in a crumpled heap on our bunks. Suddenly the men nearest the corridor called out: "Attention, the guards are running in our direction!"

Before we realized what was going on, they had already dashed into the room, elbowed their way through the mass of people, striking the butt ends of their guns against the bunks and the protruding boots. They bellowed like men possessed: "Everybody run out into the yard! Leave your things on the bunks!"

What was going on? Why the commotion? In the yard a long row of guards was already standing from wall to wall, cutting the camp compound in half. We were all told to fall into packed rows in the northern part of the grounds behind their cordon. They surrounded our barrack and other sheds in which the officers had been crowded.

We stood in the rain and mud for one hour, for two. . . . It was not until late afternoon that rows of oil lamps flickered inside the cow shed and the guards admitted about fifty officers. For a long time we waited tensely. The first men to enter the shed began to emerge. They deliberately passed near us, conveying by whispers and gestures that they had been subjected to inspection and deprived of all their papers, documents and money. The guards herded those who had already undergone inspection back to the barracks.

At the same time, other guards carried mountains of stuff from the barracks to the cow shed. This was the loot netted by their plundering of the remains of our misery. Soaked through and through, we shivered from the cold and indignation.

Everybody was thinking which of the documents on his person he should conceal, and where. Soon there was not a hole in a board or a tree within the reach of our hands which was not stuffed with crumpled wet documents and banknotes. Few were the lucky ones who were to find their papers and money the following day, for these hiding places were seen by hundreds of pairs of eyes, among them the eyes of the dishonest. Besides, our efforts did not escape the notice of the guards!

I had all my documents with me. This was a private matter, which everyone had to settle for himself. Nobody was familiar with the documents of his neighbour, even if that neighbour was a close friend. Nobody asked his neighbour's advice about what was to be done. I waged a long inner battle before I arrived at a decision. Should I conceal my documents in a hole, should I press them into the mud with my foot and destroy them or should I keep them on me? I finally resolved not to give in to the panic of destruction. After all, a military document, or for that matter even a civilian one, had to carry some weight even in these unusual circumstances. I could at least prove my identity and my rank. Why should I hide these facts, especially here, in this Soviet desert, and become, as in the case of so many, a pauper stripped even of his name.*

I had so little Polish money on my person that it presented no problem. But I did have the odd sum of fifteen American dollars in two bills: a five and a ten dollar bill. I had taken them out of a desk drawer when I was leaving my apartment in Warsaw. Inasmuch as I had got them this far, I decided to try and save them. I would not be risking anything, for the inspectors would certainly take them away from me anyway. So I worked the bills into a box of matches, using one hand inside my coat pocket. Then I nonchalantly lighted a cigarette with what was ostensibly my last match and dropped the empty box into the mud. With my heel I made an indentation in the clay, pressed the box deep into the mud and stamped the surface over it. I made a mental note of the exact spot.

Not long afterward I was called before the examining commission, seated at long boards in a deluge of papers, documents, notebooks, photographs. The shed swarmed with guards.

I happened to hit upon a young *komandir*, whose black wavy hair

---

* The question of military identity papers was frequently under discussion, for it was a well-known fact that they should be destroyed in the event of being taken prisoner. But officers even of the highest rank did not always act in accordance with this view when actually taken prisoner by the Russians. They felt that knowledge of a prisoner's rank was not a matter of consequence to the Russians since Poland was not at war with the Soviet Union. On the other hand, they feared that a lack of identification could have a disastrous effect upon the prisoner's fate. It was left up to each individual to decide this question for himself.

peeped from underneath his cap. He snapped: "Put all your military and civilian documents, notebooks, snapshots and money here on the table."

I thrust my wet hands into my coat, which was soaked through like a sponge, and pulled out my papers. I felt as if I was tearing off my shirt and standing completely naked. I handed over my officer's military book, a few loose papers, several Polish banknotes, a couple of snapshots and finally my civilian passport with its many European and overseas visas. The *komandir* gathered them all up, glanced at them, then studied me a minute and finally pushed my documents to a soldier sitting near him. "These two," he said pointing to the officer's book and the passport, "go into the envelope!" The soldier obediently slipped them into a thin greenish envelope. He jotted something on it. Then he threw the rest of my papers and the photographs into the big pile. The dark one nodded. I judged it to be a sign informing me I could go, that the inspection was over. But someone's hands forcibly tore my coat from my back and then pulled off my jacket. The guards were carrying out a personal inspection. They ran their hands over my whole body, they turned my pockets inside out. They found nothing, for there was nothing to find. Having fulfilled their duty, they shouted at me: "Get dressed!" When I had put my things on, they pushed me toward the table again.

The dark one held a small slip of paper. As he handed it to me, he said: "This is the number under which your documents will be kept in the camp headquarters."

The operation was over. The tiny scrap of paper bore a pencilled number and a round stamp: NKVD – Starobyelsk.*

It was close to midnight. Like a beaten dog I dragged myself to the barrack. For a long time I lay on my bunk staring dully at the ceiling just over my head, until sleep overcame me in the small hours of the morning.

My comrades were returning from inspection and gradually filling the dark room, leaving tracks of mud on the floor and bunks. The unpleasant odour of wet cloth permeated the barrack. The others felt as defeated as myself. They conversed in whispers. They looked through their things which had been gone through by the guards during their absence and silently cursed at the signs of theft. A

---

* Perhaps subconsciously I already then sensed the importance of that scrap of paper. Perhaps that is why I treasured it so carefully in the months that followed until one day, fearing to lose it, I burned the mysterious number and the date of 4th October, 1939 on the inside of my cut-off boot uppers. And wonder of wonders! Two years later, these figures which had seemed to be dead suddenly spoke with the crushing force of evidence, evidence for which I had long been groping . . . .

multitude of essential odds and ends had disappeared – the remaining hidden penknives, knives, papers, snapshots, even leather straps and belts that had been hanging on nails separately.

I was indifferent to everything. I failed to get upset by the loss of my knife or my snapshots. Only one thing appeared before my eyes, one thing resounded in my ears. I saw the figure of the delegate from Moscow in his tobacco-coloured jacket and I heard his melodious speech. And I arrived at just one conclusion.

His real answer to Felo Daszynski's question was – inspection.

Next morning Major Zaleski's liaison officer appeared in our hut to announce that the Soviet authorities would start registering officers that day. The job would be carried out by the *politruks* with the aid of our men. He then read out from a piece of paper the various questions we would have to answer. He also said that Major Zaleski had waged a long battle with the authorities concerning the questionnaire and had succeeded in getting it shortened.

Despite the Major's attempts, however, we were required to answer a number of searching questions which were bound to reveal to the authorities the details of our life in Poland. We were expected to disclose, for instance, the names of our parents, our mother's maiden name, our military duties and the locality and date of our capture by the Red Army. We also had to describe the job we had done in civilian life and give all relevant addresses, and finally, a somewhat unusual question, we were required to state our political affiliations.

There was a rising tide of anger in the room as each question was read out and many voices of protest were raised. Those most opposed to the questions were understandably officers whose homes were in parts of Poland now occupied by the Soviets. The mere thought of disclosing their addresses made them tremble with fear for the fate of their families.

But what were they to do? To tell lies? This was practically impossible now that the NKVD were in possession of stacks of documents with which they could check all our statements!

Once more I saw the smiling face of the delegate from Moscow who only the day before had assured us that all international conventions would be observed.

The wave of protest abated after a while. Common sense was getting the better of us. It was all very well to protest but who should the protests be addressed to and who would pay the slightest attention? Finally, who would put it all down in writing? Let us stop being gullible and let us stop tilting at windmills. Let everyone work out his own salvation according to what he thought best. To reveal a home address is no doubt a risky thing. Agreed. But what would be the position if in the future we were allowed to communicate by post with our own families? The authorities would easily find our addresses then. And they would learn a great deal from the contents of the letters. . . . The delegate from Moscow taught us this lesson yesterday. Isn't that enough?

We were soon joined by a host of *politruks* and officers of the NKVD, accompanied by their own clerks and interpreters. They sat down at tables made with planks taken from our bunks.

Right from the beginning they were faced with all kinds of problems. One problem was a lack of writing paper. As it turned out, they had such a small amount that, even if they had written in the smallest handwriting by looking through a magnifying glass, they would have still been unable to carry out their task.

Paper is one of the most valued materials in Soviet Russia. There is one standard type of the worst possible quality. It serves various purposes, such as for writing, sketching plans and rolling up cigarettes of *makhorka* (although in this last case strong competition is provided by newsprint with its comparatively fragrant smell, drawn, probably, from the ink used in printing the newspapers). The paper is supplied in huge rolls. According to need it is cut into small sheets or made into exercise books. Should one try to write something the ink will form large blots and if a pencil is used the writing is invisible unless one pressed hard, thereby perforating the paper. As if these disadvantages aren't enough, the paper needs to be carefully handled as it tends to turn into dust, destroying anything that has been written on it. Ink is rarely available in the Soviet Union. The shortage may be remedied in a way by splitting open an indelible pencil and dissolving the graphite in water. There is always a way for everything!

But there was another unexpected obstacle in store for our "benefactors". How should the names of officers be listed? According to rank? Good. And then proceed with their names in alphabetical order? Right, but this is where the drama began. Neither the *politruks* nor their scribes had any knowledge of either the Latin alphabet or the sound of Latin characters. They started by writing our surnames in Russian characters, which are derived from the Greek language, and soon got bogged down.

I shall not bother the reader with all the comparative intricacies of the two very different alphabets. To illustrate the grotesque obstacles put in the way of the unfortunate *politruks* one only has to give a couple of examples. The letter "W", as we all know, finds itself at the far end of our alphabet. In the Russian alphabet, however, it is third from the beginning. The letter "C" offers the reverse example. Vowels are a complicated matter too. So, to illustrate this in practice, all the Wisniewscys and Wolskis and others with their surnames starting with the letter "W" had to be summoned in great haste to be put at the head of a long queue, while the Celinskis, Czajkowskis and the like were allowed to wait in peace for a long time. I leave it to all those readers attracted by "quizes" to find a solution to the problem of transposing such an alphabetical phenomenon as the surname of "Jezewski". There was also the trouble, albeit on a somewhat minor scale, with the spelling of Christian names. Jan, for instance corresponds in Russian to Ivan, Tomasz to Foma, Tadeusz to Faddyey. Despite these problems, a *prikaz* (decree) had been issued that all our surnames and names as well as those of our parents were to be put in Russian characters in an exact phonetic transposition.

The above system was bound to consume a great deal of time and it resulted in a lot of scribbling, correcting and bickering. To the delight of many of us it was not possible to check who had and had not been registered. Finally, after many attempts and many threats, the Soviet authorities gave up using their own men to register us. Consequently we were ordered to do the job in the way we thought best. It goes without saying that after we got hold of an adequate supply of paper everything proceeded smoothly. However, there was not much point in the operation because at that time the prison population was constantly expanding with the arrival of more groups of officers. All the same, the idiotic procedure of compiling innumerable lists of officers which then had to be modified went on and on. For this was what had been decreed.

It was not until mid-December, when the number of officers at the camp had stabilised, that the idea of having a list of officers acquired a certain amount of sense as far as we were concerned. But by that time the Soviet authorities were able to dispense with our help. The morning and evening roll calls now sufficed for checking our numbers. And as for obtaining detailed particulars of prisoners, the NKVD finally perfected a system compared with which all previous methods were like friendly little chats. This was the famous system of interrogation known as "doprosy".

We had meticulously compiled a directory of names for our own use. Written in Russian it contained an alphabetical list of all the camp inmates — 4,000 men in all, on 200 pages. It represented the approximate position as from mid-December 1939. This stayed roughly the same until the 5th April, 1940.

I happened to be the one to whom Major Zaleski had entrusted the task of compiling the list. With the help of a few companions I completed it in a month. The Soviet authorities knew of our directory and since it was useful to them they also referred to it. They were impressed with it, as with many other things of a practical nature for which we had been responsible. The list was amended as changes occurred in the camp. I would cross out the names of people who had died, and also the names of those who, critically ill, were taken to hospital. Although I wrote "temporarily absent" next to their names I knew that it was most unlikely that they would return. I would also cross out those who at night – it was always at night that it happened – would be rudely awoken by the ominous sounding order: "Nyemedlenno sobiraysya s vyeschchami". (Get ready with your things, right away.) After passing through the gates of the camp, usually with one or a few companions, they were never seen again. Their ultimate fate was known to them only.

In place of those crossed out I would enter the names of newcomers. In the very depths of a snowy winter, men, or rather ghosts of men, in small groups, sometimes single, in a state of unbelievable misery, were still arriving at the camp.

This book served as a mirror of the changes that took place in the camp. Although the atrocious paper of which it was made was disintegrating and words became obliterated as a result, it almost survived my period of imprisonment. It remained under my constant surveillance and I never let it out of my hands until the very day when my turn came to leave the camp. The Soviet guards were searching us in the central church and found it – my treasured book which I had been trying to save at all cost.

11. EVERYDAY CAMP LIFE

The day after the general search ordered by the delegate from Moscow I set out on an expedition to look for my valuable match box. It was still raining cats and dogs. Almost ruining my only pair of boots I waded through mud and puddles for a considerable time. Damn it, this *must* have been the place where I was standing and where I hid my treasure! Nothing doing. Frustrated and feeling like a fool I went back to my hut. But I would not give up. I continued to try my luck during the next few days, albeit with diminishing hope. It was only when a severe frost had congealed the sticky soil and dried up the muddy puddles that I noticed, this time by sheer chance, the tiny brim of my box sticking out from the frozen ground. No doubt about it, this was my treasure. The green, rolled up bills had stood the test of humidity and frost. I gazed at the effigy of Washington with a feeling of deep thankfulness and then sewed the two rolls into the folds of my greatcoat.

I was awaken suddenly at night by testy voices arguing in Russian: "And I'm repeating it to you, idiot, he must be here somewhere! I've been looking for him everywhere. A long, thin man with a little beard, dressed in a leather jacket. He must be here. Jevo zowut Dashinskij. Nu davay jevo iskat poskoryey." (His name is Daszynski. Now let's look for him without further delay.) This was a messenger from the Camp Commandant, talking to the night *vachtyor* in his queer, squeaking voice. The messenger's name was Kopyeykin, a name which smacks distinctly of Gogol. Short and thin, with a skin pitted by smallpox, looking like a baked apple – he could have been anything from 20 to 40 years of age.

I nudged Zygmunt and he woke Felo – the man they were looking for – who was snoring at his side. He whispered into his ear: "Attention, Felo, wake up, attention!"

"Wh . . . wh . . . at's the m . . . matter, leave me alone," he stammered.

A general commotion had erupted by that time. The *vachtyor* woke up the officer in charge of our barrack, Colonel Saski, and asked him about Felo, threatening that if he did not indicate Felo immediately he would chase us all outdoors and do the checking there . . . . There was nothing we could do.

Kopyeykin finally lay his hand on his quarry. He was squeaking and croaking: "*Dashynski!* Nu szto szutki ustraivayesh! Nu davay, pozhyvyey, sobiraysya *Dashynski!*" (You're making jokes, aren't you? Come on be quick and get ready!)

Felo was getting ready without undue haste. He was laughing and joking, pointing out that he did not understand a word of what this fathead was saying to him. He finally added: "Don't get over-excited about me. Should I not come back you can share out my possessions among yourselves."

Feigning to be half-asleep and on the pretext of having to go outside to the latrine, Olgierd, clad only in his underwear, climbed down from his bunk and followed in Felo's steps. He then told us what he had seen: "They took him to this little house fenced off with barbed wire – just at the side of us. This is the office of the camp's NKVD and is called osobyj otdyel', (special branch), besides you probably know . . . . "

As it happened we knew nothing in those days (at least my closest friends and I). But Olgierd was always a bit ahead of us.

There was no question of sleeping – we waited for several long hours.

He came back in the small hours of the morning. His face was pale, and a kind of artificial smile stuck to his lips. He clambered up silently to his bunk and sprawled out flat. Did he go to sleep or was he just pretending? I do not know. Later, when morning came, we asked him: "Well, Felo, let us know something – tell us now – how did it go?"

"There's nothing to say, I came back and that's all," he cut us short tersely.

We thus became for the first time witnesses to the strange phenomenon of the invisible curtain which, dropping by its own weight, would come down to screen those of us returning from nocturnal interrogations. An unwritten regulation said they should be left alone, their frayed nerves left undisturbed. As time went by and many of us came to know from our own experiences what being interrogated by the NKVD really means, we also appreciated the protection secured by this general rule. And should it happen that one of us was bursting with an overdose of garrulousness he would then restrict himself to describing incidents of a humorous nature – for there was no lack of them also – and refrain from saying anything which might induce feelings of terror.

What I knew, however, and others knew too was that the summoning of Felo to the "special section of the NKVD" was an answer to the question he had dared to put to the delegate from Moscow.

Matters of routine, matters connected with construction works and also problems about the running of the camp kitchen were gradually becoming the responsibility of Major Zaleski and his team. He had, at the same time, been burdened with the duty of assigning a number of men for various manual tasks. The Soviet authorities insisted on a daily contingent of one thousand men and presented him with the so called "robochyj naryad," a kind of plan from which he could estimate how many men were needed for each kind of work to be done.

Half of the contingent were usually taken outside the gate under heavy escort to unload huge logs from railway wagons. These logs were destined for sawmills, to be returned later to the camp in the shape of boards for use in the construction of new barracks. At first, however, we were not inclined to believe that the wood was to be used for such a purpose.

It happened that several times I found myself one of this group. Sometimes we were made to march along a roundabout route under the cover of morning darkness to a distant side track of the railway line, returning home at dusk. Sometimes we would be taken to the site in trucks. When I first saw the enormous logs coated with ice, probably brought to this woodless country from the far Siberian forests, I became possessed with laughter. The mere thought of my being able to lift and roll such a load seemed ridiculous. But nothing is impossible in this world. And it would not be for the first time that logs were moved by human force alone without the help of mechanical devices. When erecting the pyramid of Cheops the Egyptians were faced with much the same problem and the pyramid was eventually built. And the impossible happened here too in this God-forsaken, windswept, Ukrainian place. To my great astonishment, though only after many unsuccessful attempts, the enormous logs finally started rolling down from the high wagons with a great crash and we then succeeded in arranging the logs into neat piles after trying out various techniques of manipulation.

At other times our work consisted of loading the same logs on trucks which had trailers attached. The logs were taken on these to the sawmill. Everybody was of the opinion that loading was far more difficult than unloading. Whether they were right – I really do not know. Perhaps they were. But by now I felt I could brandish a twenty metre log as though I was Charlie Chaplin twirling a walking stick.

Apart from Zygmunt, a professional forester, there were among us other practically-minded men who were able to organize work even in these primitive conditions. Our *Vakhtyory* who stood back in the trees, sheltered from the wind, were watching our progress with much interest. Shaking their heads they did not try to conceal their astonishment at the sight of rough work being carried on so expertly by the "white-handed officers."* But it was not always like this. Sometimes we were so completely worn out from exhaustion and hunger that we would lie down side by side on the frozen ground as a sign of protest. We also objected because our uniforms, the only ones we possessed, were being ruined by this kind of work – seams on the shoulders snapping, sleeves tearing, and so on. The guards would then proceed with much gusto to *their* kind of work – by yelling and kicking they forced us to resume.

Some bread and a bowl of oatmeal dispensed early in the morning provided the only fuel for a whole day's heavy, physical work. When we returned to the camp in the evening all we would get would be a foul tasting, sour soup heated up from the one prepared for midday.

Although the heavy work resulted sometimes in accidents, such as a crushed foot or a broken collarbone our spirits were raised somewhat by doing it. This was because the end result of our labours would be better conditions for us. For it turned out, after all, that building material in the shape of boards started being delivered to our camp.

Another party of men used to be harnessed every day to work on the site of the camp. The most imperative task was the digging of ditches to make latrines. One of these when accomplished measured the impressive length of 30 metres and on the day of its solemn opening was named the "Siegfried Line." Oddly enough, we learned later that Polish prisoners of war at Kozielsk, in central Russia, a camp of which we then knew nothing had given the same name to their latrine!

Prisoners also mended damaged roofs and panelled the walls of sheds and cowsheds. They drilled two additional artesian wells and constructed a new kitchen with six big cauldrons inserted into the brickwork.

In the second half of October the process of sorting out the non-commissioned officers and the privates started – what was called *razgruzka* in Russian. What an unruly, intractable yet proud bunch

* "White handed," in Russian *byelorutchki*, was a derogatory term applied to members of the bourgeoisie: that is, those assumed to be unused to manual work.

of young men they proved to be, this tribe of peasant and working class people dressed in soldiers' uniforms. Not easy at all to get tamed. Almost none of them knew Russian. The conversed with the *politruks* and *vakhtyory* in their crude, peasant language tinged with the accents of the various Polish provinces. Whether the Soviet people understood what they were saying I do not know. However, I do know that our lads did not mince their words and did not shrink from calling them names.

"You idiot! You're not going to teach me how to dig soil. You can kiss my arse you fathead," shouted one young farmer from the Kielce region as he toiled in a latrine ditch The *vakhtyor* to whom he directed the insults could not understand a word.

The relationship of the Soviet men towards our boys was far more considerate than towards us. This was, of course, part of their political programme. Our boys were representatives of the proletarian classes whereas we – the officers – were supposed to be their oppressors. The funny thing was, however, that the boys were obviously clinging to us the "tyrants" as if we were their own fathers! This phenomenon just could not be understood by the Soviet authorities, even by the cleverest of them.

They tried hard to get our soldiers onto their side. They refrained from forcing them to go to work, they tried to use simple, uncontroversial methods for registering them – just putting down their names and dates of birth. All this was to no avail. Our boys were scoffing at them, opposing all their advances, refusing to be won over. No wonder. Instead of filling up their empty stomachs with good food the authorities fed them with political propaganda talks and Soviet films.

A "motorised" projection apparatus mounted on a car would arrive, a screen would be hung across branches of trees and they would proceed to try and entertain our boys, who, if they wanted to stay and watch, had to stand in sticky mud or shiver and freeze in the cold. The films shown were not the few made for export but those produced on a massive scale for interior consumption. Countries outside Russia have never seen such trash! All centred around an unbearably monotonous strand of the crudest possible propaganda.

The attendance which, owing to sheer boredom, was quite heavy at the beginning shrunk after a certain time to a negligible number of eyes squinting through openings in the tents. The subject would always be the same – gory scenes showing with a maniacal obstinacy the Soviets defending their country against foes who attacked from all sides. The enemy could be some dwarfish, long-toothed Japanese somewhere in the Far East or a wicked Chinaman hiding in the thickness of the Amur woods, or a monocled British spy lurking among the evil Mongols on the border of Afghanistan. The enemy conspired under the guise of white-collared capitalist engineers plotting to blow up the Caucasian oil-fields, or he assumed the uniform of some undisclosed navy and worked secretly to destroy Sebastopol and Odessa, or he masqueraded as a fat (why should he always be fat?) American capitalist, smoking a huge cigar, who, helped by his dollars, aimed to destroy the Soviet regime. And finally in order to fill to the brim our cup of bitterness they showed a mighty "class" enemy personified by Poland. She was caricatured in a most insulting manner. Life in Poland, her regime and her people, all this was vilified to the utmost extreme. This proved to be too much. The last of the few "assiduous" film-goers left the constantly shrinking audience. Those who remained were a few new converts to the ideals of Red propaganda of the sort who had started raising their heads at that time. Still the scarcity of their numbers probably persuaded the Soviets that they were not having much success and they discontinued the films for a while.

Some time later I happened to discuss the subject of films with one of the *politruks* who seemed to be less narrow-minded than some. His name was Stepanov. He was astonished and even resentful that we should not have appreciated the quality of the Soviet films and the values they presented. I asked him whether he had ever seen any European or American films. Yes, he did see *The Great Waltz* and also one with Deanna Durbin and Stokowski. He described them as "nitchevo syebye" (not so bad) but "kuda im do nashich filmov" (no comparison with our films). At this our discussion ended. How was it possible to talk to a man with his mind completely blinkered by Soviet chauvinism and who, it seemed certain, really meant what he wasy saying?

I had seen the American film he had mentioned twice, once before the war and for a second time during my captivity. This presented me with the rare opportunity of comparing the two versions. The Soviet version had been severely cut – to such an extent that the meaning of the action was often lost. Also, the Russian sub-titles deviated considerably from the original and this made the story even more distorted. It was obvious why the films had been released in the Soviet Union because in one of them there was a funny episode showing a palace revolution in Vienna, which viewed with the Russian sub-titles acquired the character of a great historical upheaval. The other film showed, according to the Soviet interpretation, the oppressed and unemployed masses in the USA fighting for survival, apparently a rampant and constant phenomenon in that country. All in all this was exactly what appealed to the authorities.

One day small notices showing the names of all the *voievodship* in Poland were found stuck in the ground in various parts of the camp.* At the same time it was officially announced that privates and non-commissioned officers — "poyedut domoy" — would be sent home. All they had to do was to register at the sign bearing the name of the *voievodship* where they were born.

And this is how our rebellious boys were finally caught. On seeing all those names so dear to their hearts they lined up meekly in long queues, gave their surnames and Christian names in the shortest possible version and prepared to depart. The first batch of men from Silesia marched off through the gate the next day and a few days later a big group of high-spirited men from the Lwow region followed singing songs. And so their number started dwindling until finally on the 15th November, with great sorrow in our hearts, we bad farewell to the last group of our boys from Warsaw.

A total of seven thousand left the camp. They took along with them thousands of messages destined to be handed over to thousands of our families. Since there was no question of taking down any notes, they had to memorize the gist. We trusted them to deliver the messages to their destinations.

The fate of the messengers is not known so far. They never returned to their homes and our messages remained undelivered.

A long time after they had left we heard various vague rumours concerning their whereabouts. Some of the men, it was said, had been seen working in stone quarries along the River Dnieper. Others were supposed to be constructing military aerodromes in the western part of the Soviet Union. There were also other vague rumours about penal camps in the far north of the country. One has to realise, however, that between 1939 and 1941 about 300,000 Polish soldiers found themselves in Soviet captivity. This enormous mass of men was spread out over the whole immensity of Siberia and other parts of the Soviet Union. If they survived, our 7,000 boys could have been absorbed by the 300,000 and sent who knows where in this vast area.

It took me a long time to say goodbye to Kazik. He knew my family and my friends very well indeed and so there was no problem of "remembering" any messages. At the last moment he presented me with a woollen scarf.

* Pre-war Poland was divided into 16 administrative regions known as "voievodship" (wojewodztwo).

Major Zaleski outdid himself in his efforts to alleviate the difficult camp conditions. He was constantly at war with the Soviet Commandant and with the quartermasters, trying above all to improve the standard of health in the camp. Thanks to his exertions and the work of our doctors, a clinic and a hospital with fifteen beds were organised. The hospital was located in a crooked small-frame building bearing the number 4 and next to the main camp gate. Some of the beds – no bigger than a child's – were placed in two tiny rooms. The rest were ranged in the narrow corridor. The clinic was in a fairly large room that was adjacent to an open veranda. Patients stood in line for hours on this veranda, shivering with cold, as they waited for a new dressing, medicine or medical advice.

The health officer for our camp appointed by our command was Major Henry Levittoux, an eminent Polish surgeon and director of the University Clinic in Warsaw. Dr Levittoux surrounded himself with a group of doctors, specialists in various fields, who worked day and night with selfless devotion. Actual control over the hospital rested in the hands of a young Soviet physician and a few nurses. This young man possessed neither sufficient knowledge nor medical experience, but to assert his authority he wielded a dictatorial hand, ignoring the recommendations and advice of his older professional colleagues, silenced through captivity. He alone, or during his absence one of the nurses, decided who was to be admitted to the Hospital, who was to be discharged, and whose state of health warranted transfer to the municipal hospital. He was so jealous of his power that he personally supervised the distribution of one aspirin tablet, one drop of iodine or a piece of bandage. Our own doctors knew only too well about the need to conserve these elementary medicaments, which were worth their weight in gold.

And yet this humble little hospital was an oasis of cleanliness and warmth in comparison with the darkness and filth of the camp's sleeping quarters. I visited my dear friend Joseph Czapski there when, fever-ridden, he was coughing up tubercular blood. He was glad to see me. His sunken cheeks were unhealthily rosy and his long legs extended far behond the rods of his miniature bed. He spoke in a whisper with effort: "You see, though I'm sick, I feel as if I were in paradise here. Look! Clean bed linen, a clean shirt. It's warm here and we have light. What else does one need?" His long bony fingers tenderly stroked the plain yellowed muslin sheet and the rough blanket. "I hope they don't send me to the city hospital. Here at least our own doctors are looking after me. God knows what they'd do to me in the city place. But you know what? Nurse Natalia Vasilevna is good and kind. When that brute Yegorov is away, she behaves very differently. She's pleasant, smiles and talks like a human being. As soon as Yegorov shows up, she puts on an idiotic mask of indifference and zeal. The devil only knows which of these roles is the real one," he added with a smile. "I think with terror of coming back to you to those bedbug-infested bunks when I finally get over my illness. I dread leaving this bed . . . and especially this quiet, this wonderful quiet! To return to that eternal monstrous bedlam and hubbub seems worse than anything to me!"

Holding his thin trembling hands, I tried to comfort him: "My dear fellow, you'll find the camp in much better order when you leave here. Ever since the enlisted men left, it's been less crowded. New barracks are being built. Zaleski and his fantastic team of engineers are working real wonders. You'll see for yourself soon. Kirshin was mumbling something about correspondence this morning. He said that tomorrow or the day after they would permit us to write home! If this turns out to be true, you'll see how quickly you'll get better. Everybody's spirits will improve right away!"

His head sank back on his pillow, he let his eyelids fall over his eyes and lay there quietly for a moment. He tried to show by the smile on his parched lips that he was not asleep. I felt fascinated by that head of his, as if I were seeing it for the first time in my life. What a subject for a painter! Only he was the painter, not I. A tremendous skull, elongated, with a high forehead, a bony aquiline nose jutting out of the sunken eye-sockets and the sunken temples. And his greying long red hair blending with a several weeks old growth of beard. He looked like a saint.

"Don't go yet," he whispered. "Listen:
'Je sens vibrer en moi toutes les passions
        D'un vaisseau qui souffre;
    Le bon vent, la tempête et les convulsions
        Sur l'immense gouffre
    Me bercent. D'autre fois, calme plat, grand miroir
        De mon désespoir!'
"That's from Baudelaire. *La Musique*. Listen some more. . . ."

He was racked by fever. He added a verse from Apollinaire, then almost inaudibly recreated a scene from Proust, whom he adored.

Suddenly he became stiff and almost rose from his bed. He seemed to be a giant. A terrible coughing seized him and choked him. He smothered it, pressing a blood-stained rag to his blue lips. His spasms continued for a long while. The other patients watched him horror-stricken. One of them called for the nurse.

Using her fat buttocks to propel her way through the narrow passage between the beds, the Soviet nurse came up to Joseph. It was not Natalia, but the other one, the short girl, ugly as sin, whose name I did not know. She looked at my friend with complete indifference. She did not even bend over him or hand him a glass of water. Giving me a poke, she hissed angrily: *"Nu,* that's enough of that gabbing! Get the hell out of here before I chase you out!"

It was cold outside. There was a heavy snowfall. The square in front of the Church glistened with a clean downy blanket and its immaculate freshness had a magnetic allure.

The musical French language and the beautiful poetic words vibrated in my ears. During my brief visit to my friend. I had become suspended in the transcendental sphere. Now I was getting back to earth. I gaped at the monumental church, lighted by the only arc-lamp in the camp. In the wind the lamp swayed and cast an eerie shadow on the Church's tan brick facade.

I don't know why, but I never failed to see in the front wall of the church the gigantic features of a big fat woman — a witch if there ever was one! The whole edifice was her head, her eyes were the two stained glass windows, her nose and toothless mouth merged in the entrance arch leading to the main nave. The huge blue cupola along with the four small cupolae created the impression of a kerchief covering that horrible horned head. Though I laughed at this vision, it haunted me at all times.

It pursued me stubbornly until those memorable April days when, out of the throat of that female Moloch, there began to issue a daily stream of our officers. It pursued me until the day the remaining officers crossed the last few steps of Camp Starobyelsk and vanished from view outside its mysterious gate.

Another result of Major Zaleski's concern for our general health was the decision to restore a public bath which was on the site of the old monastery. It was a small brick building, comprising two rooms, and the interior was covered with old, rusty pipes, looking like an overgrown Virginia creeper. It was also filled with a number of disused cauldrons.

The public bath or *banya* is an institution in Russia. Every ten days since time immemorial the people of "Mother Russia" have cleansed their shameful bodies in its steam and hot water.

Our habit was to strip down to the waist in order to wash ourselves. On several occasions, while washing at a railway pump on the journey or, later, at the camp well, we saw some *boyetz* or even a *politruk* watching our public ablutions with disgust. Speaking in a superior tone, they would say: "You wash yourselves like swine!

Aren't you ashamed to do this half-naked in public! "Wied' ete nie kulturno! Strannyje wy ludi!" (This is not decent! What strange people you are!)

With these comments in mind, let us turn once more to the Russian way of washing. What happens in the nine days before and after the banya? Every morning all over Russia people of all ages and both sexes get up, dress hastily and then, only then, when they are ready to leave for work, proceed to their washing functions. But remember, only running water is used, *never* stagnant.

Special contraptions made of iron are manufactured in their millions to produce running water. The small container, which has a capacity of around two gallons, is filled with water and hung on the wall. (Tap water, by the way, is the privilege of a tiny number of people, mainly living in the cities.) On pressing a small, weighted rod water will trickle down into one's palm. It is then splashed against the face. And that is all – "prosto i ostroumno", as the Russians put it. If a cauldron isn't available an ordinary mug will do. All one has to do then is to take a mouthful from it, spill it into the palm of the hand and spatter it over one's face. "Prosto i ostroumno." But God forbid that it should be done with stagnant water – this would not be decent.

I had seen these morning exertions performed countless times, in the First World War as well as at the camp. A soldier in a green blouse buttoned up to his neck, a belt clasping the blouse tightly to his waist, would spit water from his mug into the palm of his hand and literally wash just the top of his nose and his eyes, without the use of any soap.

I have to be fair however. This wall container was not an entirely stupid invention. It proved to be workable and practical in the most backward conditions. We had one installed later in our room to serve the twenty-five inhabitants. It was astounding how, after having acquired the necessary skill, it was possible to wash oneself relatively decently with an infinitesimal amount of water.

In contrast the *banya* is a formidable institution. Here the traditional ritual of mass cleansing takes place in thick clouds of steam. Only within the humid walls of the *banya* can the Soviet people forget their mutual sense of shame and they expose their naked bodies for hours to the tropical temperature. In this way they scrape the dirt which has accumulated on their bodies during the previous ten days.

I have never been able to establish who were the last beneficiaries of the antiquated *banya* on the site of the ancient monastery – whether it was the priests, for instance, or the soldiers or prisoners who were there after the Revolution. The fact remains, however, that its official name was still *banya* although for many years it had housed people. The last occupants were our soldiers. They had to live there in most inhuman conditions – lying side by side on a cement floor or on bunks fixed to the rust-eaten pipes.

After our soldiers had left the camp and it had became somewhat less crowded a large team of builders and engineers under the leadership of Major Zaleski set out most energetically to construct new barracks and to repair the old ones. Their main task, however, was restoring the *banya*. Plans were made and estimates prepared of the building materials needed for the purpose. These were submitted to the Soviet Commissariat for approval. They were criticised and rejected. New plans and new estimates were then made and again approval was sought. This, after long consideration and discussion, was eventually granted. We immediately started on the work of straightening pipes, repairing the cauldrons and so on. We had to do all this work ourselves, with the aid of tools we had made. The first consignment of materials that we had requested arrived two weeks later. The whole lot was useless. Taps, connecting elements for pipes etc. – nothing would fit. So this meant new plans, new orders and new approval. Still, by the New Year the bath installations had been restored to working condition. It should be noted that this was achieved with the aid of materials 90 per cent of which had been made by ourselves, in the most primitive conditions. The inauguration which followed was a joyful occasion.

When carrying out the final inspection all the Soviet functionaries, headed by the commissars Bereschkov and Kirshin, nodded their heads approvingly. Kirshin himself tested the taps, the pump, the showers, investigated the drainage system, and enquired about the number of people who could use the bath in any one day. After all this rigorous inspection he graciously expressed his appreciation to the builders and engineers in the following words: "Da eto kharasho, eto kulturno. Kto nye rabotayet tot ne yest! Tak dolzhno i byt' w Sovietzkom Soyuzie." (This is fine, it is right. Who does not work does not eat. This is how things should be in the Soviet Union.)

Of course, it greatly benefited the Soviet Union to get hard, heavy work done by "paying" prisoners of war a daily "wage" of a slice of bread and a bowl of *kasha*! Altogether a very economical and profitable way of doing things. No doubt the Commandant, the commissars and the wise industrious *politruks* would receive due acknowledgement from Moscow.

Until the public bath was restored the camp inmates had to rot in filth. No warm water was available for washing ourselves and our clothes. There was neither room, utensils, nor fuel. Our doctors would appeal regularly to the authorities to allow us the use of the municipal baths and implored them to install mobile disinfectant cauldrons in the camp. The doctors, among them famous professors of Warsaw, Poznan, Cracow and Lwow Universities, would also warn Commander Bereshkov and Doctor Yegorov of the danger of epidemics breaking out. Cases of typhoid fever and amoebic dysentery already had been recorded.

The word "epidemic" is not a popular one with the Soviet authorities. An epidemic is a nasty, punishable thing. The number of victims does not matter — this is a mere trifle. What matters is that for its outbreak, which, after all, cannot be hidden, somebody has to be made responsible. Whether it should happen in the camp of Starobyelsk, in an agricultural *kolkhoz* or in the penal forced labour camp in the Bolshezyemyelskaya Tundra, beyond the Arctic circle, is immaterial.

Surprisingly our doctors' warnings had worked. Messrs Yegorov, Bereshkov and Co. got into a state of jitters. And so one morning at the end of October, news went round that we were being taken to the town's public baths. The instruction said two batches daily of three hundred men each. All seven of our group hastened to join the first party. An autumn rain was pouring down mercilessly. Despite a strict order which forbade using hot water for washing one's things, I hid under my overcoat a change of clean linen and in another bundle my *onuce*, a few dirty rags and some handkerchiefs. We went out through the gate under a heavy escort which was armed, as usual, with rifles and bayonets. We marched along Kirov Street, the street we had come along when arriving at the camp. Swearing in their characteristic way "po matyeri"* the *boytzy* forced us to keep to the middle of the unpaved road where our feet sank up to our calves in mud and puddles. But it was not so much my feet that I pitied as my wretched ski boots and the loose tops. However, one reaches a stage when nothing really matters. And so, in a white rage against myself and everybody I fought my way ahead through mud and water.

In such filthy weather the townspeople were too busy avoiding getting wet to stare at us. Besides, what would have been the point? By then they knew very well what the "monastery" contained and had got used to the fact. Apart from this, our appearance was disgustingly repellent — we were unshaven and hairy like apes — that not even the wretched people of Starobyelsk would look at us. Some

---

* A much used, obscene Russian expression harping on one's mother's sexual misbehaviour.—Trs.

remnants of a ridiculous vanity always linger in a human being, however humble his circumstances.

My thoughts were interrupted suddenly by the strident blaring of a horn. Like some amphibian vehicle an army truck was ploughing through water and mud in front of us. It was a Soviet-made copy of an American Ford. Written on the radiator in red enamelled letters were the initials "ZIZ" which stands for "Zavody Imyeni Stalina" (Stalin Works.) "We have everything in our country and everything is of better quality" – the well known, worn out, refrain began buzzing in my head. We dispersed like frightened hens to both sides of the road. On seeing a fountain of mud rise from under the truck's wheels to splash our faces and uniforms, the driver and his passenger grinned with delight.

After covering a good mile we reached the outskirts of the town. Standing on a bend of the River Aydar was a vast one-storey red brick building. A blue signboard bearing the inscription "Gorodskaya Banya" (Town Public Baths) told us we had reached our destination. We had left the last inhabited cottages a long way behind us. On the other side of the Aydar were vast stretches of reeds and rushes, moving in waves like some great sea. Farther still lay open country covered by a grey blanket of rain.

A short fat man appeared on the threshold of the building. He was dressed in a *tyelogryeka*. The jacket is made of dark linen cloth padded with cotton wool and there is no collar to it but just a little band. The trousers are made of the same padded material. No wonder that a man in such an attire looks like a beer barrel. The *tyelogryeka* is used universally in the dry winter season and is light and extremely warm. On the other hand in rain it is useless as it gets soaked through like a sponge. Why the man chose to dress in this garment on such a rainy day remains a mystery known only to him.

The man was gesticulating wildly, shouting and issuing various orders to the *boytzy* who had brought us here. As it turned out he was the boss of the place and it was clear that his word was law.

The *banshchik*, as he was officially called, proceeded to carry out his task according to the instructions he had been given. After selecting from the front of our column two batches of fifty men each, he ordered them to step forward. One group was to busy itself providing fuel from a nearby dump of twigs, branches and roots, chopping it and stoking the furnace. The other group was to provide water for the boilers. Since the pump happened to be out of order they had to draw it from the river using ordinary buckets. The remaining men were to go inside the building.

I found myself in the first group. The wood was miserably wet, the axes blunt and the edges of the saws jagged. And of course we had to work outdoors. Rain was streaming down my collar and I soon became soaking wet. I cast a glance at our companions down below to see how they were faring. Their lot was probably worse than ours. To reach the river they had to skate on their bottoms down a steep, sticky bank, about ten metres high. They then had to zigzag back up the bank carrying buckets filled with water. Next they had to clamber up some wooden stairs to the roof of the building where they emptied the buckets into a pipe leading to the boilers.

It was not even possible to roll a cigarette in that weather. Besides, we were the object of constant obscene insults and also ridicule because of the clumsy way in which we chopped and sawed wood: "A vot vam tak i khorosho, sukin vy syny – byelorutschki proklyatyje! Nu davay, davay, pozhyvyey" (It serves you right, you S.O.B. – you damned *byelorutschi*. Come on, come on, hurry up). Experiencing this serfdom, we were in the depths of despair.

After some two hours the boilers began to get hot. One more hour and the first group finished their bath and came out of the building. It was our turn now. First we had to undress in a room cold and sticky with mud which was supposed to serve as a cloakroom. After that everyone had to make a bundle out of his uniform, overcoat and dirty linen and tie it up with the sleeves of the garments. The *banshchik* would then throw these miserable rags into a cauldron to be disinfected and to get rid of lice. I watched this operation with a feeling of terror, wondering whether there would be anything left of my clothes.

A gang of Soviet striplings suddenly fell upon us, pushing us, naked and shaking from cold, into an adjacent room where lines of benches were standing on a cement floor. The *banshchik* announced: "All of you are to sit down on these benches and have your hair shaved. Should anybody disobey I shall not let him into the bath."

I can remember vividly the scene which followed, even today. Zygmunt, George, Olgierd and I were objecting violently, shouting in chorus at the wretched youngsters: "What the devil are you doing? We shall not be treated like this, shorn like a flock of sheep. We are not criminals, damn it. Don't you know, here in this damned bath of yours, that we are officers – prisoners of war?" A burst of laughter and insults was the only answer. I could stand it no longer: "Pashol von (Off you go) and keep your hands from my head!" I roared when one of the "hairdressers" tried to make me sit down on a slippery bench and hit my neck hard with his hair trimmer. I was struggling with all my strength but because of all the wet slippery mud mixed with the cut-off hair there was no way in which I could get a hold with my naked feet on the slippery floor. A second "hairdresser" appeared on the scene. Getting hold of my waist he threw me onto the bench and pressed his knee hard against my body as if I were a piglet. My companions called out that I should stop resisting and calm down. In fact, any further opposition appeared hopeless. As the rest of my companions had resigned themselves to their fate I could do nothing but follow their example.

The trimmer was tearing at my hair mercilessly. This was in fact more of a pulling out than a haircutting session. I was shaking with cold and watched with fury as my hair fell into the mud. I had always been so fond of it! I had never shaved it off before and now I had to suffer the ignominy of having it done here, of all places. I was now staring blankly ahead of me, failing to recognise my friends. The loathsome nakedness of their emaciated bodies and of their shorn skulls made them look exactly alike. Once more the familiar nauseating apathy with its numbing effect was taking hold of me. Nothing mattered much any longer – to hell with everything – let the earth disappear from under me.

After this humiliating experience I was admitted to the proper bath. Hot water after nearly two months! Its invigorating effect restored me to consciousness and I regained my real self. I also succeeded in washing the dirty clothes I had smuggled in! Everyone's clothes were in a hugh, stinking, steamy pile and I had to make a long search in order to find my garments. They seemed dirtier than ever and were crushed beyond recognition. My only hope was that the lice had perished! In the mud of the icy cold cloakroom my feet got dirty again and there were no facilities for washing them before putting on my boots. Anyway, was there any point in it? Before I could reach my hut a mile long stretch of mud lay in front of me.

On our way home, close to the public baths, we ran into another party of three hundred men heading towards this "sanctuary of cleanliness". Their spirits sank visibly after we had warned them of what they were going to experience.

The vast majority of the prisoners, from the colonel down to the private, was suffused by a warm wave of patriotic and religious feeling, which probably reached its peak in this period. Neither misery nor hunger nor filth could dampen the fervour of these feelings. Misery was that fertile soil on which thrived the blossoms of faith in God and in a better future.

The chaplains of all faiths represented in the Polish Army conducted services in overflowing barracks. They would don the sorry vestments of their priestly estate that had miraculously weathered imprisonment and would lift up their voices in prayer in front of altars improvised out of a few boards covered with a piece of white linen, and those prayers would be more beautiful, more sublime and closer to the Almighty than any the finest temple on earth had ever celebrated. Fiery sermons imbued with pristine thought, simple and to the point, free from any suggestion of (clerical or) mentorial tone, swept the faithful into the kingdom of faith and love.

Never in my life had I seen so many heartfelt tears as streamed down the faces of the young and the old, the strong and the weak, and even those seasoned warriors who had seemed impervious to all sentiment.

That the need of common prayer was a great and compelling one may be seen from the fact that prisoners of war of the Hebrew, Protestant and Orthodox faiths attended Catholic services in great numbers and at the end of the sermon joined in the brotherly choral singing of hymns. Catholics similarly took part in the religious services of other faiths. Zygmunt, Laud and I would often go to the so called "Circus" where one of the pastors would deliver wonderful sermons on the uppermost scaffolding of that hideous barrack. Or we would go on a Friday evening to the threshold of the pitiful shed, bearing the No. 17, where hundreds of Jews, under the leadership of Dr. Steinberg, chief Rabbi of the Polish Army, intoned Hebrew prayers in a state of concentration bordering on ecstasy.

All of these religious leaders – and they totalled some twenty-five Catholics, Protestants, Jews and Orthodox Church priests – were heroes of those memorable days. For it was suicide to reveal the very spirit of religious faith or to feed the flame of revolt openly at a time when, as we all knew, the ranks of the worshippers included informers. The red cap of the *politruk* stole in during every service and our own domestic variety of tale-bearer was present during every sermon. The termite of betrayal had already begun its work. And though there were few traitors, one sufficed to disturb the peace of mind of one hundred of us.

This was doubtless a test period. During these first five or six weeks the Soviet authorities probably deliberately relaxed their reins and made it a point not to oppose a mass demonstration of the patriotic and religious feelings that had welled up within us. Such a policy afforded them an excellent opportunity to gauge our frame of mind and draw appropriate conclusions. . . .

And so, the NKVD Special Detail on 24 hour duty in building No. 20 had its eyes and ears open at all times and diligently registered reports coming in to it. . . .

One Sunday early in November, I was sitting hunched up on my upper bunk, touching the ceiling with my head. Kneeling or squatting near me were my friends from my group of seven. George was holding a small prayer book that had somehow not yet been confiscated. Though he was reading from it in a soft voice, I could catch snatches of the prayer.

At least 300 people were crowded into our room. The press and the stench were unbearable. Below me I could see only the top of Father Adamski's head as he celebrated Holy Mass in front of a wooden cross hung on the wall between tiers of bunks. Young chaplain Adamski was a native of Lwow and resident of my own barracks, one tier of bunks lower. Of a gentle disposition, often jolly, with the Lwowian's gift for music, he would frequently sing for our benefit, and in the evenings at the request of his immediate neighbours he would pray in a murmur.

As the priest began the Lord's Prayer, the silence was suddenly rent by Kopyeykin's rasping voice, coming from the hallway: "The service is to stop at once on order of the camp commandant!"

A deathly stillness settled over the room. No one moved, no one uttered a word. The priest slowly turned away from the altar, looked at Kopyeykin, let his glance travel over the roomful of worshippers, raised his hands as if for quiet, then turned his face to the cross again and in a firm resonant voice concluded his prayer with the words in Polish:

"And forgive us our trespasses as we forgive those who trespass against us, and lead us not into temptation, but deliver us from evil. Amen."

At that instant George's strong basso intoned the words of the ancient Polish hymn, *Boze cos Polske*. And 300 voices took up the powerful melody:

"Oh Lord, Thou hast to Poland lent Thy might
And with a Father's strong protecting hand
Hast given fame and all its glory bright,
And through long ages saved our Fatherland.
We chant at Thy altars our humble strain,
Oh Lord! Make the land of our love free again."

This magnificent hymn, written early in the nineteenth century when Poland lost her independence, had been sung for more than one hundred years in its unchanged version. Not until 1918, when Poland did become free again, following World War One, was the last line changed to:

"Oh Lord! Keep the land of our love free."

And now, in the autumn of 1939, when the lid of bondage was again clamped down on the Polish nation, the Poles spontaneously reverted to the original verse penned 140 years earlier! And in the fetid odour of our barrack, under the impact of the drama of these words, our voices broke and weakened, for none could summon the strength to keep back the choking tears . . . .

This was the last Holy Mass and the last chorale to be directed to God in Camp Starobyelsk in Soviet Russia.

On that very night my nerves were so on edge that I didn't sleep a wink. The round logs and unplaned boards of my bunk pressed painfully into my body, and it wasn't my turn to share a part of Olgierd's sheepskin which we used to do in rotation — I was freezing cold. Bugs were walking over my head, neck and ears. I had reached such a degree of perfection in killing these pests that even in my sleep, I could crush a bug bloated with blood by a single slap against my head. Lice were more partial to the middle of my chest and my shinbone. Due to my constant scratching those spots were always covered with scabs.

Water from our well made life a misery. It possessed unimaginably strong diuretic properties which would result in endless nocturnal pilgrimages. At every hour of the night some unfortunate victim, enduring the painful pressure no longer, would leap from his bunk and, in a state of semi-consciousness, would stagger barefoot into the cold of the night. As the latrine was some hundred metres away it was impossible to reach without disaster striking first. And so, later, after severe frosts had set in, yellow icebergs would form around our huts and although regularly destroyed, new ones would spring up in their places.

Among our group of seven I was the only lucky one to possess ski boots which, when it came to putting them on, presented no problems. All the others had boots with high tops. Tight and constantly wet it was impossible to pull them up quickly over one's legs. We therefore decided that my boots, ready for any emergency, would be positioned every night on a particular spot on our bunk so that any of our seven wishing to go outdoors could use them.

To my great astonishment I once learned from *politruk* Stepanov, the one with whom I had discussed films, that Starobyelsk was a well-known spa in Soviet Russia. This was something that even George did not know.

"Da, da," Stepanov was saying, "in summer, but in winter too, even from faraway places people will flock here to Starobyelsk to take waters which have unusual salutary properties." Interrupting him I asked: "All right, but where do these people stay? When I went through the town I had a glimpse of part of it, but to me it seemed overcrowded and from what I saw of the houses they looked rather small. . . ." I did not want to go on criticizing. Stepanov, however, went on explaining imperturbably: "Everywhere in our country there is plenty of room and in Starobyelsk too. Besides every patient who comes here is in possession of a *rozryeshenye* [permit] issued by the sanitary authorities and, of course, a proper billeting order. Accommodation therefore has to be found – it's as simple as that."

Quite simple indeed and what a shame I did not think of it myself! Who knows, maybe the patients stayed at the old monastery, so very suitable and comfortable for sick people! Ending our conversation Stepanov added, raising his voice: "And so remember how lucky you are in being able to benefit from the health-giving waters of this 'spa'." Having said this he turned on his heels and marched off.

Lummy! Somebody would have to pinch me or I might have ended up believing all this! I could already see here a pump-room, down there a promenade, a coffee house and a casino, over there sports grounds, even a beautiful park.

The *politruk* Stepanov was always dressed most meticulously. He wore a military-style blue overcoat tightened with a belt. His round face, well shaven, was usually powdered white and, when passing him, one would get a whiff of sweetish perfume. His long black boots were well cleaned and were encased in a pair of big shiny goloshes. Wearing them he would appear out of the blue in a place where he was least expected to be.

When entering a room he would stand for a good while turning his head and shifting his gaze from left to right. And should someone greet him with a "zdrastwuytye" – "good morning" – he would acknowledge it with a condescending nod of the head only. Usually, as a matter of principle neither he nor any other *politruks* returned our greetings.

On that night when most of us were asleep and I, hard as I tried, could not follow them, I suddenly heard distinct steps in the corridor and hushed voices in Russian. I nudged Zygmunt. He used to sleep as sound as a baby, but after waking up his mind was so alert that he could immediately solve the most difficult of problems. We both cast a glance at the door and in spite of bad lighting recognized immediately Stepanov's broad shoulders and head and next to him, from beneath the cap pulled onto his forehead, the wrinkled face of the tiny Kopyeykin as well as the tousled head of the night *Vakhtyor*.

I realised at once that they had come for somebody's soul. A shiver ran down my spine. I grasped Zygmunt's arm.

Without any searching they went directly for their quarry. Standing on the bunk boards Kopyeykin pulled himself up to the second level and squeaked in a half-whisper, tearing at the victim's legs: "Ey ty tam Adamskij! Vstavay seychas. Sobyeraysya s vyeshchami. Zhyvo." (Hey you there, Adamski. Get up immediately. Take along your things. Hurry up.)

And so what we most dreaded had happened. They had come after our army chaplains. The ominous addition "s vyeshchami" left no one in doubt as to what this meant. What was beyond the camp gate God only knew.

Our priest rose obediently from his bunk and stood in his underwear, barefoot on the muddy floor between the bunks. He was dressing silently and collecting his things together. His moving lips probably betrayed that he was saying a prayer. By now all of us were awake and a light murmur of voices rose to a crescendo. Prisoners were sitting up on their bunks watching the goings on and quite a number of them were saying goodbye to the priest in a loud voice.

"Vsye lozhys Molchat!" (Lie down all of you. Silence!) Stepanov roared furiously, thick with rage. And then, pushing the priest brutally, he spat out the excess of his guile: "Nu davay, pozhyvyey Adamskij. (Come on, hurry up, Adamski.) Or else you will want to propagate further your idiotic, pious *yerundu* [rubbish], your idiotic bourgeois sermons. . . ."

A total silence fell when the priest, ready to leave, slung his beggarly bundle on his shoulders, raised his right hand high and by the sign of the cross said goodbye to his petrified companions. The scene reminded one of a "tableau vivant" when the eyes of one hundred and fifty officers focused on the narrow passage where the *politruks* and the priest were standing.

"May God be with you! Blessed be Jesus Christ!" were his last words on leaving the room.

"For ever after, Amen," came the lugubrious murmur from all bunks.

An hour later we learned through the grapevine that at about the same time of night other men sent by the Camp Commandant had plucked out from various huts twelve army chaplains and taken them outside the gate.

A few nights later they took away what remained of them. Now there were no priests left. Not one had succeeded in concealing from the NKVD his sacerdotal status.

The army chaplains were not the only dedicated advocates of patriotism in the camp. Others too held meetings and spoke on various subjects. The whole camp was buzzing with such occasions, which were held nearly every day.

The talks had to be delivered from memory as no one possessed any paper on which to write notes: Talks and lectures covered areas such as the natural and social sciences, history, economics, linguistics, etc. But the most popular talks, attended by the largest audiences, were on topical matters and political problems. There were some well-known journalists amongst the inmates who excelled on these topics. These speakers would always follow some patriotic theme in their talks. Their aim was to try and bolster the flame of faith in a better future and to incite us to fight oppression and tyranny. Heated discussions and arguments would follow what they said.

The same fate befell these hot-headed speakers as befell our spiritual leaders. The methods were the same. They would be picked up in the dead of night and taken to an undisclosed destination. And finally the same happened to the organisers of meetings – a small group of a few Colonels and Majors known as the "Scientific and Cultural Circle". This supposedly conspiratorial cell was well known to the whole camp so no wonder its activities were eventually discovered by the NKVD's agents.

The camp became as if paralysed. The tragic experiences seriously undermined its morale. But this did not last. Although public displays of patriotism had to end and this included meetings and mass prayers – the spirit of independence did not die. Our activities did not stop, they merely went underground, and in the shadow of conspiracy they became more effective and productive.

Soon after the liquidation of the first group of "rebels", Commissar Kirshin called a meeting of our senior officers and all block commandants. He chose the clinic, which was the only "free" space in the camp, as the place of the meeting. The long line of patients waiting to be seen by the doctor that morning was simply dispersed.

Kirshin had the officers wait for him a long time before he showed up with his deputy Petrov and NKVD Major Lebedyev, the head of the Special Branch.

Smoking cigarettes with long mouthpieces, they seated themselves comfortably at the table, while we thirty officers, headed by Major Zaleski, stood facing them in a semi-circle. Kirshin – his sleek appearance suggesting he had enjoyed a hearty breakfast – unbuttoned his brown leather jacket and became absorbed in reading from a sheet of paper covered with fine print. He read slowly, as if briefing himself on what he intended to say.

Petrov, a tall gaunt figure, bony featured and long-nosed, clad in an old army coat, removed his red-bordered cap and revealed a balding head. His light glassy eyes came to rest either upon us or upon the ceiling. Sucking his cigarette with twisted lips, he nervously puffed out the smoke. He looked like a decided consumptive. Lebedyev, a corpulent giant, sat with legs stretched out before him and his small eyes, embedded in fat, surveyed our group with utter indifference. I saw these two gentlemen for the first time and I learned their identity only when one of our staff officers whispered the information to me.

Finally, after becoming familiar with the contents of the printed sheet, of which he himself probably was the author, and after having subjected us to the tense wait prescribed by NKVD etiquette, Kirshin let his keen glance travel over us and addressed us in a level, almost monotonous voice: "I am informing you that from now on the camp will be bound by strict regulations. The text of the regulations in the Russian language will be tacked on the bulletin boards. And you, Zaleski, will immediately have the regulations translated into Polish to avoid any misunderstandings, is it understood?" Zaleski nodded, whereupon Kirshin continued: "The regulations forbid the conducting of any kind of religious services, the saying of prayers, the singing of songs, I repeat, the singing of any kind of songs, whether religious or national or any songs suited to any occasion, understand? All meetings, lectures and discussions are forbidden, all, I repeat, even so-called scientific meetings," he added with a sneering accent.

"It is forbidden to assemble on the camp grounds and to walk in groups of more than two people. It is forbidden to change one's living quarters, that is, to move from one block to another. Those making such a change as well as the commandants of the blocks in question will be held accountable for any such transfers. Visiting other blocks is not permitted. Reading books aloud is forbidden.* No one may keep a diary or make notes. I warn you that if we find any material of that sort, we shall confiscate it. You are forbidden to play cards. Cards will also be confiscated, I warn you. It is forbidden to smoke in the barracks. It is forbidden to put out the lights at night. No one may leave the blocks after eight o'clock at night, except to go to the latrine. No Sundays or other holidays of yours will be observed and on those days you will be expected to work as usual.†

---

* This injunction referred to the Polish and other books that the prisoners had brought to the camp.

† There were no Sundays in the Soviet Union at that time. The rotating five day work period followed by one free day had been introduced. A year later the Soviets

"All Soviet officers are to be saluted when passed on the camp grounds. Violation of any of the points listed in the regulations will be severely punished, is that understood?"

Lebedyev sat on unmoved, staring sleepily at one point – a button on the coat of one of us. Not a muscle twitched in his fat face. Petrov, on the other hand, squirmed like an eel, nervously twisted his twisted lips, on which a venomous smile hovered, mumbled something as if in approval of the litany of injunctions and smoked one cigarette after another.

Kirshin paused briefly, then continued: "Radio loudspeakers will soon be installed in every block in the camp. Soviet newspapers will be distributed among you free of charge – *Pravda, Izvestia, Red Star* and others, as well as Polish-language newspapers." Noticing the tremendous impression this bit of information made upon us, Kirshin added with a faint smile: "Yes, yes, the *Lwow Red Banner,* the *Wilno Red Banner* and the *Soviet Voice,* which is published in Polish in the Ukraine. You will soon have a library too and a lending library of lawful and cultural games – chess, checkers and dominoes."

Zaleski suddenly exploded with uncontrollable laughter. For the first time Lebedyev moved his tremendous carcass, pulled up his legs and winked like an awakened alligator. Kirshin rose from his chair and shouted in a voice quivering with rage: "Why is Zaleski laughing? What's so funny?"

"I'm laughing because I recall that I must have been about eight years old when I last played dominoes. So it strikes me funny that I should now have the unusual opportunity of going back to my childhood days in a prison camp. . . ." he roared with laughter flashing his white teeth. Zaleski spoke a superlative Russian, which he had mastered during his pre-World War One studies at the Polytechnic in Petersburg.

"That'll do," growled Kirshin, "and just you try to play your card games! That capitalist game is good in bourgeois countries, but not in the progressive Soviet Union. Card playing is forbidden everywhere in the Soviet Union and no exceptions will be tolerated here!"

Kirshin had spoken his piece. After the command to disperse, we headed for our barracks, feeling very dispirited indeed, to acquaint our comrades with the start of a new order.

The announced regulations were no surprise. They were in line

---

returned to the 7 day week and Sunday became a day free from work. Its previous church name of *Voskresenye* (Resurrection) was restored. The purpose of this switchback was an increase in productivity: nine days were gained inasmuch as there are 52 Sundays in a year while the number of free days in a six-day week is 61.

with the deportation into the unknown of our chaplains and "lecturers", which had in itself been an event of the utmost significance. The sum of the injunctions read off to us indicated that the prisoner of war rights which we had been guaranteed at the outset and which we had desperately wanted to believe would be respected, were slipping away from us. The screws were being steadily tightened and our life was becoming more and more like the existence of ordinary prisoners rather than prisoners of war.

The new order which would force an old Polish colonel to salute any Soviet officer barely out of his teens was too humiliating for words. And none of the Soviet camp authorities ever addressed us in any other way except by name. Even the elementary gesture of showing respect for military rank did not exist here. Ourselves and our country were constantly insulted by such expressions as "You former officers of the former Polish Army," or "Poland did exist, but it won't any more." The "rotten democracies" was an epithet applied to all the allies. For seasoning, such individual phrases were coined as "imperialist old effigy" (Great Britain), "old disintegrating whore" (France). America, our then potential ally, was dubbed a country of capitalist terror, dictatorship of the dollar, and President Roosevelt was described as an oppressor of the unemployed and the Negroes. The war was at that time consistently referred to as the Second Imperialist War waged under the auspices of "bloody aggressors". Never a bad word about the Germans or Hitler. Peace and harmony reigned supreme, crowned by friendship and good neighbour relations along the frontier drawn through the middle of Polish territory by the notorious Ribbentrop-Molotov pact which was signed in Moscow on 28th September, 1939.

This daily moral flagellation either by a stupid little guard or by the perfidious Kirshin was a hundredfold more painful than our hunger and misery.

On a late evening at the beginning of November Major Skarzynski, an emissary of a small conspiratorial group of senior officers, sneaked into our block. This sickly and haggard man well into his fifties had, by a quirk of fate, found himself in the camp of Starobyelsk with his fourteen year old son. He had spent many years in the United States, where his beloved boy was born. Some years before the outbreak of the war he went back to Poland where he had settled for a time and had done quite well. However, after some time he had lost his rights as an American immigrant.

Skarzynski was in a frenzy. He kept calling on Bereshkov and Kirshin, writing petitions all the time to the highest Soviet authorities and to the American Ambassador in Moscow — all this to obtain the release not so much of himself as of his son who had undeniable rights to American citizenship. I happened to know about this state of affairs, for he would talk to me about his problems and we also shared a soft spot for America and the English language which, for the purpose of practice, we always used when speaking to each other.

On that particular night he slipped onto our top bunk and squeezed himself between Felo Daszynski and myself. In a state of great excitement he whispered: "Listen. I know positively that tomorrow in the morning the American Ambassador in Moscow, Laurence Steinhardt, assisted probably by Consul Angus Ward, will be coming here in order to carry out an inspection. He will be accompanied by delegates of the International Red Cross. America, as you know, has taken over the representation of Poland's interests and he is therefore our direct representative and protector. This information came to the ears of our group of Senior Officers. They have sent me to you because of that. . . ."

"Mister Major," I interrupted, "what sort of a yarn is this! What makes you so sure of this alleged forthcoming visit or that America is taking care of our interests in Soviet Russia? Confound it, don't make a secret of it. Don't you know what happened to Felo because of his excessive curiosity?"

Skarzynski would not listen however and went on talking. The rest of our group was now listening avidly to the mysterious conversation. "We have worked out with the Colonels the text of a petition in Polish. We must translate it right away into English and have at least ten copies of it made. . . . Don't interrupt, I implore you. The Ambassador's and the Red Cross's party will be coming here in two cars. They have already arrived in Starobyelsk where they are spending the night. . . . Don't interrupt, damn you. . . . Let me finish! There is a possibility that they will drive in here through the gate and halt in the square in front of the church. We must be ready for anything. The ten of us will be holding the petition and we will try to hand it to the Ambassador or to Consul Ward. If we are thwarted in this by the Soviet authorities we'll have to pass it on to someone else in the party, the chauffeur for instance. We can push it in someone's pocket or throw it into a car. I have here a few sheets of paper — we'll cut it into smaller pieces. . . . So don't let's waste precious time any longer, let's get on with our work!"

My impression was that Skarzynski had gone completely mad. However, I must admit that the petition, which was read out in a whisper, did make sense. It was short and to the point. It stated our rights as prisoners of war and on the basis of them demanded our immediate release from Soviet captivity, enabling us to leave the Soviet Union, with whom Poland was not at war, and join the ranks of our Allies in the fight against Germany.

Together, Skarzynski and I translated the text into English, after which Felo and I got down to writing it. Before Skarzynski slipped away from our room I arranged with him to meet me at the crack of dawn in the latrine on the "Siegfried Line". Here I would hand him the ten copies of the petition.

Squatting in almost total darkness, breathing the stench of the upper bunk, the only place where we could evade the attention of the night *vakhtyor*, Felo and I started to copy out the petition. Using an indelible pencil which we had to wet with the tip of our tongue, we wrote every character separately in a calligraphic writing. We finally completed our laborious task just as dawn was breaking. I dashed with the precious little bundle of paper to the fixed place and passed it on to the delighted conspirator.

When morning came the electrifying news swept like wild fire through the camp. Masses of prisoners were circling constantly around the square facing the church as if by pure chance. A long day was passed in waiting for the gate to open to let the diplomatic cars in.... Evening came and a rumour went round that the visit had been postponed for one day but that the visitors would arrive tomorrow without fail.

The mirage rose slowly and then faded into the desert sands.

All of us had given up any hope. Only Skarzynski, with some sick obstinacy, kept believing in a prompt intervention by the United States. His son said goodbye to his pathetic father and with the approval of the Soviet authorities joined the last batch of privates leaving the camp. What happened to this young lad I do not know. I used to see the father during the next two months quite often. To me he seemed to have gone insane.

He continued writing incessantly to the highest Soviet authorities in Moscow including Stalin himself, as well as to the American Ambassador. The poor man was deluding himself that he would receive an answer and did not understand that all his petitions went into his personal file at "Tovarishch Lebyedyev's" office and never went any further. One night however Lebyedyev and Company decided to liquidate this irritating gadfly. Kopyeykin came, sniffed out his quarry asleep somewhere on the fifth tier of the bunks at the Circus, squeaked into his ear: "Nu Skarzynski, sobyeraysya s vyeshchami" and took him outside the gate . . . and that was that.

The story of the "visit" that never materialized appears somewhat faded and pathetic today. At the time, however, it was something different, an event of great importance. But it became obvious that it was nothing but a Soviet manoeuvre, a feeler put out, not for the first nor the last time, to measure the general mood in the camp and to set a trap to catch the leaders of our "freedom activities". The day of reckoning followed soon after. After protracted nightly interrogations by Lebyedyev in Block 10 some twelve suspects were thrown into the newly "inaugurated" cooler for a stretch of two weeks on a diet of bread and water only. Our poor Felo happened to be among them. A few were taken during the night outside the gate. Luckily, they did not find out about me!

Normally the Polish National Day of 11th November was celebrated at this time. As a warning and a reminder the text of the Camp Regulations issued by Commissar Kirshin was pinned to a special board in front of the church, together with a whole series of big posters extolling the merits of the Soviet Constitution, known as the Stalin Constitution. These posters were illustrated with colourful vignettes symbolizing the riches of the country, the Communist regime's achievements and the general happiness of the Soviet people. Spilling from golden cornucopias came wreathes, hammers and sickles, ears of all kinds of corn, tractors, timber, domestic animals, game, fish, fruit, wine, flowers, deposits of coal and metals as well as factory chimneys belching smoke. All these blessings were shown falling into the happy outstretched hands of the *trudolubivyje* (people fond of working) and the equally happy hands of the *grazhdanye* (citizens), their faces glowing with joy. Predominant amongst these posters, however, were huge coloured pictures of the spiritually inseparable trio – Lenin, Stalin and Marx.

Despite the fact that no more army chaplains and political speakers were present among us, great preparations were made in a mood of excitement to mark the annual Polish "Day of Independence". Secret instructions were issued by our senior officers and brought to the attention of junior officers. Despite all restrictions and prohibitions we were to respect the anniversary, refuse to work on the day and arrange for suitable speeches to be made, followed by the singing of the National Anthem. We were told that if all of us behaved in such a forthright way we would not suffer retribution at the hands of the authorities.

November the 11th came and early in the morning we were standing as usual in a long queue facing the field-kitchens waiting for our normal portion of oatmeal. It was snowing heavily and the dry snow flakes got into our eyes and collars. Coming from the direction of the church and running towards us a group of *boytzy* suddenly

147

appeared. At the head of them we recognized some well known *politruks*. Among them the thin figure of Petrov with, as always, the inseparable cigarette in his crooked lips and our "good old friend", the freshly perfumed and powdered Stepanov. Petrov was shouting: "Commander of barrack number 8. Provide one hundred men for work immediately! They are to assemble in front of the Church!" Leaving a few *boytzy* to supervise the execution of his order he continued on his mission. Similar scenes of forced recruiting took place in every nook and cranny of the camp.

Within half an hour about two thousand men were ready for marching off outside the gate. They came back in the evening half dead from exertion and cold. From Zygmunt and Olgierd, who happened to be in that party, we learned that, once more, they had had to carry enormous logs of timber. Since no engines were available they had to shunt manually from one railway track to another dozens of wagons loaded with timber.

The remaining 3,000 odd men (there were about 5,000 men in the camp on that day) had to form one huge line, two men deep and heavily guarded by the *boytzy*. After two hours of waiting we, who were at the rear of what was now a moving column of men, saw the vanguard moving slowly out through the gate. Being at the far end we had no inkling of what was going on at the front. When at last we arrived at the gate we realised what lay in store for us. There was a passage between the outside of the wall which ran along Kirov Street and a palisade of barbed wire surrounding the whole of the camp. It was so narrow that a single man could squeeze himself through only with the greatest difficulty and not without tearing his clothes on the sharp barbs. We were all pushed separately by the *boytzy* into this passage and they would then see that we kept on moving along. When some of us got entangled in the wires and stopped the column moving, they would prod us with their bayonets from outside the fence to get us going again quickly.

Not all of our men possessed overcoats. Looking like old female beggars some of them were wrapped up in rugs and a few poor wretches shivered with cold in their light summer uniforms.

There happened to be a few passers-by on the other side of the street. Most of them were women tucked in shawls from under which the tip of the nose only would protrude. Shod in soft winter *valenki* — a kind of footwear made of thick felt — they trod lightly in the fresh, puffy snow. They watched with amazement as the inmates of the "Monastery Camp" were pushed through the barbed wire tunnel. Despite the fact that the *boytzy* would disperse them with shouts: "Nu, khodi, provalivay" (*Nu*, off you go, get a move on), they would halt for a while and their whispers would then reach my ears: "Look at that, look at what they are doing to them. It's simply a shame, a disgrace!" and quite a few of the elderly women would wipe away a tear.

Moving as I have described, we walked at a snail's pace round the whole of the camp wall, a distance of about one kilometre. When I and my companions were finally nearing the gate again, almost at the end of our trip, we could still see the far end of our column in front of us. Before we crossed the gate on our way back, our ordeal nearly finished, we were counted by our "solicitous protectors" who tapped each of us on the shoulder. They apparently feared that some of us might have escaped while doing the round.

This spiteful and despicable "game" had lasted a whole day. We came back to our barrack at dusk, frozen to the marrow and in torn overcoats.

Since our cooks had also suffered this macabre experience the cauldrons were empty. And so it was only at about midnight that we were given a bowl of the watery soup *schchi*. This is how the inmates of Camp Starobyelsk were allowed to celebrate Polish Independence Day on the 11th November, 1939.

12. PRISONERS FROM SHEPETOVKA

Hardly had the gates closed behind the last batch of privates when on the next day – the 16th November – a new large party consisting of officers only arrived at the camp.

A thousand hungry men, a thousand officers of all ranks except that of General, a thousand haggard, bearded faces, a thousand miserable wretches. This was a truly shattering sight. I can see all this as vividly as if it had happened today – all those men who dispersed all over the camp like beggars with frostbitten limbs and bundles on their hunched backs, in search of a warm corner and a piece of bread.

It was only after days and weeks, depending on how long it took each man to recover, that a brother would meet his own brother, a son would recognise his own father, a friend would come across his pal. The party, numbering about two and a half thousand men, arrived at the railway station in Starobyelsk in one formation. Thirteen hundred men were detrained at the station, of whom one thousand were taken to the Monastery Camp immediately. Three hundred, as it turned out later, were taken to the local prison and held there for three weeks. Only then were they allowed into the camp.

Twelve hundred men were left locked in box-cars. In May 1940 we learned that from the Starobyelsk railway station they were transferred to the Kozyelsk Camp, another big prisoner of war camp for Polish Officers, situated in Central Russia. Presumably they went there because there was no room at Starobyelsk Camp. At the time we had no idea that the Kozyelsk Camp existed.

Since the Soviet guards had split the whole party of 2,500 men under the cover of darkness and in a quick and chaotic manner, those who had crossed the gates of the Monastery were unable for a long while to tell who happened to be in the camp and who had been left in the box-cars. We were informed by the newcomers, however, that there were among the transported prisoners several Generals and a large group of Colonels. Prominent among the group of

150

Generals was the venerable figure of Stanislaw Haller, one time Chief of the General Staff of the Polish Forces. He was the brother of General Jozef Haller who during the First World War had been in command of the Polish Legion recruited in the USA.

During the march from the railway station to the town all the Generals and Colonels were suddenly separated from the main column and directed into some side street. That was the last anyone saw of them.

About a week later, when I was queuing for a bowl of oatmeal, a tall bearded man embraced me, calling me by my Christian name: "Dearest Bron, don't you recognise me? You look so thin and so changed, particularly without your hair. Still I could tell right away that it was you! That we should meet here of all places and in such conditions. . . . Oh my God!"

I was staring at him not believing my eyes. In fact I now recognised him, though not by the features of his face, which had been unshaven, nor by his deeply sunken blue eyes, nor by his uniform, which still displayed remnants of the ensigns of the 1st Lancers Regiment, but by his voice only. This miserable beggar was Jan Sedzimir, the husband of my cousin Hela, whom I last saw briefly in Lublin sitting on top of a rack wagon with her children and a mass of bits and pieces, all of them driving into the unknown.

From that moment on Jan and I became inseparable. The poor devil had found a temporary shelter in a little shed, known as the "potato shed", constructed with poles and covered by a thatched roof which was peppered with holes. Secretly, I got him away from there and found him accommodation on my bunk among my hospitable group of seven friends.

Later, for long hours, he would tell us of his own adventures and would describe in vivid detail the sinister goings on in the so far unknown Shepetovka transit camp.

"I had been wounded by the explosion of a German shell. This happened on the Vistula river not far from Deblin. Transferred to a hospital in Kowel I spent ten days there recovering from my injuries. On hearing that the bolsheviks were to enter the town we did a bunk with a few companions strong enough to walk. . . . They didn't get far. They were caught by the *boytzy* on the very same day. I saw it happen. Luck was on my side, however, and I succeeded in escaping. I hid for a while in the woods. After a few days I ran into a fairly large group of survivors of our army. I joined them and we went on hiding in the thickness of the forests. We moved during the night only directing ourselves southwards, hoping thus to escape to Hungary. There was, however, still a long way to go . . . and we were not in fact to get very far. One morning when, exhausted from hunger and cold, we were still fast asleep when we were suddenly awoken by shouts and shots coming from all directions. A few of our men were killed on the spot. All we could do was to try and seek cover behind the tree trunks. Putting up a resistance was of course out of the question. Some two Soviet infantry companies armed with machine guns were closing in on us. We were about fifty men strong with ten officers among us. . . . They took away arms, they pinched our watches, tore off our epaulets, our eagles . . . . A young Soviet officer, presumably in command of the detachment in question, burst suddenly into our group of men on a small, foaming Cossack horse. He ordered the officers to come forward. Pounding with their butt-ends the *boytzy* pushed us out. Suddenly a shot was heard. Whether it was a *boyetz* or one of our own men who discharged, I don't know. Anyway, no one fell and no one had uttered a cry. Almost at the same time there was another shot right at my side. It was the Soviet officer on his horse who, using his revolver, had fired between the eyes of a young Second Lieutenant of the 53rd Infantry Regiment standing a few steps away from him. He shot him dead. In a savage frenzy, spurring his horse so that its sides bled, shouting in a deep voice the worst obscenities he ordered that the rest of us should be tied to the trees. . . .

"Every one of us became the prey of a few *boytzy*. They were yelling and swearing, but like wild beasts after they had smelt blood, showing their teeth with cruel and fierce delight. Pressing our bodies hard against the trees they used our belts to tie our hands behind our backs. I was howling with pain – not only were they twisting my wrists and arms, but I could feel my wound, hardly healed, parting again. When the nine of us were ready for execution, the officer, still on horseback, advanced towards us and spat out more or less the following words: 'You dirty swine, you SOB. You should have given yourselves up a long time ago to the Red Army, not hidden in the forests like bandits, fuck your mothers! I am now going to show you how the Red Army punishes those guilty of disobedience!'

"We were all protesting desperately – we, the officers tied up to the trees as well as the privates who were standing around. The Soviet officer wasn't paying the slightest attention, however. He bent down from the saddle, talked a while to some of his non-commissioned officers and then an execution squad was formed. Our executioners moved towards us . . . .

"Trees in a forest, as you know, do not grow in straight lines. The victims therefore were in a zigzag line and I counted them, starting from the right hand side. As far as I could make out I was the sixth. The squad halted in front of the first victim. The command 'load, present, fire' resounded through the forest. Inert, the first officer slumped down and remained hanging on his tied arms. His cap dropped from his head and blood gushed from his shattered skull. I closed my eyes and felt a numbing sensation of weakness in my legs. I also tried to pray. A second deafening salvo followed. At the sight of this monstrous crime our soldiers went almost mad. They were invoking God and protesting violently .... A third salvo was fired and then a fourth one. I lost any notion of time, I didn't know whether a second or a minute had passed. ...

"The patter of a horse's feet and a piercing cry in Russian: 'Perestan strelat!' (Stop firing!) woke me from my prostrate condition. I opened my eyes. The execution squad with their rifles ready for firing were positioned a few steps away from my nearest neighbour on my right hand side. Looking in front of me I noticed the other Soviet officer, presumably of a higher rank, who had reared his horse and was talking in a hushed voice to the younger officer. I did not understand what they were saying, but I couldn't fail to see that something was happening, that some orders were being issued. After a while the firing squad marched off and the *boytzy* rushed to untie the hands of those still left alive."

"Good God! You just missed a ghastly death by a hair's breadth from the hands of those brigands! What happened next. Go on!" I interrupted, unable to stand the suspense, squeezing his hand. He continued his grisly tale: "Yes, fate had treated me mercifully, no doubt about that. But reminiscences of this massacre are like a nightmare — they keep haunting and tormenting me all the time. The bodies of my unfortunate companions were left in the forest. The Soviet soldiers would not allow us to go near the remains, so that we could at least cover the bodies with some earth. 'They are to stay exactly as they are, as a warning to others,' snarled the Soviet officer.

"A long excruciating march followed. At the end of our tether after two days without any food we staggered back to Kowel where we landed in a jail. When I was searched I had to strip completely naked and they took all my money and documents from me. This uniform and greatcoat are all I was left.

"I was thrown into a tiny little cell already full up with about twenty-five other officers. The lack of space and the stench was unbearable. We sat in semi-darkness — a tiny grated window high up in the ceiling let just a thin shaft of light in. There was nothing to lie down on — no bunks, not even straw. We had to pile up, one upon the other on the bare floor. A bowl of soup and a slice of bread was our daily pittance. Twice every twenty-four hours we were all taken to the lavatory. This was sheer torture. Some of us had to relieve ourselves on the spot.

"After six days of this torment came the words of the command which you know only too well: 'Davay sobiraysya s vyeshchami!' We were taken from our cell into the prison courtyard where we were made to join a group of some two hundred officers. Under heavy escort we left for the railway station. A thousand or perhaps more privates were standing on the platforms waiting for the train. They loaded us at night, packed together like sardines into box-cars, and after a few hours the train set off.

"Various rumours went round – some good, some not so good. We tended to believe in the first ones according to which we were being taken to the city of Lwow where we would be set free. We tried to find out the truth through the slits in the boards of our box-car. It appeared that we were nearing the Soviet frontier as the border stones could already be seen. . . .

"They shunted our box-cars in all directions and it was only late at night that our train pulled out of the border station and gathered speed. Here I should explain that from the Polish frontier to Shepetovka there are two railway tracks one of which is the normal gauge as in almost all European countries, the other being the wide Russian gauge. Those two tracks were originally constructed to make a shuttle service between the two countries easier. This led us to a misapprehension since, as we knew the Polish box-cars in which we were travelling could not be pulled along the wide Russian tracks we imagined that our train had been turned back at the frontier and was heading towards Lwow. When, however, the train halted after a few hours and shouts of 'Vylizay s vagonov s vyeshchami' (Get off the train with your things) could be heard, our illusions were shattered!

"We were at Shepetovka and the date was the 3rd October. We had to march from the station in rain and ankle-deep in mud. The miserable little town, sunk in darkness, was asleep. After half an hour the outlines of a long building loomed in front of us. We went through the gate, passing a strong body of guards and found ourselves in barracks constructed by the bolsheviks apparently not long ago. But what an unbelievably shoddy piece of work they were. The plaster was falling off, window panes and frames were broken, stairs were rotting due to the constant mud, in short it was all in a state of complete decay.

"Inside there was an innumerable multitude of men – I would guess about twenty thousand!

"Conditions were simply appalling. Here in Starobyelsk things are far from being ideal but at Shepetovka they were a lot

154

worse. The enormous halls were without bunks so everyone had to lie down side by side on a bare cement floor where there was always plenty of mud but not even a bit of straw. The latrine was totally insufficient – night and day long queues stood in front of it. The only water for twenty thousand men was from two wells. It was impossible to wash oneself or one's clothes. All this goes to illustrate our misery.

"We all suffered severe hunger. Sometimes we didn't get a hot meal for two or three consecutive days. Not even hot water was available as fuel was scarce. The only kind of food we could rely on was bread – the same ration as here, that is half a loaf, about 500-600 grammes daily. Lice were devouring us and dysentry was rampant. There was no medical help and men about to die were taken outside the gate. After a few weeks mortality increased to such an extent that up to ten cases of death were registered every day.

"At the same time we were constantly fed with encouraging news! First we were led to believe that privates would soon be set free and that this would be followed by the release of officers. In fact, after a while the authorities began to separate the ranks – just as they did here. After secretly changing their uniforms and insignia of rank, some twenty, perhaps more, officers joined the privates and left. They took a big risk. I too struggled with thoughts of doing the same, but finally decided it was wiser to stay put. After all, there was no evidence that the convoys would be directed westwards and not to some other destination. I decided to stay with the rest of the officers. Perhaps I was right, who knows. . . .

"After the departure of the privates only officers – about 2,500 of them – were left in our camp. And so for another six weeks we had to endure our miserable conditions. Until the 13th November when early in the morning we were raised from our sleep by the well-known shouts of: 'Davay, sobyeraysia s vyeshchami.' Once more we had to march to the station to be entrained like sardines in a number of box-cars and taken off to an undisclosed destination. The rest you know well. And you'll fully appreciate now why we looked like real scarecrows when we arrived here!" He uttered a laugh, but soon continued in a worried voice: " . . . I shall never forget the towering figure of the senior officer – old General Haller. I can see him now in his civilian light overcoat, his faded hat and his boots worn to holes, patiently waiting in a queue in the rain for his bowl of soup or lying down to rest his aching old bones on the cement floor of our appallingly overcrowded room, or when, amidst a barrage of insults and swearing, he was picking up the rest of his meagre belongings to be marched off into the unknown. He bore all these privations without a murmur or word of complaint and all humiliations with unparalleled dignity.''

Of the many primitive workshops organized out of nothing by our provident Major Zaleski, which were gradually being put into operation through the ingenuity and hard work of our willing comrades, the first to begin to function was the carpentry shop.

One additional duty of our carpenters was that of making coffins.

The "order" for a coffin was generally put in without warning, for most of the dead departed this world outside the camp walls. Many of them died in the municipal hospital with which our own doctors had no contact. The messenger boy of the Soviet Command, Kopyeykin or someone like him, would dash into the carpentry shop and announce: "One coffin to be made right away!" exactly as if he were ordering a toothpick.

At the very beginning, when the first victims began to pass away, our carpenters would ornament the coffins with a cross and would engrave the letters S.P. (of Blessed Memory) on it. They would even engrave or carve an artistic replica of the Polish national emblem — the Eagle.

Major Zaleski battled with Commandant Bereshkov and Commissar Kirshin over the human right to honour the memory of the dead. At first he insisted that the Soviet authorities agree to the presence of a delegation consisting of one Colonel and one Second Lieutenant at every funeral ceremony to represent the dead officer's comrades. When this proposal was rudely turned down, the Major requested that at least the names of the dead be submitted and that permission be granted to have them carved on their coffins. When this too was denied him, he implored the Russians to give us at least the numbers of the graves in the cemetery, where the dead were buried. But even this request met a refusal. Our captors maintained that the question of who died, where he died and where he was buried concerned only the Soviet authorities and no one else!

Finally, one day, when our carpenters were busy nailing a wooden cross to the lid of a coffin, Deputy Political Commissar Petrov came on the scene. Chewing on his inseparable cigarette, he pointed to the cross and barked: "Remove that stupid decoration at once! There are to be no letters, inscriptions or nonsense on the coffins. Our command is doing you a big favour allowing you to waste good wood on coffins. If you don't obey us, we shall bury your dead in sacks, understand?"

From that moment on, trucks, horse-drawn vehicles or sleighs carted away from the camp carpentry shop clean, well-planed snowy coffins that bore no cross and no name, but that exuded the fragrance of fresh pine.

In the same room as me in Block 8, except he was at the other end, on the lowest bunk, lived an old little man by the name of Terlecki. He must have been about seventy-five years old. How did that poor fellow get to be among us in the officer prisoner of war camp? The rags in which he was clad did not betray any recent army membership. Furthermore, he was stone deaf and half-blind, so that it was next to impossible to pry from him the secret of his presence among us. (It was said that he was the uncle of Szymon Terlecki, the well-known Polish painter and alpinist.) Nevertheless, we treated him with the greatest respect, as would befit a retired General.

Winter began in earnest in the early part of December. Grandpa Terlecki was very tall, stooped a little and was fantastically thin. He was gnawed by hunger more than were the young people. We fed him extra pieces of bread, for which he thanked us with a kindly smile from under his long white moustache. The diuretic well water gave him especial difficulty. It was a heart-rending sight to see Grandpa climb out of his bunk in the evening before we fell asleep, and in his ankle-length white underwear, wrapped in a fragment of old blanket, patter barefoot along the dark corridor and then down the broken stairs into the snow and toward the latrine. This pilgrimage must have been repeated every hour all through the night. The poor man groaned loudly as he moved toward the door, unable to stand the sharp pain in his bladder. Whenever we heard this painful moaning we all knew that old Terlecki was hurrying outside again.

One day at dawn, Terlecki's bunkmates became alarmed at his absence. At first, accustomed to his periodic nocturnal trips, they did not notice that the old man's place had been vacant for some time. When the realization finally dawned upon them, a few of them immediately hastened to the latrine to investigate. They searched for a long time until to their horror they saw the old man lying inertly in the ditch we called the Siegfried Line. He had apparently tumbled into the dung from the ice-covered pole on which he was perched and had frozen to death! The dung was frozen solid, which kept the body on the surface. Otherwise Terlecki would have been swallowed up and some dung collecting equipment of the future would have come upon the remains of a human being at the bottom of the pit.

We notified our own and the Soviet Command of the tragic accident. Before our carpenters, prodded on by the Soviet guards, could build a new pine coffin, we placed the old man's body on the clean snow close to our barrack and covered it with a Polish army blanket. When we were lowering it into the coffin, before the lid was clamped down, I stealthily slipped my hand underneath the blanket and placed a small wooden cross on the bony chest that was covered only by a ragged shirt.

At nine in the morning, whispering a prayer, we carried the coffin to a horse-drawn sleigh. The kind-looking driver helped us deposit our comrade on the sleigh. Then, at a Soviet NCO's command to cover the coffin, the driver placed an old sack over the white boards, sprinkled them with straw . . . and carted the nameless body away.

Terlecki's death was only one picture out of many. A few of the prisoners died in the barracks suddenly of a heart attack. One young officer hanged himself from the branch of a tree during the night. A captain was shot like a dog from the sentry tower for approaching the "forbidden" three-metre strip that ran like an invisible ribbon along the inner part of the wall. At least fifty died in the camp hospital before the Soviet authorities had had a chance to transport them outside to let them die beyond the camp according to time-honoured custom.

Whenever a death occurred in the camp, our carpenters at least knew for whom they were making coffins. But the coffins which were ordered in relatively greater quantities for the "deceased" from the city, remained an unsolved mystery. We never really found out how many of our people died in the city. One of the officers employed on coffin construction was once struck with a bright idea: Perhaps some of these coffins for the "outside trade" were used not only to bury our prisoners but also to haul away local burdensome Soviet citizens, prisoners or other enemies of the people whom death had mowed down unexpectedly. Who knows? After all, what could be more convenient, speedy, inexpensive and safe from detection than to make such use of the carpentry shop hidden inside the walls of the Monastery camp?

For in that vast subcontinent called the USSR, anything and everything is possible.

13. LAVOTCHKA, THE GREEN BOX

One morning in the latter half of November, a sensational bit of news spread through the camp like wildfire. "The *lavotchka**** has arrived! The *lavotchka* has arrived!" was passed on from person to person. Its motor wheezing and axle-deep in mud, the Zis truck rumbled through the gate and parked in the square in front of the Church. A big, green wooden box stood on the truck's high platform. The box looked like a little house, or rather like a huge dog-house. It had a sloping roof while one of the walls was a double door held in place by an iron rod and padlocked. With our bare hands we transported the Zis's mysterious load to a wooden annex of the Circus. This annex was really the skeleton of what remained of a summer veranda adjoining the walls of Block 5. The joke of the hour was that the green box contained a new shipment of wild monkeys for the Circus.

But we all knew that the truck had brought supplies for the *lavotchka* that had been promised us. It also brought a big staff to service the *lavotchka*. The unloading of the box was supervised by the commissary's director, who bore the title of "tovarishch diryektor". He was a well-fed civilian in a warm quilted overcoat, an imitation fur cap with ear-muffs and oversize goloshes. This director was aided by two male assistants and by one middle-aged and plain woman. The *lavotchka* personnel was completed by a light black-moustached bespectacled man who was rather shabbily dressed and had the swarthy colouring of a Georgian. The director himself treated this unimpressive looking individual with great deference, addressing him either as "tovarishch kontrolyor" or what sounded even more mysterious, as "tovarishch kalkulator".

A few hours elapsed before the supplies were arranged on a few improvised shelves and the overflow was stacked on the floor and before the gates of Sesame opened to admit the first lucky prisoner in a line that must have numbered at least a thousand.

The things that that commissary had in stock seemed to us something out of this world, rivalling Macy's in New York or

* Small shop, in this case a mobile one – Trs.

Harrods in London. There were needles with small and with big eyes, there was black thread and white, there were metal buttons for our underwear and black wooden ones for our outer garments, there were safety pins, coloured combs, tiny mirrors the size of a half-dollar, long shoelaces, razor blades (There were no razors, shaving brushes or shaving soap), toothbrushes and toothpaste, shoe polish (but no brushes), slivers of dark gritty soap for laundry purposes and perfumed face soap, heavy ladies' (why ladies'?) perfumes in decorative vials, scented toilet water, fragrant white and pink powder (no lipstick, what a pity), cloth suspenders, cloth belts, *onuce*, pencils (but no paper), cigarettes with long mouthpieces of the Bielomor Kanal brand, pouches of loose tobacco, matches, and, last but not least, hard-boiled sweets.

No wonder our eyes sparkled greedily at the sight of this magnificent array and were riveted by the coloured sweets that glittered like Indian jewels. With a deft knock of a rod, the saleswoman broke loose the sweets which had become glued together into a hard pyramid, and then weighed them into 500 gram (one pound) portions on old-fashioned rusty scales.

The temper of our people, who had been irritable and impatient when they started queuing, improved steadily as they drew nearer the magic window. Whether at the sight of the woman or the sweets or the feminine perfumes and powders, they laughed gaily and joked with the saleswoman. And when they left the window with a hatful of acquired items, they gratefully threw her a polite *spasibo* (thank you). At first, she maintained a stony demeanour but under the impact of an endless stream of sincere words of appreciation, she thawed out a little and would say softly, *pozhaluysta* (you're welcome), or would even wish us good health, if none of her *tovarishches* (comrades) was within earshot.

After a while, as the first customers began to leave the *lavotchka* clutching their purchases and loudly sucking their sweets, others gradually began to drop out of the queue with long faces. For it developed that the items were sold only for roubles and not for Polish zlotys, which many of us still had despite the inspection. Hardly anyone had roubles in his possession. Those officers who had come from Shepetovka were somewhat better supplied with Russian money for they had had the opportunity of exchanging the zlotys for Soviet roubles at fantastic rates. But what, for instance was I to do with my 80 kopecks, with which I had been presented by the old peasant woman at the Kupyansk station?

But another circumstance dashed our hope of purchasing these precious items. The *lavotchka* had enough stock to take care of the

160

needs of 200 people while our camp population exceeded 4,000!

The quarrels that ensued, therefore, were understandable. The chief bone of contention was that the principle of first come, first served ruled out a fair distribution of the items. But this time it was already too late to settle this issue. All of us, including our superior officers, were completely taken by surprise by the arrival of the *lavotchka*. Besides, no one could have foreseen what the *lavotchka* contained or the prices or the fact that only roubles would be acceptable in payment. When in the future, the *lavotchka* was again to descend upon us like a meteor, our camp command and block commandants would be prepared with a key for the equitable division of the goods. We would purchase the entire contents of the green box in bulk and would then proceed to distribute the goods proportionately among the various buildings, where in turn a peaceful individual distribution was to be made. We would usually draw lots and frequently by mutual consent, the article in question would wind up in the possession of the most needy.

Meanwhile, the *lavotchka*'s stock melted away and there was no way of restraining the buyers. Anyway, what could be done if there turned out to be only 50 razor blades or at most 100 baby size toothbrushes or 25 tubes of hopelessly petrified toothpaste, or about 100 fragrant cakes of "Carmen" soap manufactured by the "T. Zh." soap and perfume factory in Leningrad? As far as I know, the Carmen brand soap is the only one of its kind in the Soviet Union, for I never came across any other. Its green wrapping featured an oval adorned with colourful flowers out of which peered a fiery damsel with raven tresses, bared bosom and a blood red rose stuck in her passionate lips.

It soon became evident that all the remaining articles, including the sweets, were stocked in the same proportions. Hence, a few hours later, the *lavotchka*, denuded of its last button, closed its door.

The prisoners of war were not the only clients of the *lavotchka*. One by one, virtually all Soviet camp functionaries, young and old, slipped into the store by way of the back door that led from the Circus to the veranda, and left carrying impressive quantities of goods.

Though I did not queue up with my 80 kopecks, I hovered close to the *lavotchka* out of sheer curiosity. I could not help noticing many interesting things. As far as the *lavotchka* stock was concerned, the one item I longed for most was a toothbrush, which I had not seen in two months. To be sure, I had learned to manage without it. First, I would massage my gums with the crust of dark bread (I had been advised to do so by the very likeable dentist, Dr Leon Slower of

Wilno, who later became my friend), then I would remove particles of food from between my teeth with a splinter of wood, and finally I would wash out my mouth with soapy water . . . *ad nauseam.*

I observed the workings of the *lavotchka* with more than passing curiosity. I realized that living as I did completely isolated from the outer world, I had a rare opportunity to catch a glimpse of what may appear to be a small, but a very revealing, sector of actual life in the Soviet Union.

When I could see through the broken panes of the veranda the familiar faces of Lebedyev, Petrov, Stepanov and a dozen other *politruks,* and following their example, several score younger members of the camp police, stealthily making purchases through the back entrance, I felt my blood boil at the lawlessness of it.

Even Colonel Bereshkov and Commissar Kirshin, though they did not dare do their shopping in full view of the prisoners, fidgeted about in the square in front of the church to make sure they would get the articles their messengers had gone to purchase for them. I could see perfectly well that whenever the messengers approached their higher-ups with bundles under their arms, they would all disappear through the *"prohodnaya budka"* (the passageway for pedestrians near the gate, built in the shape of an L and sheltering the sentries), probably crossing Kirov Street and entering one of the two large two-storey buildings housing the Soviet camp command.

This scene would recur whenever the green box reappeared in the camp at intervals of two or three weeks. Invariably the Russians were the first to get their hands on the stock, picking out the best items with no less eagerness than was exhibited by us who lived in abject poverty.

Little by little I learned a number of things. I did not have many clues to go by, but step by step I would get at the heart of a question. It was in this way that I learned the meaning and function of a *lavotchka* in the Soviet Union, and how I understood why our guardians were so greedy in their plundering of the contents of our green box.

Everybody knows that this immense country has for years been suffering want, that for years it has been in the throes of a chronic shortage of essential commodities. Inefficient farming methods or faulty distribution of agricultural produce lies at the root of the food shortage; inefficient manufacturing methods create a clothing shortage; and the same shortage applies to the commodities which the *lavotchka* displayed to us so temptingly. For these buttons, needles, safety pins, scented soaps bearing the image of Carmen and toothbrushes are not to be found in most parts of the USSR. Our "artisan" officers had already learned the problem presented by finding a nail, a piece of wire, glass, or tin, an electric cord or bulb, a quart of kerosene, a sack of coal, firewood, brick or cement, a spade, a pick-axe. . . .

How falsely now rang the words we had heard so often in Poland when we were being driven eastward: "U nas wsyo yest," "U nas vsyevo mnogo!" (We have everything. We have plenty of everything.)

The *lavotchka* articles were sold at official prices. That was why *tovarishch* controller and calculator had to be present. The articles and their prices were a great temptation to the Russians. We could see for ourselves that the prices were relatively low, even if we took as our measuring rod the official rate of exchange of the rouble (five roubles to one dollar). So far I did not know anything about prices in the so-called free market which I had heard existed. But I was soon to get a good deal of information from Major Zaleski, who, thanks to his constant contacts with the Soviet authorities, had the chance to fathom the mysteries of life beyond the camp gate. Stretched out on a narrow bed that was fashioned out of a few boards nailed together, in a room measuring nine feet by seven, which served as the headquarters of the Polish command, Major Zaleski launched into a reply to my question. Nearby was another room, perhaps about two feet bigger, in which eight of Major Zaleski's closest collaborators lived. The two rooms comprised the crooked hundred year old cottage marked with the number "1". As the Major's legs were covered with festering wounds, probably because of faulty diet, he would raise them whenever he could.

"So you want information," he began in his usual hearty manner. "Do you think I go into town and drop into bars for a stein of beer or spend my free time in the company of young ladies? Or do you think it's such great fun to talk to those scoundrels every day and fight over every single thing? Oh, all right, all right, what are you after, prices on the free market? They're more or less ten times higher than the official prices in the *lavotchka,* but even at these prices it is difficult to get the most primitive articles."

"Could you tell me, Major," I continued my questioning, "how the *lavotchka* happened to come around to us?"

"Well, you see, it's like this. From the very beginning, I begged them to make available to us such odds and ends like thread, needles, buttons and what not. I had no idea of the existence of the green box and was just as surprised as the rest of you when I saw it for the first time. But now I recall various snatches of conversation among Bereshkov, Kirshin and Company, which, when pieced together, give

163

the following picture: Apparently some high economic agency in one of the big cities like Kharkov or Voroshilovgrad has declared our camp to be a place entitled not only to food, but to a government supply of luxuries such as the thread, buttons and sweets. A *naryad* or requisition undoubtedly had to be drawn up by the camp authorities. I don't know how they did it. I was not consulted. I suppose they gave the total number of the "inhabitants" of the camp and probably did not specify that it was a camp for men only. Anyway, who cares way out in Kharkov? Our camp is of interest only to the Moguls of the Lubyanka prison in Moscow. That may explain why they sent us those heavy perfumes, powders and soaps. For that matter, who knows? Since there is a great shortage of commodities at official prices, since it is difficult to buy tobacco in town, not to mention soap, why should Deputy Political Commissar Petrov deny himself this exceptional opportunity and not stock up on tobacco? And why should *politruk* Stepanov not spirit out a package of sweet-smelling stuff if he is so fond of it?

"And Messrs. Bereshkov and Kirshin undoubtedly have wives and daughters for whom soap and sweets would be nice presents. Who is to check up on them or accuse them of not being good little boys? We certainly won't!

"It's a business that can't fail. So don't think it was out of a feeling of altruism for the poor 'former Polish Officers' that Bereshkov and Kirshin put in the requisition for a *lavotchka*. They did it merely to suit their own ends. I know only too well what is going on under my very nose here in the quartermaster's office. As soon as a good hunk of meat or a good barrel of fish shows up, before you know it, the stuff is whisked off through the gate, probably to the Soviet Command across the street.

"What makes me most angry," he went on, "and infuriates the Soviet civilian workers as well — I know because I often talk to them when they are building new barracks — is that all these NKVD people are a privileged class and live a life of plenty. None of these Soviet carpenters or cabinet makers would ever be allowed to enter the veranda by the back door and buy themselves tobacco or sweets. They've got to keep away!

"Don't forget that this state of poverty and economic chaos has lasted continuously from the days of the last war. The Soviet infant learns at its mother's breast that it will have to always search for food, for clothing, for the thousand and one notions of which there is an endless shortage and which it is so hard to get by ordinary legal means.

"Well, I've talked rather a lot . . ." he paused.

Kopyeykin's furrowed face appeared at the window. "Zaleski! The Commandant wants you!" he croaked.

Muttering a curse and slowly buttoning his jacket, Major Zaleski bent almost double to get his tremendous frame through the low doorway and went out into the cold without his greatcoat.

Our boots were rotting at a frightening pace and what is strange, this was due more to snow, even when dry, than mud! Evidently, the properties of worn-out leather are such that snow permeates it more easily than wet clay. After prolonged and intense requests for a consignment of goloshes which would help to preserve our boots, 800 pairs arrived unexpectedly in mid-December. I am repeating 800 pairs! Major Zaleski was overjoyed – it was through his endeavours. Every fifth officer would get one pair. The official price – I have a vivid recollection of it even today – was 14 roubles 85 kopeks a pair. (This was at a time when roubles made their appearance in the camp, of which more later.) This was a considerable amount of money to us but the importance of a pair of goloshes was immeasurably greater.

A row broke out about who was to have the precious goloshes, but we eventually came to an agreement. We then took stock of the state of our footwear. It was decided that those men whose toes were sticking out of their boots would take priority in purchasing goloshes.

Before we had lined up in the queue – I happened to be one of the privileged ones – we learned that two hundred had already been sold under the counter and had found their way outside the camp by way of the "prokhodnaya budka."

Major Zaleski, who at first had been beaming with joy, was now in a raging temper. He gave the Soviet officer on duty as well as a few *politruks* a good dressing down. Among them was Petrov who having recruited a few *boytzy* was eagerly busying himself with getting the loot outside the gate. I feared he overdid it this time.

More confusion and new quarrels were the result of our failure to reclaim the two hundred boots and a new process of elimination had to be devised. It was now a matter of choosing between boots with lesser and bigger holes. I managed to maintain my privileged position, however.

When after several hours of queuing I eventually reached the shed in which the goloshes were tried on and sold, I found that only miserable oddments were left. They no longer formed pairs and neither did their sizes match. I suddenly noticed amongst a heap two goloshes which were unmistakably a pair and pounced on them with the swiftness of a bird of prey. Their shape was rather strange – elongated with sharply pointed noses slightly upturned and reminding me of Arab slippers. The bottom part strongly arched against a protruding heel, the ankles high and wide. They were undoubtedly a pair of ladies' goloshes. I grabbed them without further reflection as one more moment of hesitation and I would have been left empty-handed. But putting them on my boots was absolutely out of the question. They just would not stretch over them. Still I found a solution to the problem. My worn out boots landed on my bunk for a rest and I put the goloshes directly on my feet! Furthermore, I stuffed the heels and the pointed toes with paper, bandaged my feet with two pair of *onuce* and in order to move about I tied the goloshes to my feet with shoelaces.

The contours of my feet soon became well known all over the camp and a constant source of jokes. Despite my companions' ridicule I became very attached to my "ladies' goloshes". They served me faithfully in conditions of both snow and mud. Although my soles would freeze up they never got wet. The goloshes also served myself and my closest friends as night slippers. I said goodbye to them fondly after two years constant wear when they were practically dying of old age not to mention wear-and-tear.

An incident happened the night after their purchase. I had placed them purposely on the edge of the upper bunk to have them ready for any emergency caused by the diuretic well water. The fresh, black lustre of the lacquer shone brightly in the light of an electric bulb and this must have attracted the attention of the night *vakhtyor* who, after waking me up by pulling at my feet, said in a whisper: "Eh, these goloshes are yours?" Somewhat frightened I said yes and asked him what was the matter. "And how much do you want for them?" Astonished at this unexpected business proposition put to me at the dead of night I explained to him that they were not for sale and that I myself was in great need of them.

"*Nu.* I'll give you 150 roubles, and mind you it's a good price . . . " he was clutching my goloshes, viewing them intently and even sniffing them. Petrified I thought I would never see them again. I repeated that I was not prepared to sell them at any price and that he should return them to me forthwith. Other men were now waking up and there was a murmur of voices. After some reflection the *vakhtyor* replaced the goloshes on the bunk. Perhaps he was, after all, a decent fellow. On going to sleep once more I made a mental calculation to find out what sort of profit our "protectors" would have made on those two hundred pairs taken outside the gate.

Apart from the normal consignment of foodstuffs supplied to our kitchen about once a month we would get delivered another extra consignment of particularly valued articles which were for sale at official prices. The goods would sometimes arrive with the *lavotchka*, sometimes directly. About three or four times we had a delivery of sugar, usually two, at the most three sacks. One used to vanish immediately into the "prokhodnaya budka"! After a meticulous division of the remaining quantity, carried out as though it was being served in a chemist's shop, the share that each of us received of the precious stuff was at the most, one-tenth of a pound. On another occasion we were brought two barrels of beetroot jam of which, again, one disappeared straightaway beyond the gate. What was left for each of us was just a teaspoonful — a mere sensation on the tongue of this sweetish but on the whole tasteless stuff.

One of the consignments contained a few pieces of calico. Never in my life have I seen anything of such poor quality and at the same time in such loud colours. This material was probably manufactured for the benefit of some eastern peoples of the Soviet Union but by some twist of fate it had found its way to our camp, of all places. Since we dressed in rags the opportunity of having a shirt or underpants made of it was tempting even to the most discerning of us. There would be no end of laughter when some unshaven prisoner with a long beard would hold the material against himself as though in some ladies' fashion shop, wondering whether he would look better in bright blue pants with yellow spots or in a pair of orange ones with green polka dots.

But there were others who burned with desire for these coloured fabrics. Just like the goloshes, sugar, jam, etc., half the consignment of calico disappeared mysteriously and swiftly beyond the gate, no doubt to enliven the wardrobes of our good, brave protectors' wives and daughters.

All the buildings, big and small, of the Monastery camp were open to us, with the exception of the biggest one, the monumental Orthodox Church. The huge front door, adorned with iron-work, was boarded up with heavy rods. So was the smaller door in the rear that probably led into the vestry. We were all intrigued by the mysterious character of this edifice. Various rumours circulated throughout the camp about the secret hidden inside the temple's walls. Some claimed that the church had not been entered since the days of the Revolution and that it contained hoards of gold and silver stored there by the priests. Another version maintained that the church served as a site for executions and that its dungeons held mountains of human skeletons.

And then, one day, a huge truck lumbered into the square. After having executed a series of complicated manoeuvres, it backed up the first three stone steps leading to the entrance, and came to a halt. The Soviet officer on duty that day rounded up about one hundred and twenty of us, including myself, and told us to equip ourselves with spades and shovels, of which there were no more than ten in the entire camp. Then, surrounded by a few guards, he mounted the steps and like the doorkeeper of an ancient castle, opened the temple's creaking rusty double door.

The pleasant though rather choking smell of grain assailed us from the dark interior. Only a few steps away from the door rose a tremendous mound of beautiful Ukrainian wheat. So the secret treasure of the Orthodox church was neither gold nor human bones, but grain.

"Load the wheat onto the truck!" the command rang out.

Prisoners of war are insatiably curious. So we were all very interested to find out where the trucks were taking this beautiful grain.

On the other side of Kirov Street rose a big three-storey building in red brick, its windows barred and screened like in a prison. The building was so tall that the Monastery wall could not hide it from the probing eyes of the prisoners. Its façade bore a metal inscription marking the date of its erection − "1910". Somewhat lower was another inscription that read "Municipal Bakery". On the window ledges lay thick layers of dirty flour that looked for all the world like snow-drifts. Once or twice a week, this old soot-covered building, which usually seemed deserted, would suddenly come to life. We could hear the dull roar of the machines, we could see black smoke issuing from the chimneys, and if the wind happened to blow in our direction, the pleasant smell of freshly baked bread would be wafted our way. And once or twice a week, in the pre-dawn icy hours, we could hear the din of many human voices, chiefly female, and the measured stamping of many cold feet. That was the bread line − the line of the patient people of Starobyelsk waiting for their daily bread. But sometimes their patience would come to an end. The nocturnal stillness would be broken by the sounds of mass fighting, by shrill cries, moans and cursing. However, this rebellion would last only a moment, for it would quickly be quelled by a mighty and commanding voice shouting: "Shut up! Order! Get back in line!" And then a murmur of low frightened voices would get through our Monastery walls.

We naturally supposed that the grain left the church to be ground across the street in the building, which, in addition to the bakery, housed a power-driven mill. But the time between each truck's departure with the load of grain and its return for a new load was so incomprehensibly long that it completely upset these suppositions.

The method we had used to empty the church of grain turned out to be the sensation of the day. And not only among the prisoners, but particularly among the sizeable handful of Soviet workers – the cabinet makers and carpenters, the potters and drivers – who visited the camp daily.

Zygmunt was a woodcutter. All day long he chopped fire wood in the small square in front of the kitchen, if indeed the term "wood" could be applied to the collection of roots, gnarled stumps and dry branches. Nearby worked a carpenter, a Ukrainian named Fomenko, a tremendous peasant specimen in the prime of his life. With mechanicial precision, philosophical calm and without the slightest haste he hewed thick round blocks to be used as a foundation for new barracks. Soon Zygmunt secretly became friends with this engaging carpenter. It is easier to talk with someone outdoors without fear of being noticed. When we were in the barrack in the evening Zygmunt would report to us his conversations with Fomenko.

Like the rest of us, Fomenko had not known that the Church hid a warehouse of grain. When this fact became public knowledge, Fomenko would glance at the spectacle of the grain being taken away, shake his head, mutter something and spit feelingly. He said nothing for about two days until he finally yielded to Zygmunt, who kept asking him over and over again: "Tell me, brother, where are they taking that grain, across the street to the mill? Will they bake us bread out of it?"

Fomenko exploded furiously: "Oh, all right, I'll tell you, only keep your mouth shut about it. . . . I thought you might guess where these sons of bitches are taking our Ukrainian wheat. They're not taking it to any mill, but to the railroad station, and they're loading it onto freight cars and then they're going to send our grain to Germany to Hitler, the motherfucker. The whole town is talking about it. They saw it with their own eyes, they were at the station. . . . They're stuffing the bellies of the German sons of bitches while our people go hungry. Now you have your information, now you know where the grain is going. Nice times we've come to."

He spat into his hand, planted his feet on either side of a log of wood and gave vent to his healthy peasant anger by some powerful swinging of the axe.

This bit of news, which was confirmed from various sources, plunged our entire camp into gloom.

Bread was distributed to us every three or four days, one, or if we were lucky, two loaves per person – a method of rationing which was wasteful and hardly conducive to good health. Famished gluttons devoured a four day ration in two days and then went hungry. Stored in the dirty bunks in the midst of rubbish, dust and vermin, the bread went sour and disintegrated. Depending on the quality of the flour used sometimes the bread was good and sometimes it was sticky and barely edible. Because there was dampness literally all over the camp, the bread was generally already mouldy when it was handed out to us.

This was in the early spring of 1940. With the approach of warmer weather the bread grew increasingly bad and more and more mouldy. It was a common occurrence to bite into a well-baked cockroach, brown or black, in the bread. But this was not so bad as having a well fed and stinking bedbug find its way into our mouths from the breadcrumbs on our bunk!

The pile of rotten bread mounted daily. We did not know what to do with it. Even the stray dogs would not eat it. Our Camp Commandant asked the Soviet authorities to take the mouldy bread into town. He suggested that it would make fine nourishment for the hogs and that the population would certainly welcome the gift. For his pains he was told that this was none of our affair. We were ordered to dig a deep hole and bury the bread.

Shocked though we were, we did dig a big grave for the bread on a slight incline near the bathhouse. The order was obviously prompted by the necessity of concealing what was going on inside the camp. For if the populace had witnessed these huge quantities of mouldy bread being shipped out of the camp, it might have thought either that we were being fed inedible bread or, even worse, that we were being overfed. Both conclusions would have aroused general indignation. It was much simpler to bury the bread.

The strange grave we dug swallowed up at least two tons of spoiled bread.

14. ROUBLES

Zygmunt used to supply us regularly with news from the outside world obtained from the Ukrainian carpenter Fomenko. Fomenko had to live in a communist country since he could do nothing about it and since he loved his native land, the Ukraine. Of the other countries outside the Soviet Union he knew next to nothing. But he possessed an innate flair for recognising people for what they are and he came to see us as human beings and not the enemies he had been told we were. He did his best to show us sympathy and complained bitterly about conditions prevailing in the world outside the camp. He admitted to earning 225 roubles a month and said that his rations were inadequate. He and his family had to suffer the cold in his cottage as the bucketful of heating oil he received once a month wouldn't be sufficient to fuel his wife's primus for cooking if it was used for heating as well. His wife was a sick women unable to go to work. His son, who was nineteen, had been conscripted a month ago and sent to the Finnish front but there were also two toddlers at home in freezing and hungry conditions. Even bread, which was rationed, was scarce as was the *makhorka*. And to buy food on the free market with butter or lard costing 25 roubles a pound, was beyond his means. (That was the position in December 1939, in the summer of 1942 butter cost 150 roubles a pound.) And boots, clothes – where would he get the money for these? Fomenko went on lamenting: "And so as you can see – all this goes on and on despite our radio and the newspapers telling us all the time that things are all right and are going to get even better . . . !" Zygmunt interrupted: "Good, but now tell us something about this 'free market' where you are supposed to get everything you want."

"Well, it's like this. Members of a *kolkhoz* after having paid their dues for every hectare are allowed to sell part of the surplus on the free market. The rogues charge you impossible prices so that they can buy themselves boots and clothes – at very high prices too, of course. . . ." Zygmunt interrupted him: "Right, but tell us how do boots and clothes get on the free market?"

"It's very simple. Either a poor wretch sells his own rations or else the *artyelniki** pilfer and sell their loot."

Once Fomenko carefully produced from under his jacket a small package which he presented to Zygmunt. Wrapped up in a piece of white cloth it contained two little bricks of butter in the shape and size of an egg. "Here, I brought you this small trifle.... Very expensive it is too – five roubles each piece. To get it here was not easy either. Those sons of a bitch will search you in the "prokhodnaya budka". No, I don't want any money for it. I know you haven't got any. If you can, you just give me a little *makhorka*."

A week later the good Fomenko, having outwitted the guards, presented us once more with two bricks of butter. This proved to be the last time, however. He did not report for work next morning. In vain Zygmunt would watch for him day after day. We never saw Fomenko again. Some scoundrel must have denounced him.

The amount of food each of us received in the camp was supplied according to some category in which we had been placed by the authorities. Whether this was a category worked out specially for "byvshye polskye oficery w sovyetzkom plenu" (former Polish officers now in Soviet captivity) or a category worked out a long time ago for some underprivileged class of the Soviet population, in which we were included, we never found out. It was a fact however that our bread ration was slightly superior to that of an average citizen of Starobyelsk who, on the other hand, was probably better off in fats, meat and fish. Our kitchen would be supplied regularly every ten days with foodstuffs in more or less the same amounts. Every man received a bowl of cooked oatmeal for his breakfast, which was served between 7 and 8 a.m. Whether it was fit for eating depended on the number of hours it had been cooked. If it had taken the six hours that were needed the stuff was good, and if less – which owing to lack of fuel used to happen quite often – it was good too, but for domestic fowl only. Once a week we would get a portion of meat, in most cases horse but once or twice a portion of frozen fish. Meat or fish as well as some cabbage provided our lunch in the shape of a soup to be shared out from 1 to 2 p.m. That was all. In the evening and in the morning we would get a mug of boiling water.

On top of that the kitchen would be supplied with a tiny daily ration of white flour to be used as seasoning for the soup, some sunflower oil for dressing our *kasha* and a measure of salt.

For many years sunflower oil has been the staple fat used for cooking in Russia and should any housewife in western countries be

* Workers in a collective enterprise of light industry or trade.

unaware of the fact I can assure her that it is a good and nutritive fat, provided one gets used to it. It once happened that Felo Daszynski, who used to work in the kitchen, brought along to our barrack half a mug of the stuff. We pounced on this "delicacy" like hungry wolves. I ate with great appetite a few slices of bread soaked in it despite the fact that when raw it has a rather unpleasant taste. And then, the next day, it all happened. I became the victim of a violent diarrhoea which lasted for ten days. I really thought I would die in the latrine. I lost some twenty pounds. It then took me a long and arduous time to restore my lost strength. I pulled through, however, and as time went by I not only got accustomed to the oil but even came to like it, although I never took it in raw form again.

The oil and the other things I have described were provisions for the kitchen. Apart from them we would be supplied every ten days with so-called "dry rations", dispensed to each of us individually. Unlike the rations we received for the kitchen, which were supplied at regular intervals, we could never rely on a regular supply of dry rations. When we did get them they consisted of:

Sugar – one and a half lumps a day.

Tea – three pinches every ten days, or alternatively *Fruktovyj chay* (a kind of black sticky fruit extract) – two cubes of the size of a cubic inch.

Makhorka – one or two packets to last 10 days. But to an average smoker one packet would be just right for two days at the most.

Cigarette paper – for rolling cigarettes we used newspapers and saved the cigarette paper for taking down notes.

Safety matches – small quantities on rare occasions. We suffered a constant shortage of this article and would therefore light cigarettes from each other's. This ever-burning source of fire would last for twenty-four hours as even at night there would be somebody wanting to smoke.

Cheap, "grey soap" – a tiny scrap every second decade at the most.

A new kitchen, which we constructed ourselves, was inaugurated in mid-December when winter was already in full swing. It was a vast improvement compared with the field kitchens. Now our "chefs" were in a position to improve the standard of food. Vegetables could be properly washed. Fish could be soaked in water for a whole day to remove the unbelievable amount of salt which if left rendered the fish uneatable. The *kasha* could be well cooked. For this task volunteers were recruited from our ranks. Standing high on the brick stoves above the bubbling cauldrons, and using enormous wooden poles with oar-like blades, they would mix the oatmeal for six hours – from midnight until early morning. These untiring workers were known popularly as the "gondoliers".

In spite of all limitations and the bad quality of the ingredients our cooks did their best to bring some measure of culinary relief if not enjoyment to our palates. They let us know, for instance, that according to their investigation the infinitesimal amount of white flour which we received in our day's ration failed in any way to enhance the taste of the soup. Should it be possible, however, to save the ration for a couple of weeks a great surprise would then lie in store for us – a substantial portion of tasty fritters. Similar savings were suggested regarding oil (an important component of the above dish) and later fish and meat.

A unanimous resolution passed by a general vote resulted in us giving our resourceful cooks a complete *carte blanche*. This was soon followed by the appearance of the promised "surprise." Instead of scraps of overboiled fish which when prepared with vegetables tended to smell offensive, once a week every starveling would get a nice portion of well fried fish. A portion of smoked fish prepared in an ingeniously constructed kind of smokehouse would be another treat aimed at introducing some variety into our diet. Every few weeks we were served with a big portion of goulash with *kasha* saved on our morning breakfasts and about once a month came the great feast – fat fritters made of white flour.

It goes without saying that all this was nothing less than a trick played on our stomachs, as obviously no one can pour anything from an empty vessel. But justice was being done to our palates, which had been longing for better food. It should not be surprising, therefore, that we were immensely grateful to our benefactors – the whole indefatigable team of "gondoliers", curing experts, those who washed fish, carried water, made the fires, cut wood and particularly the culinary artists, who, with so few ingredients, were able to perform wonders in frying four thousand portions of fish, four thousand portions of fritters . . . not to speak of other miracles. On the occasion of every such feast our dreary barracks would ring to the sound of loud cheers and "hurrays" as everyone expressed their deep appreciation and satisfaction.

On principle the Soviet authorities did not interfere with what went on in our kitchen and did not stop us saving up our small daily rations. But watching the Sisyphean labours of our cooks they could not comprehend what on earth it was all intended for. Inwardly, however, they could not help being impressed by the achievements of our officers, or, as they used to call them, the *byelorutchki* (white hands). More than one *politruk* would lick his fingers after being given some tasty fritters. Even Commissar Kirshin himself, of all people, would not scorn a piece of well fried, and what is stranger still, unsalted fish. I once caught him stuffing himself with it in the course of one of his inspections of the kitchen.

As usual he would move within the compound of the camp unaccompanied. One always had to watch out for him. Camouflaged in his unassuming brown jacket and at times wearing a civilian cap, he would easily get lost among the mass of inmates. During his tour he might check on progress in the construction of the new barracks, or nip surreptitiously into a workshop, then perhaps vanish into the dark abyss of the Circus or other barracks. Recently he had become particularly interested in the running of the newly constructed kitchen. There had never been anything like it in the Monastery Camp. It was undeniably attractive and well laid out. No wonder that when he saw this splendid addition to the camp's facilities Mister Commissar Kirshin was very pleased. Probably, at the same time, he was also devising plans for the future. Once the tiresome Poles had left the camp, he must have thought, their useful bequests would be left for the camp's next inmates.

And so walking around the kitchen he would inspect the larders and watch the scrubbing and rinsing of vegetables and the cleaning and preparation of fish on the long tables. Much interested in our arrangements for cooking large quantities he once even clambered up on the stove to peer into the steaming cauldrons, and he watched our "gondoliers" at work for a long while.

He paid no attention to a group of at least thirty men who were lined up outside in deep snow from the entrance of the kitchen to the hand-operated water pump covered in ice. Using the chain system they were passing buckets filled with water from the pump to the kitchen, a distance of about fifty metres. Until then I had never realised how much water was needed in the kitchen. As I had always used taps I had never had the chance to measure water by the bucketful. But here we were faced with a different situation. Every bucketful of water had to be paid for − either with frostbitten fingers or with soaked coats converted instantaneously into planks of ice by the frost. And the kitchen needed two thousand buckets a day. An attempt to supply water during the winter along a wooden trough was, of course, bound to fail. It turned to ice almost immediately.

On seeing this huge food-producing works in full swing Kirshin expressed his approval condescendingly to our chief "chef". In civilian life this thirty year old Reserve Lieutenant was a small farmer in the province of Pomorze. His name, Antoni Aniol (Anthony Angel), had an angelic sound. No wings sprang from his wide shoulders and his face was adorned with a shaggy red beard, but since his labours produced nothing but goodness and comfort we all came to believe that he had descended to the earth from heavenly heights. We therefore called him our Guardian Angel or Saint Anthony of Padova.

Said Kirshin to the Angel: "Nu da, da. Vot eto rabota kultur-naya . . ." (All right. All right. This is a civilized piece of work. The running of the kitchen and the delegation of work is satisfactory. . . . Still it's very hard to understand why you bother to store so much food.) He made an allusion to our saving white flour, sunflower oil, etc. – "Why all these unnecessary measures? After all we supply you with enough good provisions. So why try to improve on them? I do not understand this. What a strange people you Poles are. . . . The devil himself wouldn't know what to make of it!"

On the subject of food one thing should be mentioned here. It was unbelievably difficult to get used to having our meals in the barracks. There was no canteen or anything like it in our camp. So orderlies would take the food to the barracks in buckets. Often nearly cold when it reached us it was then shared out, using ladles. This was done in the constant din and stench of the barracks and we had, of course, to eat sitting, or crouching, on our bunks as there were no other facilities. Dust, grit and even particles of mud would drop into our food from the upper bunks and this would understandably enough, lead to frequent protests and squabbles. But what could we do? To eat outside, in the cold, was not possible, although my closest friends and I would do it sometimes – only to be as far away as possible from all the noise and filth. After about two months, conditions improved a little, when around Christmas the new barracks were opened. My bunk in the new hut to which I had been transferred now measured 70 centimetres in width, nearly double the width of my old bunk. When the lavotchka first visited the camp clever, crafty Olgierd, one of the seven in our group, was found standing in the front of the queue. In this way the rogue revealed that he was in possession of roubles. How and from what source he had got them was known to himself only! When questioned he laughed gaily, telling us not to worry and that everything he laid his hands on would eventually be shared among us. After he had reached the counter I moved up close to help understand what the saleswoman said in Russian. He bought a bit of everything. Later, seated with him on a bunk, we eyed his acquisitions with great interest like children at some funfair

Olgierd gave me two safety razor blades, a toothbrush and tooth paste. What bliss it was to clean one's teeth and to actually shave!

But the quality of the blades proved to be so poor that after the first shave I had to try various ways of sharpening then, such as honing them on the palm of my hand, on glass or my leather belt. Because of the quality of the blades and also the fact that our soap produced very little lather I could only bear to shave once a week. But I never allowed myself to grow a beard, unlike many of the inmates. I feared, perhaps subconsciously, that this would lead to some kind of moral surrender, easy to fall into but difficult to overcome.

In anticipation of further visits from the *lavotchka* our chase after roubles intensified daily. The rate of exchange – roubles for zlotys – increased in logical order. The price of a rouble on our "money market" started at 2 zloty to a rouble and then rose gradually to 5, 20, 50 zlotys. Rumours went round of deals transacted with Soviet workers, even *politruks*. One worker had apparently purchased a watch, another, it was said, had bought a gold holy medal and yet another an attractive leather wallet. These rumours culminated in the shattering news that a *politruk* by the name of Khvalin, otherwise a little-known personage, had acquired a gold wrist watch for the astronomical sum of 600 roubles. The news of this amazing transaction reached the Soviet authorities with lightning speed. An almighty row was the result. Commissar Kirshin, alarmed and seething with rage, summoned the Polish commanders of each barrack to a special parade and announced heavy penalties for those who dared to do business again with Soviet workers. The Polish officer who was found guilty of the "crime" was jailed for three weeks and his money was confiscated. Whether the *politruk* Khvalin was left with his watch and the workers with what they had purchased remained a secret. All we knew was that, as if touched by a magic wand, they never appeared in the camp again.

Still, something had to be done. Prisoners were in desperate need of roubles. An enticing quantity of watches, rings, medals, etc., lay in their pockets. The authorities could have them confiscated – easy enough, but would it be advisable? It could not be like the first encounter with Polish troops on the front line when after all everything was permitted and so easy. Still something had to be devised – something sensible and within the regulations. Bereshkov, Kirshin and Co. set down to thinking, and after two days they finally came up with a project which seemed to be simple and indeed clever!

When early in the morning our orderlies came back from the kitchen with the buckets of *kasha* they informed us that some unknown civilians had been seen hanging about near the summer veranda adjacent to the Circus. Soon, Kirshin called a parade and made an announcement, which satisfied our curiosity: "I am going to prove to you further how the Soviet authorities care for your well-being. Following a request by the Commander of the Camp a special body known as the "Trust for the Acquisition of Objects of Jewellery" has arrived from Voloshirovgrad. Its aim will be to purchase from all of you at official prices valuables in your possession, such as watches, rings, watch-chains, fountain pens, etc. You will thus be able to provide yourselves legally with roubles which, as we know, you lack and which you will need for further purchases at the *lavotchka*. A maximum sum will be paid out to every seller and the rest will be deposited with the camp commander. Once a month you will be allowed to draw on it to the amount of fifty roubles."

On ending his speech Kirshin stressed the point that by making the *lavotchka* available to the prisoners the Soviet authorities had given us proof of their great benevolence and that this had been further confirmed by allowing us to acquire roubles. Of course, the great promises made by the delegate from Moscow during his memorable visit on the 4th October had long been forgotten. We had then been told that we would draw our officer's pay!

The Jeweller's Commission, consisting of five scruffy men, set up on the veranda the tools and equipment of their trade, including scales, weights, special keys, pincers, pieces of cloth and bottles containing acid. A long queue of impatient prisoners soon formed, waiting for the counter to open.

The summary calculation that we made seemed to indicate that despite all the robberies to which we had been exposed since our capture, about 50 per cent of our men still possessed watches, chains, rings, medals and fountain pens. This represented enormous potential "capital." What we did not know, however, was how the Commission would value these objects. Neither did we have any idea of their "market" value.

Those of our companions who had done business with the Commission told us how they had got on. One of them said: "I've bamboozled them all right! What consummate fools they are! Without saying a word they paid me 150 roubles for an old damaged wrist watch. At home I'd never get more than 2 zlotys* for that rubbish."

The next man seemed less enthusiastic: "They offered me 450 roubles for a gold Longinus watch with a double case. I couldn't make up my mind and didn't sell it – it seemed to me to be such a low price. But I managed to flog a ruined fountain pen for 20 roubles.

*Less than two pre-war shillings (i.e. less than 10p.)

178

Normally I wouldn't get a penny for it. Well, better that than nothing!"

We soon learned – I mean the whole of the camp – that the views of the Jeweller's Commission" completely differed from ours and that the objects were valued accordingly. But it was not easy to make head or tail of their system. We found out for instance that, as in darkest Africa, the better polished and shinier the objects were the higher the prices they would fetch. If a watch was in "working condition" the price would be higher. No wonder then that in all the barracks men became frantically busy with repair work. The metal parts would be cleaned and polished and the mechanisms given a superficial face-lift. Our locksmiths' workshop became particularly popular and locksmiths turned on the spur of the moment into seasoned goldsmiths! With the dexterity of professional craftsmen they would solder tiny cracks, replace missing links in a chain and give a new lease of life to the mechanisms of watches which had been defunct for ages. For what mattered was that a watch should tick for just half a minute, the time of the inspection by the Commission, and to hell with what happened after that! It was like a horse market when at the last moment the owner would feed his asthmatic horse with fresh carrots or give him a shot of some stimulating stuff. In our huge community of officers, who in civilian life had been part of the intelligentsia it would have been hard to find a non-represented profession. We had among us, therefore, a few proper watchmakers who would perform real wonders. I have a particularly clear recollection of the most clever and helpful of them who with great agility would hide himself right by the veranda to arouse the watch at the very last moment by some mysterious manipulation, so that it was ticking as his companion passed it to the Soviet experts. . . .

The Commission offered the highest prices for wrist watches – either gold, silver or plain steel ones. For nothing looked more attractive and fashionable nor embellished one's wrist so well! A few lucky ones among us managed to get the fantastic sum of 700 roubles for their gold watches (the watches were, in fact, in good condition), but this was the limit. Others had to content themselves with prices varying from 150 to 500 roubles at the most. Pocket watches, even when gold, were not so much in demand despite the fact that they contained considerably more of the "yellow" metal. There was a standard price of 50 roubles for signet rings, and fountain pens, no matter whether trash or costly Parker pens, would fetch 20 roubles only.

When setting out to war I had two watches, a wrist and a pocket one which was an old family heirloom. Both were stolen by the *boytzy* when we first fell into their hands. I carried the pocket watch in a suede pouch in the upper pocket of my tunic and this is where the paw of the *boyetz* found it. But I carried the chain for the watch in a side-pocket and, miraculously, it survived.

It was an old and most atttractive gold chain with a little pendant. For a long time I resisted the temptation of selling this, the only valuable object in my possession, but I finally gave in. Watch chains and pendants are not in fashion in the Soviet Union and there is hardly any demand for them. This is what I was told by my companions before I reached the counter. I handed in my treasure to the expert of the Commission with somewhat shaky hands. He took a look at it, weighed it and gave his verdict in a loud voice: "Sorok pyat roubley!" (Forty-five roubles.) After a second of hesitation and with much difficulty I stammered out the word "khorosho" (good). The man counted out four *tchervoncy* (ten rouble notes) and five green single ones. I walked swiftly away and like a dog with his bone hid myself in a remote corner of the camp. I then proceeded to carry out a lengthy amd laborious mental calculation resulting in the conclusion that for the sum I had obtained I should be able to buy at the *lavotchka* various goods such as soap, buttons, thread, needles, *onuce* and, of course, sweets. I suddenly felt rich indeed.

There remained one object which by virtue of some unspoken, unanimous agreement among prisoners was not to become negotiable. Gold wedding rings, as far as I know, were not being exchanged against roubles. No one wanted to part with them.

The Jeweller's Trust had been at the camp for three days. The queue to the magic counter on the veranda, rather long at first, was gradually shrinking until, finally, it vanished. Everybody had got what he wanted. The pockets of the camp inmates became swollen with rouble notes and the officials of the Trust, after having loaded several heavy boxes on a truck, went off pleased with the result of their hunting expedition.

Twenty-four hours had hardly elapsed when hundreds of alert eyes noticed our watches on the wrists and our rings on the fingers of the *politruks* and even of some of our guards. They did not seem to be the least embarrassed − on the contrary they were parading with their loot without any attempts at concealing it. Why should they after all? They had purchased everything in an honest and legal way. We also noticed that our top "protectors" had provided themselves with the best and most expensive watches. Why not? Messrs. Bereshkov and Kirshin had no doubt made sure that they had priority when it came to acquiring the best stuff. They had, after all, been the initiators of this transaction so profitable for the State, for Soviet society and ... well ... also for the Polish prisoners of war. And so everything went well — "prosto i ostroumno".

With so many roubles now in prisoners' pockets trade inside the camp began to flourish even though Kirshin strictly forbade such transactions in the name of some unknown morality. Overnight clever middlemen sprang up who served as a natural link between the sources of supply and demand. Though they functioned in secret, their identity was soon a matter of general knowledge.

An unusually droll personality, Reserve Second Lieutenant Joseph Will of Warsaw, soon came to the fore. Short, neat, clean shaven, he was a great specialist in barter procedure. In civilian life he was a modest bank official. Here he suddenly became a commodities expert. With the ease of a pawnbroker he appraised the market value of articles submitted to him, thanks to which he soon became the oracle of the commodities market. He was satisfied with a small commission, adhering strictly to the golden maxim of a big turnover and a small margin of profit. His sharp eyes were all-seeing. He remembered who had valuable timepieces and hence was a potential source of roubles. He also knew who did not have precious items and consequently presented no rouble value. And so, Lieutenant Will was a very busy man at Camp Starobyelsk. Very sought after, for example, was material to patch up our threadbare pants. Will was able to convince potential purchasers that a piece of old blanket was the ideal answer to this need and that a piece snipped out of a spring coat was no less practical. He made a mental note of chain smokers and of those who never touched tobacco and he was an excellent broker in this popular sphere too. A package of loose tobacco brought as much as five roubles, which was at least ten times the official government price. In spite of the great number of non-smokers, there was a chronic shortage of the stuff. During one four week period we received no so-called "dry rations." I do not know whether this was due to the big snow, the war with Finland or friendship with Hitler. The fact remains that there was no tobacco to be had. The heavy smokers were going mad. They paid many roubles and gave up their bread for a pinch of tobacco. They smoked bark, tea leaves, and tobacco dust along with other rubbish shaken out of their pockets. They poisoned their systems and they became ill. One rolled cigarette would be shared by ten smokers. "Let me take one puff or I'll go insane!" they would cry in despair.

In the field of second hand trade, the buyer and the seller both felt embarrassed and did not wish to know each other. Under these circumstances a broker was a very useful person.

Will really had an array of the most unusual objects for sale: linen towels, badger shaving brushes of the best quality, Shakespeare complete in two beautifully bound volumes, rubber heels and soles, razor blades, socks, handkerchiefs, bags and knapsacks. His prize item was a de luxe ladies' manicuring set composed of a dozen scissors, files, nippers, etc. in a beautiful Morocco case — a Viennese product of Kärtnerstrasse. This unusual item was marked at 400 roubles.

Will, God forbid, did not assemble all these goods on his bunk. Upon request, he would bring the merchandise for inspection to a quiet secluded spot, usually to the latrine on the Siegfried Line. While seated on the rod, we could close the deal, undisturbed.

After a few visits of the *lavotchka,* and after having purchased a pair of goloshes, I got to the bottom of my 45 roubles. One day I came up to Will and asked him casually: "Tell me, how much are dollars?"

"Which ones? Green ones or chestnuts? And how many pieces?" he asked in a low voice. He feigned indifference but his eyes shone.

"I don't understand," I replied.

"Oh, the deuce, paper or gold," he added in a whisper.

"Paper. Fifteen pieces in two sections, five and ten," I explained.

His interest evaporated. He grimaced. "There is no demand for it, the price is too low. . . ."

"Why, our people, that is, those who left Lwow late, said that the dollar brought 250 roubles and more after the bolsheviks came in!"

We got to the latrine. I rolled myself a cigarette to kill the horrible stench. Will continued his explanation: "Now, look, Lieutenant, just come down to earth for a minute. What has Lwow got to do with us? From Lwow it was possible to get out of the country and use the dollars to travel with. But where do you propose to go from here? Don't you know that there are no black market currency dealings in the Soviet Union? Who needs them and what for? After all, paper money is of value only when it can be used outside Russia or when it can be smuggled out. But how? You don't think it can be done by mail, I hope. Does anybody ever leave Russia illegally? Perhaps twenty people a year. Of course there is a little business done in gold roubles and dollars through some kind of atavistic attraction for that pretty metal. . . . Well, I'll see, perhaps our boys will buy the stuff out of a sentimental regard for the dollar and because they feel that one day they will get out of here by hook or crook. . . ." he concluded his resumé of the monetary situation.

"All right, how much will you give me for them?" I asked, thoroughly worried.

"Ten or twelve roubles a piece. I'll let you know in a few days. Where do you live? Oh, yes, at number 6. I'm just oppsite from you, at number 9. Au revoir." He disappeared beyond the boards of the latrine.

I bargained with Will for a week until I finally got him to agree to give me sixteen roubles to the dollar. The transaction netted me 240 roubles. This capital had to last me for the long months to come.

All this camp trading could not be kept under cover and was of course known to the NKVD agents. I don't know why they were against it, but the fact is that they did everything they could to kill it. Just after New Year's Eve they escorted two speculators out of the Circus in the middle of the night. Fear overcame the others. Poor Will was so frightened he avoided all his clients. He made himself scarce, spending all his time in the tiny room of hut number 9. He started growing a beard and shrank to such an extent that it was difficult for me to recognize him. Then one night they came for him.

From the middle of December I lived in house number 6 with my closest friends. Our windows faced the main road of the camp, where the traffic was always heavy. Diagonally to the left led a path to the latrine, which was never deserted, even at night. Thirty of us slept in what could be called one and one-half rooms. The bigger room housed 18 of us and the small adjoining "mushroom" sheltered 8 prisoners including myself. In the small eternally cold vestibule opposite the entrance slept 4 young second lieutenants. In another part of the same house, which had its own entrance, 60 people lived in four rooms.

We always slept lightly. The lightest rustle outside, the clatter of Soviet heels on the ice and the creaking of their boots, which was different from ours, would awaken one or two of us simultaneously. "Michael, James, Peter!" — these were passwords which we changed weekly and which were uttered by the first person to notice a *politruk* or watchman approaching our house. One bright cold night Olgierd was the first to catch sight, through the ice-covered window panes, of two Soviet soldiers heading straight for house number 9. Five minutes later, they came out pushing poor little Will ahead of them. In his unbuttoned uniform, his coat and untied bag dragging along the ice, he passed by our windows on his way to the gate. I shall never forget his bloodless horrified face.

Hardly a quarter of an hour had gone by when Bogdan Janowski ran into our vestibule and cried "Michael!" This was a direct warning. We saw three soldiers stalk past our windows. A second later they noisily forced their way into the vestibule. Automatically each of us had stuffed somewhere into a cranny a slip of paper, a salvaged document, and even roubles exceeding the sum of the fifty roubles permitted. It was not Kopyeykin who called on us this time, but the two who had come for Will. They were accompanied by the night watchman.

"Daszynski! *Nu*, come on, where is he?" one of them roared. Silence. We all pretended to be asleep.

"He's a big man with a beard, I know him!" the other bellowed.

Felo was lying just below me in the so-called "mushroom". They found him without any difficulty.

"There you are! *Nu*, get out! Davay, sobiraysya s vyeshchami" they chorused.

My heart sank. So they were taking him away. They would finally punish him for the speech he had made in front of the delegate from Moscow on October 4.

They had already called Felo several times for long night interrogations. He had never given us any details, but he had always come back pale and weary. And just about two weeks before they came for him, he had written an appeal that was so stupidly hopeless. We had begged him not to do it. But he had insisted and had brought his plea personally to the Soviet officer on duty. When Felo's father, Ignacy Daszynski, had been President of the Polish Parliament in 1925, Amanullah, king of Afghanistan, had been travelling in Europe. All the capitals of the continent had welcomed the exotic monarch, and he in turn had handed out decorations generously. Staying at Warsaw a few days, Amanullah decorated Daszynski with an order which carried along with it an Afghan princely title and life-long privileges not only for the recipient of the honour but also for his descendants. My father too had received such a decoration. Felo seized upon this the way a drowning man clutches at a straw. He wrote a letter to the Afghan Ambassador in Moscow in which he reminded the diplomat that he was potentially an Afghan subject and asked for his help in getting out of Soviet enslavement.

For four months we had been inseparable. We had suffered hard knocks together, we had wished each other a good future. He was the first to fall out and make a breach in our group of seven. I looked at his beautiful head from my bunk. There was something about it that reminded me of Dickens. I knew all about his family. Felo had left his wife in Warsaw. His sister and brother were probably abroad. He in turn knew where my family was.

He packed his belongings without hurrying, paying no attention to the guards who were prodding him on. He managed to summon a smile and say: "You see, I was right. My letter did produce results. Long live Amanullah! I shall always remember you!" He came up to me, squeezed my protruding feet and whispered in English: "Just be quiet. I remember the names of your sisters in the United States and will contact them as soon as possible. Good luck, Bron!"

"Good luck, Felo," I replied with a lump in my throat.

We quickly chipped in a few roubles apiece, for Felo was penniless.

We stood with our faces glued to the frozen panes as Felo passed by and waved to us. The hard snow crunched in the stillness of the night under the feet of Felo and the three Soviet soldiers.

15. MY FIRST INTERROGATION

The second half of November marked the start of a regular wave of interrogations – the so-called *doprosy*. This is an extremely popular word in the present-day Soviet dictionary if we consider that for more than twenty years it has been applied in practice to many millions of people annually.

At first, we seemed to be called in alphabetical order, but soon, either as a result of the complexity of the Latin alphabet or perhaps for other reasons, this system was abandoned and the NKVD messengers called us out at random. But one thing never changed – the interrogation was always at night. Hence, no one knew when his hour would strike. The muffled cry, "Michael is coming!", that agreed upon signal of alarm at the sight of a messenger, would tear at our nerves in the dead of night. Then there would follow a tense moment of waiting: Which name would we hear first? And would the command be only "Sobiraysya s vyeshchami"?

My turn finally came too. It must have been around midnight. The messenger dashed inside and called out a name. He mangled it to such an extent that about ten people who had somewhat similar sounding names sat up on their bunks. The messenger held a slip of paper with the name in his hand. One of our men helped him read it. The name was mine. The messenger came up to me and announced: "Nu, davay sobiraysya nyemyedlenno!" I relaxed because he had not added "s vyeshchami". A few minutes later I was plodding along in the mud in front of the Soviet soldier, who held his gun cocked just in case. He led me to building number 10 in which the Special Section of the NKVD was located. This was one of several places for interrogation. Another was outside the gate, on the opposite side of Kirov Street, in the buildings of the Soviet command. I later got to know that place too.

The wooden one-storey structure, marked number 10 and surrounded with a thick network of barbed wire, stood in the very centre of the camp, near the central church. Near the gate that led to what was once a small vegetable garden, an armed sentry stood day

and night. Only the smoke issuing from the chimney and the occasional smell of frying betrayed the presence of any life in that house. The windows were covered with lime and tightly shuttered for the night. I was conducted into a dark vestibule. The messenger told me to wait. I stood there for about half an hour before another soldier appeared in the low doorway and called: "Come in!" I found myself in a small room illuminated by a few bulbs, which blinded me completely. I was alone. Reproductions of the inevitable trio, Marx, Lenin and Stalin, hung on the tattered wall paper. Close to the wall stood a desk and a few chairs. I don't know how long I waited, maybe half an hour, maybe more. I was tired and sat down in a chair for a moment. The murmur of voices sounded from behind the wall. Suddenly an inside door camouflaged by wall paper, which I had failed to notice, swung open and a hatless NKVD officer in a green overblouse entered the room smoking a cigarette. I recognized him at once by his raven curly hair. It was the same young officer who on 4th October had conducted the personal investigation and had taken my documents away from me. Without uttering a word, he sat down at the desk, unlocked a drawer, pulled it out a little, removed a big revolver from it, put it on the table, then looked through some papers without taking them out of the drawer. He did not pay the slightest attention to me. Not until he was in the act of lighting a new cigarette did he look up at me, Study me for a moment, then, pointing to the chair opposite the table, curtly invite me to sit down.
me to sit down.

I felt ill and weak in the legs. The NKVD officer leaned over the table and looking me straight in the eye, asked: "Your surname is Mlynarski, your first name Bronislaw, your parents' names Emil and Anna, you are a lieutenant, a sapper, is that right?"

"Yes," I replied, somewhat surprised by the exactness of his information.

A moment later he again glanced into the drawer and suddenly declared in a high-pitched and angry voice: "You are of course in the intelligence service."

"No, I am not in the intelligence service," I shot back immediately, though I was taken aback by this question.

"*Nu*, we know, we know very well. Why lie, why not admit the truth?" he laughed loudly.

I assured him in a definite and emphatic voice: "I am a Reserve officer in the Sappers and I have never served in intelligence." And I added: "Besides, you know very well that as a prisoner of war I do not have to answer such questions."

The officer jumped up from his chair, seized his gun and cried out, trembling with rage: "I advise you not to try to teach me or lay down conditions. You are to answer absolutely all questions. I warn you for the last time!"

He sat down, regained control over himself, pulled out a clean sheet of paper and began to jot something down. Minutes passed. The bright bulb screwed into the wall over the officer's head hurt my eyes. The man puffed his cigarette smoke right into my face. I asked him if I could smoke. He replied briefly: "nyet." I was extremely angry and he knew it. He addressed a few questions to me with a casual air: in what unit had I served, where had I been taken prisoner and under what circumstances? My answers were short and edged with sharpness.

"Where is your home, where is your family?" he interrogated further.

"My home is in Warsaw, under the German occupation. I haven't heard anything about my family since the day I left Warsaw."

"Where did you work in civilian life? Did you employ many people?"

I could hardly restrain my laughter. I explained that I had been a department head in a big steamship company which was owned by the Government, that I had had people under my supervision, but that I had not employed anyone on my own. He shook his head in bewilderment and could not understand.

"Did you own your house? How big was it? How many servants did you have?" And he went on: "Did you have your own car, too?" I sensed I was talking to a hopeless case so I started off on a different tack. Patiently and calmly, I said to him: "The house did not belong to me. It was a big apartment house and there were many apartments in it. I rented three rooms with a kitchen and bath. The furniture was mine. It was beautiful furniture. I had a beautiful piano, beautiful paintings and books – family heirlooms. And I did not have a car. But I did have a bicycle." I lied on the spur of the moment. Let him prove it wasn't so, if he could!

He jotted everything down carefully. A long pause ensued again. Suddenly he asked, his face twisted into an evil smile: "Well, all right, if you claim you weren't in intelligence, how do you explain your frequent trips abroad? Where did you go and why?"

It was only now that I understood what he was driving at. Good Lord, I had given him my passport during inspection – a passport stamped with an interminable collection of visas. On the one hand, I realized that in the eyes of a Soviet official, a passport is the most incriminating document there is, for after all, nobody has been leaving the Soviet Union for pleasure in the last twenty years, those few individuals who did go abroad on government business being appropriately guarded. But on the other hand, I felt I was on sure ground. So I sailed right into the fellow with a long tirade: "Yes, I did go abroad very often. I've been doing it since my childhood days. I've been going abroad for pleasure, for study and on business. During the last few years, in my capacity as an official of the steamship company, I regularly went on business trips outside of Poland." And here I began to enumerate all the European countries I had visited, including ports and capitals. I then went on to the Mediterranean area, the Levant, Egypt and even the United States. I could see that his pencil could not keep up with my rapid dictation. I could see that the man was completely lost in the welter of names. He was constantly interrupting me. He no longer knew whether Copenhagen was in England, Southampton in France or whether Sicily was a Greek port. In conclusion, I assured him that I was not the only one to travel at will all over the world, but that tens of thousands of Poles did the same every year without difficulty and without ulterior motives.

I don't know which of us became more tired, he or I. He threw the paper into the drawer, rose, opened the small door a crack, called someone and disappeared. A sleepy-eyed dishevelled soldier came into the room, sat down in the officer's place and gaped at me stupidly. The silence began to get on my nerves. I closed my eyes to escape the glare of the bulb and to snatch a few seconds' sleep. As soon as the soldier noticed I was about to doze off, he kicked me in the ankle under the table and roared: "Don't sleep, you —! Open your eyes, do you hear?"

I focused my eyes dully on the barrel of his revolver. A long cruel hour passed. The kinky-haired officer reappeared. Perhaps he had taken a nap, perhaps he had drunk some tea. The soldier left. I asked the officer whether I might roll myself a cigarette now. He nodded his assent. The smoke revived me a little. The officer interrogated me further about my life. He asked me where I had learned to speak Russian. Again I assumed the initiative. I told him briefly about my four years in Russia during the First World War, about having completed my studies in Moscow, about my father, about music. He interrupted me: "Is all that true? Maybe you did not learn Russian a long time ago, but just recently," he drawled with a foxy expression, after which he suddenly asked me a question in the form of a definite statement: "You were in the Soviet Union after the revolution, only a few years ago. Where were you, how long were you there and what was your aim? What Soviet citizens did you get to know?"

"No, I have not been in the Soviet Union since the autumn of 1918. . . ." I replied at once.

"Why lie? You'd be better off not to lie. We know everything perfectly well anyway," he said, smiling maliciously. I was furious. "I never was in the Soviet Union, I tell you." I enunciated every syllable excitedly. I grew silent. I did not know what else to say. How could I convince him that I had not crossed the Soviet border at all in recent years and that by the same token I had not committed the "crime" which he was plainly insinuating I had committed? I was at a loss to understand this man's mentality. The suspicious nature of these people was simply beyond belief. They imagined that every person who entered Russia came as a spy on behalf of his country. For after all, every person must be the envoy of his government, which delegates him to the Soviet Union for intelligence activity under the guise of a tourist or a merchant. That was what they were taught to do in the Soviets, that's how things are in the Soviet Union. The barrier of reasoning was insurmountable.

For a long time the officer was silent, smoking one cigarette after another, an ironic smile playing on his face as he studied me. This humiliating *dopros* must have lasted three hours by now. I knew that this young man hated me, that he had contempt for me, that he considered me his class enemy. . . . I was emotionally worn out, my sense of reality was growing dim. Suddenly an impulse of instinctive self-defence suggested an idea which I wanted to seize upon and turn into words. I stirred in my chair and began to mumble something. The officer casually asked: *"Nu,* want to say something? *Nu,* let's hear. . . ."

"Do you like music? Because you see, I am a musician at heart, though I am not a professional. I live music, I love it, I've been immersed in it since infancy. And I know that all of you in this country love music. Maybe we can arrive at a human understanding on this score. Do you play any instrument or do you sing? Tell me please, will you?" I said all in one breath, stubbornly insisting on an answer from him. His facial expression changed somewhat, his ironic smile disappeared, his black eyes looked at me with unconcealed surprise. He muttered reluctantly "What has that got to do with anything?"

"Well, please answer me!" I insisted. He was taken off his guard and did not quite know how to react. There was no doubt but that our thin papered walls had additional eyes and ears. Finally, pressed into a corner, he stammered in a lowered voice: "Yes, I like music very much. I play the balalaika and I sing. But what the devil has this got to do with anything?" he added angrily. I replied quickly:

190

"Just that I happen to know several Soviet citizens whom you must also know, or at least about whom you must have heard. So if you want to prove the truthfulness of my words, to check my deposition about my life, and the life of my family, ask Professor Igumnov, the excellent pianist from the musical conservatory in Moscow. Ask Professor Goldenweiser, also a pianist in that school. Ask Mme. Nyezhdanova, the famous opera star. I'm mentioning these three because I know that they are alive, that they have been awarded the highest Soviet decorations. I heard the ceremony here at Starobyelsk Camp on the radio. These artists were associates of my father, who was a pupil of Tchaikovsky and of Leopold Auer. Later on, my father was a close friend of Alexander Glazunov, Scriabin, Liadov and many others. . . ."

He did not interrupt me. He seemed to be listening with genuine interest. I continued feverishly, reaching into my store of memories that were so dear to me: "Do you see this scar on my forehead?" I asked. "That's where I cut myself on the gravel of the park in Morges, Ignace Paderewski's estate in Switzerland, when I was five years old. When I was seven, my mother took me to hear Rachmaninoff. After the concert, we went to his dressing room. Rachmaninoff pulled me up on his bony lap. He asked me if I was studying the piano and whether I wished to play well. 'I want to play the way you do,' I told him. He kissed me. In Moscow in 1917, Glazunov often came to my parents' home. Once he caught me in the act of improvising an arrangement of a Strauss waltz. He sat down at the piano. I harmonised very well, he said. But, he pointed out, it would be better if I did thus and so, see, like this. And he wound up playing a few waltzes for me, including the beautiful Blue Danube. I remember how spellbound I was by the sight of those fat fingers of his travelling up and down the keyboard and producing the most exquisite music. In Warsaw, during the first international Chopin competition in 1927, three of your young pianists stood out among all the contestants. Surely you know the names of Shostakovich, Oborin and Ginsburg. My father was director of the Warsaw Opera at the time. He was one of the judges and the guiding spirit of the contest. My father had also founded the Warsaw Philharmonic Orchestra and it was under his baton that these fine young pianists each played one movement of two of Chopin's concertos for piano and orchestra in the semi-finals. Oborin won first prize, but his compatriot fellow contestants were not far behind him. Ask them, ask Shostakovich, who is world famous today, ask Oborin and Ginsburg, who are today professors in your country, whether they remember the home of Emil Mlynarski in Warsaw in the building of the Opera, where by special permission from the Soviet Embassy, these boys were able to spend two evenings. They felt completely at ease in our company. I shall never forget the ebullient and brilliant Shostakovich playing his new sonata, accompanied on another piano by Ginsburg, a lad of no more than eighteen who was blessed with wonderful fingers. . . ."

The officer was listening to my story intently. I continued enthusiastically, forgetting that I had before me a representative of the NKVD. "And why do you suppose those boys were allowed to stay in my parents' home? Why do you suppose they felt at ease there even though they were far from their own homes? Because music reigned supreme in my father's house. Music, the Queen of Art, which was above all man-made walls, restrictions or superstitions. That's why these young people must surely remember the Mlynarski home. . . ."

Suddenly the low camouflaged door opened. The big heavy body of Lebedyev, NKVD major and head of house number 10, stepped into the room. His shirt open, sleepy-eyed and dishevelled, he sat down in a chair, which creaked under his weight. He yawned audibly and addressed his subordinate in a lazy voice: "What's all this talking about?"

The young officer quickly reported: "This prisoner of war is talking about Soviet citizens known to him. . . ."

So I had not been mistaken. The walls did have ears. Mr. Lebedyev had been listening on the other side of the wall until his curiosity prompted him to have a look at this strange conversationalist. *"Interyesno, prodolzhaytye . . ."* he said, punctuating his words with another yawn. I was brought back to reality with a bang. I could not collect my thoughts again. So I added a few sentences that had no bearing on my musical recollections and announced that I knew no one else in the Soviet Union.

Lebedyev's small eyes, embedded in fat, bored into me for a long moment. Finally, he asked me casually: "To what political party do you belong? Come on, tell me. Perhaps you belong to the PPS (Polish Socialist Party) or the OZN (Organization of National Unity). Come, come, I'm listening!" He pronounced the Polish abbreviations with a funny Russian accent.

"I have never belonged to any political party, neither to the PPS nor the OZN," I replied shortly.

"How strange. No Polish officer belongs to any political party. They're all innocent little angels!" Lebedyev's huge frame shook with laughter. "We'll look into that later, we shall see," he added as he rose. The young officer followed suit. He lifted the revolver from the table and waved it before my head. "Anything that was said here is to remain a secret, understand?"

They left the room and a soldier reappeared in their stead. He looked at me with disgust and bellowed: "*Nu, davay, sobiraysya!*" He pushed me out through the door and then gave me a shove through the wicket-gate. "Hurry back to your block!" he spat in parting.

Thus came to an end my first *dopros*. It had lasted four hours. Again I had that beaten feeling. Now they know me in the NKVD, echoed over and over in my head. I looked up at the sky, aglitter with its myriad stars. The same sky for everyone, all over the world! Why did this miserable earth have to be so different everywhere!

Wrapped in their blankets, their long underwear shining white in the darkness, human shadows moved along the path leading to the Siegfried Line.

I threw off my boots. Soundlessly I climbed into my bunk, lay down and inhaled the fetid air.

In the morning, Zygmunt awakened me and whispered solicitously: "How was it, Bron? Did those sons of bitches keep you long?"

"Oh, let me alone, will you," I replied rudely.

He reached for my hand, pressed it hard and gave it a little pat. Dear, good Zygmunt.

The NKVD knows all about me by now, whirled round and round in my head.

At the beginning of December 1939 radios had been installed over the whole camp. In the Soviet Union a radio consists of primitive loudspeakers in metal frames covered in black paper. We named them the "black discs". In the camp they were hung in most of the larger rooms high up in the most inaccessible places so as to make any fiddling with them impossible. Cables leading to the loudspeakers were securely fixed and there were no knobs enabling us to turn the programmes off. So whether we liked it or not the radio would continue blaring without interruption from 7 a.m. till midnight.

The "black discs" – and there are millions of them in the country – can be seen hanging everywhere – in large peasants' cottages, in canteens, in the "Krasnyje Ugolki" ("Red Clubs"), in public squares, hospitals, railway stations – briefly in all places to which people are likely to flock. Are there any private radio sets in the Soviet Union? Perhaps, but I have never seen any. They are after all a kind of window into the outside world and this is dangerous. Therefore, the only people allowed to possess them are those at the top of the governmental ladder, some party luminaries and of course the NKVD.

All in all propaganda was flowing incessantly from the "black disc" in the ceiling down to our bunks. At times it would become absolutely unbearable. We would then cut the wires to stop the constant blabbering but on seeing a guard enter we would reconnect them in a flash. Particularly insupportable were the lengthy transmissions aimed at inciting the population to increase productivity. Time and again the broadcasters would sing the praises of Stakhanov and his rival, another labour "genius" called Syemivolos. Time and again they would call people to participate in the socialist competition (Socyalisticheskoye Soryevnovanye). This was a permanent institution based on the following trick: a factory, say in the region of the Donbas, would challenge another similar one in the Ural region to a "duel" in order to establish by an increase in productivity which of the two competitors got first prize. Similar competitions frequently took place between various *kholkhozes* and other collective enterprises.

As a rule the war bulletins would start with a report from the German General Staff. On such occasions, when quoting in full the German source of the bulletin, namely the "Svodka Gyenyeralnavo Shtaba Vyerkhovnovo Khomandovanya Gyermanskoy Armyey . . .", the voice of the speaker would fill with pathos and pride. This would be followed by a long description of German military activity, great stress being laid on the successes, mostly at sea in those days. The British war bulletin sounded modest – the source was given as "Britanskaya Svodka" (The British General Staff) and the report was read in an undramatic way. It amounted in most cases to an enumeration of losses sustained by Great Britain and hardly a mention of her successes. A similar tendentiousness was displayed in the Soviet press. The newspapers usually referred to the war as the "Second Imperialistic War," imputing imperialism to the Allies and presenting the Germans as the victims of aggression.

It was with considerable grief that we learned of the sinking near the British coast of the 15,000 ton Polish transatlantic liner MS *Pilsudski*. The radio newsreader announced this German success with special relish and did not miss the opportunity to vilify Poland and her brave merchant marine for being in the service of imperialist Britain.

A really vitriolic anti-Polish campaign was being waged at that time on Soviet radio. Everything Polish was denigrated with an unsurpassed hatred – the country, the population, the Polish Government and the army were attacked every day on radio. Stories would be told of various most improbable incidents in those parts of Poland where the Red Army had been on the rampage. Out of sheer despair we even laughed at one of these yarns. The story was that somewhere in the region of Stanislawow Polish officers had raped several peasant girls, strangled them and slit their bellies open to fill them with stones! This absolutely ludicrous story appeared in the press and was repeated with great relish on the wireless. In such a manner Poland and the Poles would be regularly debased, until the 22nd June, 1941 when Poland suddenly became an "ally" of the Soviets!

The only bright and soothing ray, the only consolation to our nerves was music. Music, this divine language conveyed to our world from Heaven through the genius of human race — untinged by tendentiousness, free from the poison of hatred, pure as water from a fountain. Hunched up on my upper tier bunk I would push myself as near as possible to the "black disc" so as to be in the best position to listen to music without missing a single bar and to forget for a moment all our misery and sorrows. It was not easy, however, to secure total silence even during the most interesting musical programmes. Down below, the place was always full of conversation, of heated, unrelenting debate and of explosions of gaiety, that artificial, morbid kind of gaiety which makes one think of a lunatic asylum. But it didn't matter that much. I had learned to neutralize the din and had hardly ever in my life listened to music with such intense concentration. After all, even under normal conditions, during a musical audition, say, or listening to music in a concert hall or at home on the wireless, I would be exposed to a greater deal of various distractions. Here in the darkness of my upper bunk I was not confronted with the lights of the concert hall or the glare of the spotlights, with the sight of the well or badly cut tails of the conductor, or his mane of grey-blond hair, or with all the magic lines and signs designed by his hands or fingers. I did not have to watch the comically blownout cheeks of the French-horn player, the straddled legs of the cellist nor the alluring silhouette of the harpist plucking with her long fingers the strings of her instrument. I did not have to watch Don José's belly constricted by a corset, the bosomy Isolde in a long night shift, the frolicsome leaps and bounds of the wicked Faust's Mephistopheles or the lachrymose face of Leoncavallo's deceived Pagliacci. The attractive profile of a beautiful woman in the row in front of mine with her big ear-rings — how many carats and how are they measured? — did not distract my attention nor did the sight of a fat merchant with his head slumping rhythmically either from sleepiness or sheer boredom. . . . What is his line of business? Cement or ladies' underwear?

And even at home, in front of my wireless, there would be the telephone, the dog, the front bell, a book, a game of patience, a "we are served" or "hurry up, get dressed, it's time we should leave" – all interrupting the music like the slash of a razor. Here in the darkness of my bunk there was none of all this: no one would ask me to the dining room, the telephone would not ring and there was no conductor with his tails. I succeeded in alienating myself completely from reality and learned to attain a maximum capacity for concentration. I drank of the sounds of music as a lost traveller in a desert oasis would drink cool refreshing water.

The standard of the programmes was on the whole excellent, no matter whether it consisted of live transmissions of symphonic concerts, recitals and operatic performances or transmissions of gramophone recordings. The relatively few records produced in the Soviet Union are of inferior quality and hence the majority of records played on the radio were of foreign make. This explains perhaps why the names of the soloist and of the conductor were never announced, nor the name of the orchestra to which we were listening. All the announcer would say was just "You will now hear Beethoven's Symphony No. 5 played by a symphonic orchestra..." and that would be all. I was often devoured by curiosity. And who knows – maybe this mysterious anonymity contributed to a better concentration. Supposing, for instance, they had announced that Sir Thomas Beecham was conducting. I would have immediately visualised this shortish man with his small head and peaked beard. The same would have happened in the case of the majestic figure of Koussevitzky in his wonderfully cut tails, of which he used to say himself "Vyed moi fraki vsyem izvyestny". (My evening dress is well known to everybody).

On certain occasions, however, the identity of the soloist would be disclosed. I shall never forget how impressed and deeply moved I was on hearing once the following words: "Chopin's piano concerto in A-flat will be played by Artur Rubinstein with the accompaniment of an orchestra...", which orchestra remained a mystery. I knew, however, that the recording had been made by the London Symphony Orchestra under Barbirolli. As far as the great soloists of the West were concerned, Artur Rubinstein was an exception to the rule of anonymity and his recordings were transmitted quite often. The emigré Russian Rachmaninov was as a soloist probably on the black list but they were patently unable to dismiss him as a composer. On the other hand, for reasons unknown to me, the music of Igor Stravinsky was completely banned – maybe for the reason that he is *par excellence* a Russian.

Light music of "foreign" origin would be transmitted from time to time but only orchestral works and never vocal compositions, as words were likely to disclose the source. Modern dance music was always referred to as "jazz" although what they played lacked a single note of real jazz.

As for Soviet artists no matter whether they were performing in public or in a recording room their names would always be announced. All artists who have achieved a certain fame enjoy the title of "ordyenonosyetz", which means "the bearer of an order" and this is bestowed regardless of the importance or number of decorations. It always had a somewhat funny ring to it. Elderly or the most famous artists are rewarded by the highest honour, namely the title of the "distinguished artist of the Soviet Union," which the announcer on the radio would always stress with great pomp.

And this is how I learned that many friends and colleagues of my father were still alive and active. The mention of their names brought back memories of young Russian musicians – Shostakovich particularly – who took part in the Chopin competitions in Warsaw in the years 1927, 1932 and 1937. And thanks to this knowledge acquired through the "black disc" I was able to hold forth during my first nocturnal interrogation in hut number 10.

16. THE NEW BARRACKS

A few days before Christmas two new huge barracks bearing the numbers 20 and 21, in which over 1,300 men were to be housed, were completed and made available. In order to have them ready for those dates a team of three hundred of our engineers had worked on them furiously for fourteen hours a day. From the very beginning until the end Major Zaleski had been the untiring leader of the enterprise. These barracks, two unassuming, ordinary constructions would have been unworthy of any attention anywhere else but to our weary eyes they appeared as some dream castles. In contrast to the old dark and filthy ones their interiors were relatively bright and spacious, and equipped with two tiers of bunks made with smooth planks, shelves for our kit and bread, brick stoves, and here and there even some tiny tables. Each prisoner was now allotted a space 70 centimetres in width, which compared with the 50 centimetres we had been allowed previously, was a great improvement. The whole interior was damp from the timber brought from Siberian woods and fromvsture absorbed in conditions of rain, snow and mud, during the period of construction, yet these shortcomings did nothing to discourage the future "tenants", rheumatics included, from installing themselves as soon as possible within the new tempting walls.

And then came the next act – a general reshuffle of the whole camp. It was conducted by the Soviet authorities with their habitual zeal and a lot of ineffective and senseless shouting. Their idea was to segregate us into our ranks. Since this raised no opposition all went well. Colonels and Lieutenant-Colonels were thus housed in a fairly decent brick building number 14. Majors, of whom there were three hundred men, were packed tightly into a two-storey barrack bearing the ominous number 13! Barrack number 12, a gloomy, dilapidated structure, received a batch of old and sickly Captains, mostly Reserve, many of them typical "Grand daddies of the woods" as we used to nickname them. As most orders for coffins received by the carpenters workshop came from this ill-fated dwelling we called it "the old men's home" or "funeral house." Strangely enough a large group of doctors had been squeezed into this labyrinth of small, dreary rooms. Despite their samaritan profession they were as helpless regarding themselves, as they were regarding their elder room-mates who suffered from every possible bodily ailment.

The new barrack number 20 had been allotted to younger infantry and cavalry Captains. The remaining buildings, consisting of huts, cow sheds as well as the new one number 21 − all now fortunately somewhat less overcrowded − were occupied by Lieutenants and Second Lieutenants. These two junior ranks, totalling 2,300 men, constituted the majority of the camp's inmates, in those days approximately 4,000 men in all.

As I have mentioned before, as a result of the reshuffle I had found myself in hut number 6, which contained ninety men. I was lucky to be able to remain with my closest friends. For the Soviet authorities tried to break up groups of officers during all the changing around. We considered this a wicked and malicious thing to do. In order to keep our group intact we had to resort to all kinds of devices. Captains and Lieutenants would, for instance, swap uniforms and sleep for nights on different bunks − all this to disorientate the *politruks* and the *vakhtyory* so that they forgot our faces and ranks. And we did manage to bamboozle them! My group remained as it was! Only much later did we understand why they tried to break up groups. It was not merely a malicious manoeuvre − it was a precautionary measure applied to any categories of convicts in order to frustrate attempts to escape or to thwart any potential nucleus of conspiracy. I was slowly complementing my education in the matter of methods used under the enlightened Soviet penitentiary system.

All the buildings assigned to the officers of junior ranks were also used to accommodate some 50 to 100 (their number kept varying) civilians who for some odd, inaccountable reason had strayed into a prisoners of war camp. Although some of them were perhaps deliberately concealing their military ranks, the great majority was in no way connected with military service. The group comprised civil servants of various government institutions, such as the Ministry for Home Affairs, of Finance, Justice, Education and even Foreign Affairs. Those subjected to the worst treatment by the NKVD were Judges and Public Prosecutors. They would either be summoned frequently to building number 10 for interrogations lasting many hours or taken outside the gate from where many would never return.

There was among those civilians an old Jew, Moishe Finkelstein, aged seventy-five, a merchant in timber from Rowno. Of military matters he knew no more than that there was such a thing as an army. He could not, for instance, tell a Lieutenant from a Colonel. A kind, good natured and charming man he was a popular character in our camp. Using well trod paths, in the company of a few officers whose conversation he found entertaining, he used to go for a stroll every day regardless of the weather. He walked slowly, although his short legs seemed to move quite swiftly, reminding one in a way of a light canter. His light blue eyes always showed astonishment at being surrounded by so many military men – something which had never happened to him in his life before. We used to call him, affectionately, "Old Uncle" – which he seemed to like – and he would smile benevolently from under his long silver beard.

I once asked him how he came to find himself in the Starobyelsk Monastery Camp.

"It just happened one night," he said. "Those brigands came to my house, smashed everything inside to smithereens, beat us all up, took my old wife and other members of my family away, apparently to Siberia, and put me into prison – exactly as I now stand here in my fur coat. They then kept me in two other prisons for two months until they brought me here in the party of our prisoners. I keep asking them – what do they want from me as I'm not a military man, but just an old merchant in timber and why are they tormenting me. But they will only shout at me "you dirty old burzhuy, capitalist, krovopiytza* . . ." The old man stopped for a while but then started crying: "Where is my poor old wife, oh God, oh God, where is she now? If I only knew whether she's still alive." Big tears were streaming down his beard.

I was fond of standing on the steps of the central church and watching the uncommonly beautiful scarlet and pink shades of a sunset on a frosty afternoon. This was the highest observation point in the camp and it happened to be situated on its western side. Beyond the dismal gate a rise in the level of the land revealed the roofs of all the wretched little houses of the town. I always dreamt that one day I would be able to look inside them. Despite the severe cold no smoke could be seen coming out of the chimneys. One would have thought that as no fires had been made nobody lived in any of the places. This was not the case. There were plenty of folk in there, children, young and elderly people worn out after a day's heavy work. They had to suffer unimaginably cold conditions for the simple

---

* Literally a person who sucks blood. Used in the early Russian revolutionary jargon to denote a capitalist: a person who does not work himself and exploits workers.

reason that not enough fuel was available. Because their cooking was done on a primus stove and they were allotted only a few litres of oil a month by the authorities they regularly went without enough food to eat. We were told this by the Soviet workers whom we used to meet occasionally within the compound of the camp.

One evening when nostalgically scanning the western horizon I suddenly heard shouts. Two *boytzy* were pushing an old man through the narrow passage known as the "prokhodnaya budka" into the inside of the camp. He was quite tall, dressed in civilian clothes, and carrying a bundle on his hunched back. The man staggered on the ice and fell to the ground. I hastened down the steps but before I could reach him he rose to his feet and was heading blindly in front of him not knowing in what direction to go. I came up to him and asked who he was and where he came from. "My name is Michalski," he answered in a whisper. I took him to our hut and we offered him tea and some bread. He was sitting stooped on the boards of the lower bunk wrapped in the remnants of his once grand fur coat and with a black woollen stocking stretched over his head.

According to a custom which we used to observe with newcomers we refrained from asking him any personal questions. Besides, as he was toothless, he was speaking with great difficulty. Despite the greyish beard which almost hid his face a bell rang in my ears and as in a dream I gradually recognised his noble features. At last I dared to ask him whether it was possible that he was Mr. Michalski, the Majordomo of the Polish President at the Royal Castle in Warsaw. He nodded in assent. So I did recognize him after all! In fact few people from Warsaw would fail to recognise him. He was known particularly by all those who for the past twenty years had visited the Castle – the ordinary people of Warsaw as well as members of the Diplomatic Corps, attending receptions given by the Polish President. Should any of them be reading these lines they will no doubt remember clearly the imposing figure of Michalski wearing richly embroidered French court dress, silk short trousers, long white stockings and lacquered shoes with ornate buckles. Hammering the shiny inlaid floor with his long Majordomo's staff, a golden Polish Eagle fixed to its top, he would announce in a powerful voice the names and full titles of the President's guests as they arrived at the hall . . . . He had held this position for twenty years, ever since Poland had regained her independence.

It had seemed as though he had been in service at the castle for centuries, remaining as the living legacy of the old Kings of Poland. He was a human symbol, uniting the present with the regal splendours of one hundred and fifty years ago. On the other hand, one could say that dressed in his resplendent livery he was a somewhat grotesque anachronism in the less colourful environment of a modern republic.

After an hour's rest at our hut a Soviet messenger summoned him to the Commissar Kirshin. I saw him again a few days later. He then told me about his whole ordeal.

Following the exodus from Warsaw he had gone with the President down to Olyka in the province of Volhynia – the ancient residence belonging to Prince Janusz Radziwill. During this dramatic ten day journey the President's convoy was hunted and bombed by the Luftwaffe day and night – German fifth columnists were co-operating well! When on the 17th September the President fled to the West via Rumania old Michalski remained in Olyka Castle. Like a faithful dog he was to take care of the *objets d'art,* paintings, china and silver evacuated at the last moment from the Royal Castle. A few days later Olyka fell into the hands of the Red Army. The magnificent residence was completely looted and all the refugees living in the Castle – most of whom had fled from the Germans – were either imprisoned or deported to Siberia.

Michalski went through several prisons. During a series of brutal interrogations – the notorious *doprosy* – all his front teeth were knocked out and a few ribs broken. The fact that in carrying out his duties he had been in contact with the President and the unusual ring of his "court" title sufficed to feed the warped imaginations of the Soviet police with the idea that he was a big fry from whom information of the possible greatest importance could and should be extracted! Michalski had never served with the forces but the Soviets assumed without any question that his title of "Majordomo" meant that he was an ordinary army Major and they segregated him as such. This must have been why, after having reduced him in various prisons to a state of complete physical ruin, he was sent to the prisoner of war camp at Starobyelsk. After a new series of protracted nightly interrogations by Lebyedyev, the boss of the NKVD at the camp, and the Commissar Kirshin he was consigned by the latter to barrack number 13 which housed the Majors. "And so I became a real Major" – Michalski said, concluding his story with a ghost of a smile on his haggard, emaciated face. And from now on the newly promoted "Major" would be addressed as such by his fellow prisoners despite the fact that on his old shoulders he wore a now tatty fur coat and on his head an old stocking, full of holes.

17. "THANK YOU, MY FRIENDS"

While helping Major Zaleski to prepare a list of all the prisoners in the camp I worked in the tiny room in hut number 1 which served as the office of the Polish Command of the Camp. I would work there every morning from 8 a.m. to midday. On the 20th December I was sitting there as usual at a piece of furniture − let us call it a table − made of a few boards (real tables were a rarity in the camp). Half-dressed, Major Zaleski was lying on a narrow bunk − for he also lived in the office. Doctor Kazimierz Wolfram, a well-known surgeon from Warsaw, was busy rubbing some sort of whitish ointment into the repulsive-looking boils that covered his swollen legs. Zaleski seemed to be in a strange, sullen mood. For the last few days he had lost his sense of humour and his habit of telling jokes. It was clear that his thoughts were on more serious matters. He was grumbling a bit at the doctor and now and then he would utter a light moan of pain as Wolfram continued to massage his ailing limbs. Suddenly he turned to Laud and me: "Listen my boys! Since one can never know what may happen to any of us what I'm asking you is . . . well, just in case . . . pack up those two shirts, a pair of underpants, socks and my pullover into that suitcase. . . . Don't forget tobacco, and other trifles for washing. No other bits and pieces."

Laud and I looked at each other without saying a word. Laud was an old friend of the Major from the days when they were both at the Warsaw Higher Technical School, and at the camp he was one of Zaleski's closest collaborators. He stammered out with some difficulty: "Very good Mister Major."

The day was cloudy and cold. Outside the small frost-covered windowpanes, the world looked gloomy and dreary. Hut number 1 was situated along the main artery linking the kitchen with the rest of the camp. At that moment the morning portions of oatmeal were being dispensed. Hundreds of men, their heads wrapped up in scarves or pieces of rug, were passing each other on the icy sand-covered path. Some of them were carrying empty buckets, others had their buckets filled with steaming *kasha*. They were moving slowly in pairs, carrying several buckets at one time on wooden hand-barrows. Just opposite my window a long line of men was passing buckets of water to the kitchen to replenish the ever-thirsty cauldrons. The men would frequently slip on the frozen mountain around the pump which the constant hacking out of ice could not prevent from forming. The winch of the well was screeching plaintively like the wild cranes when leaving on their annual migration to warmer climes.

The Major's swollen legs looked more and more like two huge loaves of white bread. Doctor Wolfram was now powdering them with talcum powder. After he had bandaged them he helped the Major to pull up his boots which for that purpose had the tops slit open. The Major was groaning and cursing the Doctor. He eventually rose to his feet, and stood towering over Wolfram. Clasping his arm, he said: "Many thanks, dear Doctor. Let's hope things will turn out well – what matters now is to carry on until the evening. Here, have some of my *makhorka* and there's also cigarette paper or just plain newsprint – whatever you prefer" – he was inviting us all.

Doctor Wolfram, an exceptionally good-looking man, with oriental features and a swarthy complexion, rolled a cigarette and said: "A bit of patience and everything will be all right. But try, Major, to rest as much as you can, abstain from walking and remember, whilst sitting, keep your legs propped up against some chair or something . . . you'll feel more comfortable like that."

The Major burst out laughing as if his good humour had come back: "You incorrigible optimist, dear Doctor! Your good advice is very fine in theory but how do you expect me to cut out my constant tours of inspection round the camp? And can you imagine me talking for hours to Messrs. Bereshkov and Kirshin while sitting with my legs up in the air – me a poor humble servant facing my lords and exalted masters! I can assure you that I often have to remain standing as those gentlemen won't even offer me a seat. Oh to the devil with all this. . . ! He waved his hand, as though pushing the matter away.

In order to change the subject I cut in: "Have you heard the news? Since early this morning the wireless has been shouting about Stalin's birthday tomorrow. "Uncle Joe" will be sixty-one. The *politruks* and the *boytzy* are busy decorating the boards in front of the Church. Looks as if it'll be a big do. . . ." I stopped. The door opened slowly and Kopyekin appeared in the entrance. There was no telling whether the expression on his unbelievably wrinkled face showed pleasure or displeasure. Any grimace of his lips could mean either one or the other.

We greeted him with a polite "zdrastvuytye" which he surprisingly acknowledged with the same greeting. Major Zaleski immediately put on a show of joviality. Addressing Kopyekin in his excellent Russian he said: "*Nu*, what is the news from across the road tovarishch Kopyekin? (Meaning the site of the headquarters of the NKVD.) The same freezing cold as the monastery or is it perhaps even worse? How is the Commander, did he have a good night's rest? You are apparently getting ready for tomorrow's great feast — the birthday of the "people's leader"! *Nu*, take a seat tovarishch Kopyekin, and warm yourself up. Have a smoke," he said amiably offering him some *makhorka*.

Looking somewhat embarrassed Kopyekin sat on the edge of the Major's bunk. Using a piece of newspaper he rolled a cigarette with a few agile moves of his fingers. I had always been impressed (as I have never succeeded in mastering this art) by his knack of rolling *makhorka*, which was dry and loose as sand. Kopyekin puffed at his cigarette, sending out big whiffs of smoke and without saying a word stared at the floor with the expression of an imbecile. After a long pause and then stammering as if unsure of himself, he interrupted the silence in his queer voice, reminding one of the quack of a duck: "*Nu*, Zalyevsky, that will do. Stop being funny, there's plenty of work ahead. *Nu*, get dressed and off we go to the Commander!"

The Major sighed loudly, pulled down his tunic, tightened his belt and reached out for his cap. He looked round the room attentively as if he had left behind something and then looked straight into the eyes of each of us. Laud tried to help him on with his greatcoat, which he would not wear usually, so he reluctantly flung it over his shoulders.

"Hail my friends . . . and many thanks," he said, quickly following Kopyekin outdoors.

We were used to our Major spending three or sometimes even more hours at the headquarters of the Soviet Command of the camp. This time, however, his absence began to worry Laud and myself after no more than one hour. But more hours of futile expectation were to follow. As dusk was falling we told the Major's closest colleagues about his absence and scattered in all directions in search of Kopyekin. But he too, usually easy to trace, seemed to have vanished into thin air. I decided to take a risk and call on the Soviet officer on duty. On that day it happened to be a certain Lorenstein, a young, good-looking, strongly built Jew with permanently rosy cheeks. I was pleased it was him. Of the three officers on duty who worked on a rotation basis and changed every twenty-four hours, he was the most accommodating. He worked in a new barrack near the gate which was also used as the guardroom. Adjacent to this building was the narrow corridor, "prokhodnaya budka" On seeing me the guard pointed his rifle and called: "Halt. Who goes there? What do you want?"

"I want to report to the officer on duty," I said, trying to assume an authoritative voice.

"Wait here." He went inside the building and reappeared soon after. "Come in," he barked.

It was my first visit to the room of an officer on duty. There was a huge portrait of Stalin on one of the walls and opposite that one of Beria, the head of the NKVD, and one of his henchmen unknown to me.

Lorenstein, with his cap on, was sitting at the desk smoking some expensive brand of cigarette. On his uncovered wrist – perhaps displayed on purpose – I noticed a gleaming gold watch. I saluted him. He acknowledged my military greeting by a wave of his hand as if he was trying to chase off a fly from his nose and asked me in a formal voice, although relatively polite: "What is the matter? From which barrack are you?"

"From number 1, where I am employed with the Polish Command," I said.

"Ah, yes, I remember your face. And your name?"

I gave it to him and then asked about Major Zaleski, saying that we were concerned because of his prolonged absence and also adding that he had left with Kopyekin for the Soviet Command at 9 a.m. and had not returned so far. Would the officer know where he was now and when he would be back?

"I don't know," he answered tartly. "Since he went to see the Commander he must still be with him. Conferences, as you know, often take a long time. There's nothing to worry about. Is that all?" Rising from his chair he thus indicated to me that the audience was closed. I marched off.

Major Zaleski did not turn up that night. To try to avoid a new wave of depression we attempted to keep the fact a secret. Next day Laud ran into Kopyekin. Knowing him rather well he pressed him assiduously for news. Kopyekin tried to cover up his embarrassment with anger: "To hell with you, leave me alone. I know nothing, I took him to Commander Bereshkov and that's all!"

More long hours followed, pregnant with deep concern about the fate of our Major. It was only after forty-eight hours had passed that Kopyekin appeared in hut number 1. Laud, myself and a few companions bombarded him with questions. He was looking uneasy. As before, he sat on the Major's empty bunk, rolled a cigarette, kept silent for a few nerve-racking minutes and stammered out: "Pack his belongings right away and take them to the 'prokhodnava budka.' I'll be waiting there for you. . . ." He pulled his cap over his protruding ears and left.

When packing up the Major's possessions I had the feeling that we, his closest colleagues and friends, were rendering him a last service. With Laud we took the suitcase according to Kopyekin's direction. He received it without any comment.

Commander Bereshkov, Commissar Kirshin and the officer on duty, Golovanov, appeared in hut number 1 a few hours later. Their freshly shaved faces brought into the stuffy air of the room a strong fragrance of face powder and cheap eau-de-Cologne. There were five or six of us in the room — all junior officers. Bereshkov watched us attentively for a while after which he addressed Laud, who was standing closest to him, in a crisp, peremptory voice: "Who of you here, among the Polish Command, holds the highest rank after Zaleski? Is it Niewiarowski or Miller?"

Laud answered: "Both of them are Majors. Major Niewiarowski is older and also senior as far as the duration of his military service is concerned."

"Where is he? Bring him here immediately," Bereshkov shouted. All three "masters" made themselves comfortable on Zaleski's bunk. Smoking cigarettes and paying no attention to us they talked in monosyllables. After some ten minutes Major Kazimierz Niewiarowski, appeared. He was fifty years of age, a Sapper and like Zaleski a building engineer. Fair, without a single grey hair, with blue eyes and a slightly upturned nose, modest and helpful, he was liked and held in high esteem by all his companions. Somewhat hot-tempered he was also devoid of any spite so that he would seldom hurt anybody. For three months he had been working like an ox on the construction of the new barracks. He was the head of the whole building team and I would often see him toiling with an axe, a hammer or a saw in his hand.

Bereshkov came to the point right away. He said abruptly: "Niewiarowski! You were Zaleski's first deputy? Right. From now on you shall be the Polish Commander of the Camp. You know what your functions will be and you also know the regulations. You will live here in this room and sleep on Zaleski's bunk. That's all!"

Poor Niewiarowski, caught unawares, was trying to explain to the Commander (he spoke Russian fairly fluently) that he was not sufficiently qualified for the job, that he lacked administrative experience and was therefore not good enough for that kind of occupation. Besides there were in the camp other officers with a higher rank, such as Colonels for instance ... Bereshkov retorted curtly: "No arguing! It'll have to be as I said." After giving this his ultimate order he and the other two officers left, carrying with them the odour of good tobacco and bad perfume.

An hour later, a new Polish Commander, silent with a gloomy expression on his face, was displaying his miserable personal possessions on the bunk of his friend, Major Zaleski.

Major Walenty Miller, a young Artillery man and an officer in the General Inspectorate of the Polish Armed Forces in Warsaw (GISZ), was born somewhere in the Far East — in Kharbin (Manchuria) I think, where he had also spent his younger years. He had an excellent command of the Russian language and it was on this account chiefly that he had been made second deputy to Major Zaleski. Endowed with an exceptional sense of humour he would tell jokes and make biting remarks and witticisms not only among his friends but also in front of Soviet officers. In fact, he was a bit cheeky on occasions, going rather too far in what he said. He was billeted in barrack number 6, together with all the other officers working in the Polish Command of the Camp.

That the errand-boy Kopyekin should have been coming frequently to see Miller (we used to call him Walek) on official matters was, of course, a perfectly normal occurrence. Lately, however, his visits had become more frequent than ever. Kopyekin would sit down on the bunk near Walek and they would talk in whispers for a longer period than would appear necessary. This strange relationship interested me as it did Zygmunt and Laud. We did not interfere as we trusted Walek's good sense. That the clever and intelligent Walek was working on Kopyekin had by now become obvious. The change which this simple Soviet soldier was undergoing under the influence of Walek was also visible. And then at last the day arrived when Walek Miller saw fit to unveil some of the mystery shrouding his conversations with Kopyekin. For he had come to the conclusion that the matter which he had been investigating was now ripe for disclosure. He had learned from Kopyekin that further down Kirov Street there was a hut, about 400 metres from the walls of the camp, in which were held Colonels and Lieutenant-Colonels of the Polish Army — in all about a hundred men. This was the first sensational news. The second one was that further still, in a self-contained cottage situated in one of the side streets, about half a kilometre away, were housed nine Polish Generals. Walek not only succeeded in extracting this startling piece of information from Kopyekin but, what is more, managed in a most masterly way to get into contact with the inmates of the houses. He was given the names of a number of those in the "Colonels' House" and all the names of those in the "Generals' House". This proved to be the most effective intelligence coup so far achieved as regards what went on outside the impenetrable walls surrounding our camp.

The "Generals' House" was not visible from our camp but there existed a place from which one could observe part of the courtyard of the "Colonels' House" where the prisoners were allowed to take walks. From the observation point thousands of sharp eyes used to watch regularly any details of life outside our camp. But no one had ever spotted the tiny human figures moving across a gap formed by the trees which grew closer to the walls and the buildings a bit farther away. And yet those figures could be seen by the naked eye — I had watched them on many occasions. Using the Morse Code those of us with more guts tried to establish contact by waving handkerchiefs, but this met with no response from the other side.

At a later date, owing to a coincidence which set the final seal on the veracity of the information obtained by Walek, the existence of those two isolated houses became common knowledge throughout the camp. This happened when for the first time we were allowed to receive letters from our families in Poland. In the first batch of incoming mail, which we distributed ourselves among the prisoners, we found letters addressed to well-known officers whom, to our great astonishment, we could not trace in our camp. It became clear that apart from our Monastery Camp other prisoners of war were held at Starobyelsk. Our addresses, which the NKVD authorities had dictated to us when correspondence with our families was first allowed and which we in our first letters to our relatives had to give them, were written faultlessly, although our relatives had to write them in Russian characters. The address ran as follows: Name and surname without the indication of the military rank (this was forbidden), Starobyelsk, "potchtovyj yashchik" (Post Office Box) No. 15, USSR. And this is where the NKVD authorities had made a grave error. They simply forgot to fix special PO Boxes for the "Colonels'" and the "Generals' Houses" and thus all the mail arrived at the main Monastery Camp. Oil tends always to come to the surface. In spite of all their foxy watchfulness the NKVD do, after all, make blunders, although not very often.

On the 25th December, 1939, that is on Christmas Day, at 6 a.m. Kopyekin appeared in our room and crept stealthily towards the bunk occupied by Walek Miller. All of us were still asleep but I being as light a sleeper as a hare, on hearing the squeaking of some stranger's boots, woke up immediately. Drawn out of his sleep Miller sat up on his bunk.

"Good morning tovarishch Kopyekin," he said. "Why the devil have you woken me so early. It's still night and besides it's Christmas Day. . . . "

Exactly like on the morning when he came to fetch Major Zaleski Kopyekin kept silent for a long while until in a low and confused voice he finally brought himself to utter the following words: "Nu, davay Miller, feast day or no feast day, davay sobyeraysya poskoryey. . . . "

Assuming a flippant tone Walek interrupted him and asked nervously: "And so what, Kopyekin, with or without the *vyeshchi*?"

"Nu, da, pozhaluy s vyeshchami . . . Toropis. . . ." (Yes, maybe with your things . . . hurry up), he answered hardly audibly.

And again – I do not know how many times we had had this before – we had to witness an unbearably nerve-racking scene. A farewell scene to a friend leaving for the great unknown. And like many others before him, Walek with his suitcase and a knapsack went outside the camp walls through the narrow passage of the "prokhodnaya budka."

The ceiling of the room, blackened by soot and smoke, hung right over my head like some heavy lid. It seemed to me that my wide-open eyes would become covered by all its dirt and dust.

I could visualise Walek marching along Kirov Street, a street well known to me. At one end it gets lost somewhere in an open field, at the other end it finishes abruptly at the dismal building of the Public Baths, stuck to the steep bank of the Aydar river. But under Walek's footsteps it went on further until suddenly it began to give way and recede. I could still for a short moment see him stepping into some *other* road which instead of getting narrower and narrower as it faded away, started, on moving towards the horizon, to widen strangely until finally it became so wide that it transcended all earthly dimensions.

And so I began asking myself – when will my turn come?

Naturally, one asks why the Soviet authorities wanted to liquidate the two Polish Majors. After all, they had scored important achievements, the most important one being the transformation of the camp's buildings from a state of complete disintegration into conditions far more acceptable. To explain their liquidation we could only, as usual, work on assumptions. But the assumptions in this case were based not on empty premises but on experience and meticulous observation.

Both Majors had the opportunity – of which they made ample use

– of gaining a deep understanding and knowledge of what the Soviet authorities were up to. Through frequent contact and hours of discussion with the senior Soviet officers in command of the camp they got to know quite a lot about the personalities of these men. And Zaleski and Walek were brave men, even excessively brave in view of the conditions in which they found themselves. They were, after all, in the unenviable positions of prisoners of war with their backs to the wall, constantly having to fight to achieve improvements in camp conditions and to secure our rights as prisoners of war. In brief, they were too close to the centre of power and this was a dangerous thing. The bosses of the NKVD do not like and mistrust such close and intimate contacts. The two Majors were tolerated as long as they proved to be useful but once the wheels of the camp machine started rolling by themselves along well beaten ruts, they became expendable. More than that, since they knew too much they became dangerous. And so, was there any better solution then to liquidate them? The Moor had done his duty, the Moor can go.

But there were others too who had to pay their price. Some of those living over there, on the other side of the wires, on the side of "Soviet freedom."

Since the memorable morning of Christmas Day when the errand-boy Kopyekin called on hut number 6 for the soul of Miller he had vanished into thin air. We would look and watch out for him in vain. We did so out of ordinary curiosity but also because we had got quite used to him. In a way he had become a part of our life, a kind of necessary evil. Whether because of his friendly relationship with Major Zaleski, his mysterious conversation with Major Miller or some other thing, the reason for removing him from the camp was unknown to us. What we did know, however, was that it had happened at a time when he was undergoing a process of moral transformation, and, simultaneously, some sort of psychological breakdown. He had been performing most conscientiously all the dirty work imposed on him by the authorities. That is true. Gradually, however, and probably subconsciously, this uncouth man had succumbed to the influence of the enormous mass of prisoners by whom he was surrounded and with whom for three months, day and night, he had to remain in contact. Somewhere in his hard exterior a spark of compassion must have penetrated which ignited subconsciously an instinctive comprehension of the great wrong done to the vast number of strangers from the West – men who were neither monsters nor wicked. Men who knew how to laugh when in view of all the sorrow it would have been more understandable to cry. Men who once they became used to his wrinkled face and squeaking voice and were convinced that he himself did not bear any malice would address him in simple, human words.

So this is how the story of Kopyekin came to an end, the story of an NKVD messenger-boy, whom none of us would see again. I could quote many more similar instances. A night *vakhtyor*, an officer of the *lavotchka*, a chimney sweep, a carpenter had only to have one or two conversations with a prisoner, just as one human being to another, on a simple, down to earth subject, such as, for instance, what life is like in the Soviet Union or what it is like in the Western countries. Some snooper would overhear it and report this scandalous act of fraternization to the NKVD authorities. The outcome would invariably be the same. The culprit would never again report for work within the walls of the camp.

I remember one case particularly clearly.

After the construction work on the new barracks had begun a middle-aged man, about fifty-five years old, would appear regularly in the camp. His name was Pavel Syemyonovitch Plotnikov and his profession was senior master builder. He would check and correct our construction plans to the best of his ability, accept our requirements for building materials, check them once more most meticulously and submit then finally to his superiors for approval and execution.

As I have mentioned before, I used to work until midday in hut number 1. After . . . well let's call it a bit pompously, lunch until late in the evening I would be with Laud and a few other companions, architects by profession, in a tiny closet which seemed to have grown like a fungus on one of the huge walls of the building called the Circus. This is where Pavel Syemyonovitch had established his "building office" and where a few of us helped him. The structure, knocked together half and half with boards and clay, must have once served either as a lavatory or a larder – which of these it was hard to tell. After the room had been promoted to the status of an office it would contain inside – with the greatest difficulty – five men in a seated position at a table made with the help of a few planks and stacked with papers. Over our busy heads hung an electric bulb spurred to life by an alternating current from the local power station asthmatically shedding vaccillating light.

Regardless of a tiny window, half of which was protected by a shield of cardboard, and a small, warped door, a frosty wind was blowing inside the "office." It made mockery of the little iron stove. Although stoked incessantly with crumbs of wet coal its fire would keep on dying out. Pencils would drop from our frozen fingers and the watery ink in the inkstand would turn overnight into a chunk of ice.

Unless on matters of boards, nails or bricks, Pavel Syemyonovitch hardly ever opened his mouth for the first few weeks. Those blue-grey, deeply-set eyes, however, would watch us with an expression of benevolence. When listening to our conversation held in Polish they sometimes even came to life! Since he came from the western part of the Kiev region where for a number of centuries our language had been holding its own, Polish could not have been totally alien to him.

The mere fact that Pavel Syemyonovitch did not show towards us any offensiveness provoked on our part manifestations of politeness as well as of good manners. We would greet him nicely every day and ask him how he was feeling and how things were beyond the walls of the camp. We would also offer him tobacco and some bread of which he by no means disapproved. At the very beginning of our acquaintanceship he would acknowledge our advances by somewhat brusque monosyllables, but as time went by his tongue, at first paralysed with fear, eased up slowly and then he would bestow on us a more liberal measure of words.

So Pavel Syemyonovitch underwent a gradual change. He became more relaxed and cast off the bonds of fear and suspicion – partly, perhaps, because of our common misery and poverty. I sensed that he had taken a liking to Laud, myself and some other companions. Plucking up my courage I once asked him about his family, his home and the conditions in which he had to live.

He related his life story in brief but telling words.

Before the Revolution of 1917 he had been an independent building contractor. After completing his education in Kiev he settled later in Kharkov. He was doing quite well and could even afford to build himself a *datcha* (summer house) not far from the city. After the Revolution everything he possessed was taken away from him: the *datcha*, his savings, his business in Kharkov, even his apartment. From an independent position in the building trade he was downgraded to that of a mere cog in the new regime.

From then on he would drift from one place to another like a boat deprived of its rudder. He would be sent from commune to commune, wandering about over the whole of Russia and Siberia. His dream of owning a stable place of his own, of securing for his family and for himself in old age a safe existence, vanished for ever. He had been shifted a year ago from the Ural region to Starobyelsk. He was pleased at least to come back to his Ukrainian homeland. " . . . I have two rooms not far from here. There's a lack of fuel and I suffer greatly from the cold. Although I'm entitled to the full food rations and coupons for clothes – I'm always short of them. I have to dip into my meagre savings to buy at colossal prices this and that on the black market. My monthly salary amounts to 550 roubles [this sum appeared to me as astronomic] but as I have a wife and three children I can't make ends meet .... But others have even less than I, so really I have no right to complain."

I asked him about his children, their age, whether they went to school and whether they liked music. Pavel Syemyonovitch responded eagerly: "My eldest daughter, Nadya, is already twenty. Oh yes, she's very musical and plays the piano beautifully. Unfortunately she has to work to help her family. She's employed the whole day long in a clothing cooperative and rushes every second evening to her music school. It's not a very good one and lacks funds but at least it possesses a few instruments on which Nadya will practice. As she keeps saying to me, she loves music so much that she simply cannot live without it. . . . "

As he went on talking about his children he showed emotions when he mentioned his elder boy Vanya, who was sixteen and studied at the city school. He also told us with great sorrow about his younger son, the nine year old Syerozha who was weak and frail and had to be looked after the whole time by his mother, a woman worn out by a hard life.

"But do please explain to me," I said to him, "what prevents Nadya from attending a proper school where she could devote all her time to her musical studies. It is after all generally known that the Soviet authorities make a point of promoting all branches of art of which music is probably the most favoured one?"

"Well, all this is absolute rubbish. It might apply to the bigger cities, such as Moscow, Leningrad, Kiev and a few others where the authorities are in fact trying to develop talents. In thousands of the smaller towns as far as their love for art is concerned no one takes any interest in young people. It does, of course, happen sometimes that a young boy or girl is allowed to go to a bigger city for further studies. . . . " He added in a frightened whisper: "This is usually the case of a son or daughter of a powerful party official or a higher official of the NKVD. . . ."

He grabbed a pencil, his fingers blue with cold, and became engrossed in doing mathematical calculations. He did this deftly with the help of an abacus. Tossing from side to side with a short, loud bang the wooden rings threaded on thin steel rods he would thus be able to perform in what seemed some magical way all four arithmetic operations.

On another occasion it happened that the conversation which Laud and I had cautiously started switched to the subject of the forced labour camps. Of all the subjects in the Soviet Union, this is the most strongly prohibited one: that is, excluded from discussion. The reason perhaps is that it is the blackest cloud hanging over the everyday life of the Soviet people. Pavel Syemyonovitch took a watchful look outside the door and asked us to look out through the little window. He was really scared, but, on the other hand, devoured by an urge to open his heart and confide in new friends to whom, he was sure, he could entrust his greatest secrets and worries.

In the vocabulary of Tsarist Russia the word "katorga" (forced labour in Siberia) had for many centuries a sinister ring of terror. In today's Soviet Russia a new word has been substituted — a far gentler-sounding word — namely the word "lagier" which literally means a camp and in most cases a military one. This "subtle" term has nevertheless acquired a universal meaning. It has thus become a symbol of all the modern ways of torturing millions of people, no matter whether in forced labour camps, penal camps, reformatory camps or life deportation camps. . . . The word *lagier* is a curse, a term for the greatest possible terror-inspiring fear.

Pavel Syemyonovitch started his grisly tale with the above etymological preamble. His hand resting inert on the abacus he fixed his glassy eyes on the frame of the ice-covered window. " . . . It is now some two years ago when during the night men of the NKVD suddenly took away my brother from his place in Rostov on the Don. He was a quiet and a good man, a bit of a dreamer though. Literature was his main interest. He used to write short stories and poetry for the local papers — just rather nice pieces of writing. Until one day the censor took exception to one of them — there must have been something which they didn't like — whether it had to do with the style or the text, I don't know. Probably not sufficiently in accordance with the spirit of the regime . . . . Anyway, they took him away, the poor devil. Where he is now and for how many years he has been sentenced we don't know . . . he wasn't particularly strong so perhaps he's no longer alive. . . ." A short silence followed. "What worries me now is my son Vanya. He has just had his sixteenth birthday but his head is as full of ideas as that of a grown-up man. He learns at school well, but is undisciplined. I have been summoned by the headmaster several times to discuss his case. But yesterday for the first time Vanya and I had to go to the NKVD for interrogation. They assailed Vanya and me with all kinds of questions. Despite my constant admonitory remarks Vanya was cheeky and answered the questions, most of which concerned some youth organization, apparently anti-revolutionary and totally unknown to me, in an impolite manner. To me everything he said seems to be a complete yarn, for where and how could such an organization be formed among children? Children will grumble like grown-ups – that's true – about either the cold at school or hunger at home. But the NKVD will jump to conclusions and immediately read a rebellion into manifestations of displeasure, treating those simple boys' reactions as real anti-Soviet activities. Oh God, oh my God, this is simply terrible! I feel so worried about Vanya!" In a state of visible dejection he went on: "Every family in Soviet Russia knows well that sooner or later its every fifth member will be deported to a *lagier* – you can therefore work out for yourself the number of their inmates either still alive or on the point of dying. I heard not long ago the following joke: in a crowded electric tramway in Moscow a young man tried to offer his seat to a standing elderly man. Whereupon the latter said: 'Thank you, my son. Since sooner or later I shall have to sit and possible for a long time too, I prefer to stand as long as I am allowed to.'"* The expression on his face underwent a change. It was meant to be something similar to a smile, but the effect was just a jagged set of teeth.

Pavel Syemyonovitch arrived the next day completely shaken, his eyes red. He would now and then wipe his nose noisily with a dirty piece of rag. When moving the rings of the abacus his hands were trembling. At last, when I found myself in his presence without other witnesses I asked him why he looked so off colour and whether something undesirable had happened.

"My dear little Vanya . . . they came to fetch him last night." He lowered his grey head, rested it on the table and started sobbing like a child. At that moment the door opened with a squeak and an NKVD messenger appeared.

"Tovarishch Plotnikov, k komendantu" (the Commander wants you), he called.

They left. Pavel Syemyonovitch did not report for work the next day. All the papers of such great importance to us – estimates, requests for materials, etc, – remained strewn inertly on the table. Another two days passed. Building work became paralysed. Major Zaleski appealed to the Soviet Command and asked for the replacement of the "obviously sick" Pavel Syemyonovitch by another man. His substitute appeared at last, a young man, boorish and incapable of doing his job properly. He did not, however, hold his office for long, as by that time the barracks were almost completed.

I wonder what fate befell you, Pavel Syemyonovitch, you good, decent old fellow.

---

* The joke is based on a pun. To "sit" means in Russian also to be imprisoned.

18. DOGS

Human beings in their present form are – as far as we know – the most recent living creatures on our planet. In a contest, however, it would be the dogs, with their greater experience and cleverness and what is generally known as a dog's instinct, who would undoubtedly win over men! Why it is called instinct instead of wisdom I shall never understand. Perhaps it is because men wish to reserve the notion of wisdom for themselves only. On the other hand – let us all agree – as far as the good qualities of a dog's character are concerned, such as his good nature, resilience, sense of friendship and faithfulness, a dog towers above us, the "perfect" human beings.

The only way any living creature could penetrate inside the walls of the camp was through the gate. And this applied to dogs too, of which there were at least three dozen always in the camp. A cat or a mouse would perhaps get round the obstacle in some other way but a dog was unable to force a barbed wire fence nor jump a two and a half metre high wall. Dogs were perfectly aware of the fact that they were not allowed to enter the camp. They had stones thrown at them and even shots fired by the guards. But even risking their life would not daunt their spirit of enterprise and sportsmanship. I would often see a dog sneaking into the camp in broad daylight under the wheels of a horse-drawn cart, between a horse's legs or moving stealthily right between the wheels of a truck.

What really attracted them to our camp, to that huge mass of men deprived of a sufficient amount of food even for themselves? Isn't the pursuit of food the only motive animals have for staying with human beings? The answer is No when applied to a dog. Food isn't everything to him. Deprived of friendship a dog will look for it as any of us would do. And more than that. His unsurpassed instinct has taught him the notion of divine justice: he senses misery, sorrow and also disaster. Even in the throes of hunger he will himself, like a good Samaritan, flock to men, his two-footed friends, to comfort and to distract them and to warm them up by constantly rubbing against them with his coat. This is how it was at Starobyelsk too. Packs of homeless dogs made their appearance on the scene as the true friends of the Polish prisoners of war.

Right from the beginning a peculiar relationship developed between the two sides. They clung towards us and tried to endear themselves but at the sight of a Soviet uniform they snarled and the fur on their necks would bristle up. We never set them on our "protectors" — that would have been too risky a thing to do. The dogs divided their feelings into sympathy for us and hatred for the Soviet uniforms. How they could tell a Soviet uniform from a Polish one, whether this was through their visual perception or through their sense of smell, we never understood. They treated Soviet workers clad in civilian clothes with the same friendly attitude that they showed towards us.

We would give them all kinds of names. France was represented by "Foch," a big shaggy sheepdog. He used to spend most of the time in my hut and unless the night *vakhtyor* found him and chased him outdoors he would sleep gently under Zygmunt's bunk. "Sikorka," thus named in honour of General Sikorski was a distant cousin of an English Setter. "Winston" was a lean dog and apart from his two semi-protruding fangs reminded one in no way of a bulldog. "Linek" was a favourite of us all. A small, black-and-white mongrel, always in excellent spirits, he would romp about the camp. His peculiar name was a derivation of the diminutive of Stalin – "Sta-linek." This used to cause us a lot of fun.

"Linek" was the pet of Dr. Maks Labedz, the vet who, after many unpleasant experiences during the march (which, I have already related), had reached the Starobyelsk camp in one of the last batches of men to arrive. The old vet used to spend by turns a great deal of time with every dog. He not only took care of their physical well-being but also of their appearance. Using bits of tin he manufactured combs and used them for combing out masses of dirt and fleas from the dogs. We also carried out surgery when necessary. Frequently our faithful friends would come along with their heads or bellies bandaged or with a broken paw immobilized by a cleverly-made splint.

The old, shaggy "Foch" would spend five days a week in the camp and for the remaining two days disappear outside the walls to play truant. We, of course, envied him. After a few weeks the timing of his routine wanderings became almost infallible and the funny thing was that his two days of absence would fall exactly on Saturdays and Sundays. In other words, he had become a believer in that institution known as the "weekend." It soon became obvious to us that he had a master in town who appeared at home for two days in the week. This prompted us to conceal in the long hair of his neck a tiny paper roll in a little tin box fixed to a string. We repeated this attempt at using "Foch" as our messenger on more than one occasion. We put various questions on the piece of paper: "What do people think of us? How much truth is there in the stories of your colossal losses in the war with Finland? Do you really love the Germans? Do you also have to suffer from cold and hunger as we do?" We would finish our note with greetings and an imploration for an answer. But we would look for it on Foch's neck in vain! He always came back without the string and the scrap of paper. Would his master be an enemy of ours or was Foch's hair being searched by the NKVD?

It happened at the turn of winter in the second half of March 1940. "Foch" appeared in the camp after an absence of ten days looking filthy and hungry. He also bore marks of injuries. Now tell me my friend where have you been? Where have you loitered? Did you think of us as we have thought of you? I thrust my fingers into the hair around his neck. And there it was! There was the string, not ours however! Look at that boys, here is the scrap of paper and with an answer this time! How excited we were!

Sewn in a minisule bag made of cloth was a piece of cigarette paper with an inscription in small, distinct Russian characters: "Dear Friends. According to rumours you will be soon leaving Starobyelsk. People are also saying that you might go home. Whether this is true we don't know. We hate the Germans as much as you do. May God protect you." No signature. That was all.

Have you been a harbinger of good or of bad news "Foch," our dear old dog? It looked as if he was trying to say something to us by way of either his intelligent eyes or his long pink tongue. He was writhing and whining. In a manifestation of silent thankfulness we pressed our lips to his big, shaggy head.

Between the two rows of barbed wire which followed the perimeter of the camp walls there also ran a strongly-flexed steel wire. Special chains were fixed to it and then fastened to the collars of big grey Alsatians. There were some ten of them and each of the dogs guarded a sector 100 metres long. Their function and that of the barbed wire, the machine guns and the arc lights was to make sure that the camp was securely isolated from the outside world.

These dogs, being well trained, would almost never betray their presence by barking. It was only in the calmness of the night that their existence became manifest: by the rhythmic clank of their chains and the vibrating whistling noises made by the upper rings of the chain being dragged swiftly by the dogs and shifting in both directions along the steel wire. It happened sometimes that I had to go and work outside the gate. On watching their bared white fangs glistening beneath their raised lips as they trembled with rage a shiver of terror would always go down my spine.

These were wicked dogs. Wicked for they were made so by men.

When speaking of dogs I must mention an incident which took place in the winter of 1940-41.

It happened in a different camp a long way up in the north where snow and frost lasted eight months of the year. A huge dog, as big as Foch but younger and therefore more lively, attached himself to us. We christened him by a royal name — "Rex". Resembling a big, strong Airedale, Rex had no reason to spend his weekends outside the wire. Like a lost island in the midst of an ocean our camp was situated in a sparsely-populated region, containing meagre forests, stretches of fallow land and here and there meadows which in summertime would turn vivid green in patches interspersed with flowers. A few wretched chimneyless cottages dotted the great expanse of snow. The interior of the camp was visible from all sides. But no walls surrounded it like the Starobyelsk camp — there were only high fences of barbed wire. There was no real need for these either. But for reasons of safety and secrecy the NKVD authorities kept away from those miserable little huts any curious human eyes likely to observe the lives of the prisoners.

If "Rex" had ever had a master he must have forsaken him for good and chosen us as his friends. He had been with us for six months and shared with us all the everyday preoccupations of our captivity. He used to sleep in a low loft as probably it would have been too warm for him in our room and also because burrowed in a corner amongst pieces of junk he felt safer from the rifle butt of the night *vakhtyor*, whose duty for some unknown reason was to see that the dog stayed outdoors.

Once one of the young vets had to perform a surgical operation on him. Because of some infection the upper part of Rex's right leg had started rotting, so that eventually a raw bone could be seen sticking out from beneath the skin. Although the vet lacked even the most primitive surgical instruments the operation was successful. The vet also fixed the stump of Rex's leg with a permanent artificial leg and thus restored his limb to the original length. Rex would sometimes forget about his crippled condition. While leaping about he would stumble and fall, after which he would look round as if to apologize for being so clumsy. When walking over a wooden floor or climbing up the stairs he would signal his arrival by hammering with his hard crutched right paw like a blind old man would do with his white walking stick!

Rex was very good natured and extremely affectionate. Of course, he loved us, his protectors, dearly and faithfully without any reservations, but in front of Soviet uniforms he behaved correctly. He was not particularly fond of them – that is true – but he would never bark or try to attack them. Rather, he tried to avoid them and on seeing a man in an unpopular uniform he would simply step aside.

One frosty morning Major Volkov of the NKVD, the tall, bloated Commander of the Camp, accompanied by *politruk* Nyegodyayev was doing his routine daily inspection of the camp. We were all used to his visits. Major Volkov would first scrutinize all of us attentively to make sure that we had all risen from our bunks to our feet and then he would gaze assiduously at the floor to see whether it was well scrubbed and washed. In fact, the floor – consisting of old decaying, hollow boards – was the only thing which really attracted his attention. That thousands of bugs swarmed all over the walls of our room and its bunks, that rats would frolic around like some tamed animals, that fuel was insufficient, that every second window was without window panes – and we lacked any means to remedy this matter – all left him completely unmoved. The floor, however, was a different proposition. It was the centre of his attention, the supreme test of cleanliness. A clean floor was the best proof of good, "cultured" manners. But this was not only our Major's "bee in the bonnet." In all the camps through which I happened to pass in those years the floor would always attract the most attention from the camp commanders. Perhaps somewhere at the top of the Soviet bureaucracy a new cultural concept had been worked out, expressed by the slogan: "Clean floors in the USSR are the happiness of humanity."

Both our visitors were well shaven and well perfumed, and clad in long, warm greatcoats, big fur hats and knee-high *valenki* made of fine, thick felt. Both men moved noiselessly like cats. In contrast to our leather boots which on the frozen snow would creak and chirp like swarms of crickets, their footwear, ideal for dry snow, did not produce the slightest squeaking noise. Unnoticed because of this, the two inspectors appeared on the first floor of our hut and unknown to us, were intending to enter the room occupied by myself and seven of my companions. All of a sudden, we inside the room heard the most extraordinary commotion going on outside. I pushed the door wide open and just imagine my astonishment at what I saw! Standing on his hind legs with his front paws resting on Commander Volkov's shoulders and with his muzzle close to his face, our big Rex was emitting noises which were by no means hostile or any cause for alarm. Rex would almost always greet us in such an exuberant way and a man taken unawares by this manifestation of friendliness would sometimes go down under the dog's weight. Did Rex on that day mistake the Soviet uniform and take it for ours? Who knows — maybe he did.

Major Volkov, scared out of his wits, yelled something in an inhuman voice, and swearing like a trooper the *politruk* Nyegodyayev kicked the dog hard and pushed him down the steep staircase. A big turmoil followed. Accusations were levelled against us of an assault on the Commander of the Camp, and of the dog being specially trained to attack the representatives of Soviet authority. Serious consequences would follow as a result of this act of provocation but for the time being the order was given to remove the dog to the gate forthwith.

We could not help laughing secretly at this outrageously comical scene, but on the other hand we trembled about the fate of "Rex". We all said affectionate goodbyes to him and for a long while followed him with our eyes as he hobbled along gaily, as if nothing had happened, at the feet of one of our colleagues who undertook the sad mission of taking Rex to the gate.

The next morning I found myself in a team entrusted with the task of clearing the snow-drifts which had formed on one side of the road outside the wires. With spades and shovels on our shoulders, escorted by some *boytzy*, we set out behind the gate. Our visits to the world outside the wires would always leave us greatly impressed. The frosty air, shrubs and trees covered up by snow, the snowy grooves well planed by sledge winners and tinged yellow by horse droppings, paths trod by human footsteps, the footprints of foxes and hares — all this seemed so different from everything in the camp's interior. It seemed to us that all these simple things surrounding us were breathing with the freshness of freedom, with an implacable zest for life. Such a contrast to the all-pervading mustiness crawling out of every nook and cranny of the camp.

We had hardly covered three hundred metres when our blood curdled from shock and fury at seeing a few steps from the road the blood-stained corpse of Rex lying there in the snow. He seemed to be even bigger in death than in life. With his wide eyes open as if begging for mercy, it seemed from the way it stuck out that he had raised his stiff crippled paw to defend himself. They had tied Rex to a white birch tree and clubbed him to death with sticks. In an attempt to escape the deadly strokes the poor animal had visibly struggled for he had traced on the snow a huge bloody circle as he ran desperately round the tree, splashing red stains of blood against the silver bark.

They murdered Rex with sticks. They even begrudged him a bullet. No, they did not. It was meant to be like this. As a punishment for having dared to rise up and rest his paws benevolently on the shoulders of a Soviet Commander, and for the fact that he was our dog, our obedient and faithful friend . . . for these reasons he had to go first through an agony of suffering. They did not remove their victim, they did not cover the bloody traces with fresh snow — they knew we would be passing along the scene of their crime. So let the prisoners see for themselves and become aware of how severe a punishment can be when dealt by their superiors, who hold in their hands the power of life and death.

Oh Heavens. To what lengths of abasement and vileness people sink when deprived of everything human in their nature.

EPILOGUE
by Witold Kaczkowski

I ON OUR WAY TO THE NEW CAMPS

Our turn came at last. At 5 a.m. on the 10th May, 1940 the whole of our group, numbering some thirty men, billeted in a few rooms of hut number 13, were woken up by a *politruk* holding a list, known for some obscure reason as a "papuga" (parrot). It contained the names of those who were to leave the camp. There were eighteen lucky ones, of whom I was one. I heaved a sigh of relief.

Within one hour, carrying our belongings, we assembled inside the building of the former church. First we had to undergo the usual thorough personal search during which we had removed from us all instruments such as knives, razor blades, etc. After another check of our identity photographs we were taken in pairs outside the gate, loaded on a truck and driven to the railway station where a special van used for the transportation of prisoners was waiting for us on a loading platform. Ever since the series of departures from Camp Starobyelsk had started rumours had gone round that travelling on a "passenger coach" was tantamount to going to freedom. The authors of the rumours were probably the Soviets themselves.

We were crammed eight to a compartment. Grated doors leading to the corridor were shut and bolted. We felt like wild beasts in a cage. Special guards belonging to a convoy of NKVD soldiers, whose task was to see us to our destination, were posted in the corridor. But where were we going? This was anybody's guess. Travelling to the unknown in conditions like ours – in bolted compartments, when neither the destination nor the duration of the journey is known – was a most depressing and unnerving experience. Despite this our general mood was remarkably good. We all trusted that our route would take us in a westerly direction.

After a whole day's stay at the station we eventually set off on our journey. Basing our observations according to the movements of the sun we were able to figure out that our train was heading towards the west. And so despite the poor conditions in which our journey was taking place, despite our deplorable food consisting only of bread, herring and cold water, we were all in high spirits. Owing to our merriment the compartment at times got so noisy that our guards in the corridor would often command us to keep quiet. We reached Kharkov in the evening of the same day.

We had to spend the whole night at the station. Next morning, however, we started travelling towards the city of Kursk. But this was up north and not westwards. Our spirits sank. We thought nevertheless that they were directing us if not to Kiev then perhaps to Oryol-Bryansk. But nothing came of our hopes. From Oryol we were heading in a northern direction eventually reaching Tula. We now felt sure that we would be going to Moscow or possibly farther to the north or east. But after a whole day's stop in Tula our train set off up north-west. And so our hopes rose once again. Especially when after having passed Kaluga the train was definitely moving to the west.

The day was 15th May – the nameday of Sophie, my beloved little sister. Anticipating a possible prompt reunion with her I therefore spent it in a cheerful and lively mood. The next day, however, all my expectations were to be badly thwarted.

After having passed the important railway junction of Tikhoretzkoye our train halted around midnight at a small station called Babini on the Kaluga-Bryansk line where we were kept until 3 p.m. We did not know the reason for such a long stay at such an unassuming station. However, we soon learned why. A few trucks with a detachment of NKVD soldiers made their appearance. We were were ordered to get off the train, to board one of the trucks and sit down on its platform. The new guards proved to be not exactly Polite to us and made it clear that if there was any attempt to escape they would not hesitate to have us shot dead. This made us think we were being taken to some forced labour camp.

We drove for about one hour across wretched countryside dotted with miserable hamlets, sad as the whole of the land. Greek Orthodox churches, which could be seen standing in ruins, with all their crosses removed, made one think back to the excesses of the Russian Revolution. Threats and foul language used by our guards induced me almost to regret the Starobyelsk Camp and on the whole the more "decent" treatment towards us by our "protectors." The difference in the attitude towards us was so marked, the conditions in which we had been travelling on the train and now in the truck so appalling that it was only understandable that we should be expecting the worst. The Soviet Union is after all a country wrapped in riddles.

Our truck halted in front of a gate opening on to a compound of large buildings surrounded by a wall and barbed wire. Once inside we saw a rather big, one-storey house, a cowshed and other outbuildings, such as stables, warehouses, etc. All these had once formed part of a landowner's farm, and were later converted into living quarters. The place was now used as a prisoner of war camp, but a year ago, we were told, it had been a children's sanatorium. Surrounding it was a beautiful forest of old fir trees.

The place was a real surprise to us. We had, after all, expected something much worse. As it happened we had landed, we were soon to learn, in the Pavlishtchev Bor, or Prisoner of War Transit Camp. We found there nearly 300 fellow Poles including about 200 inmates of the Kozyelsk Camp as well as the whole of the so-called "special group" which had arrived from Starobyelsk some two weeks ago. A few days after our arrival we were joined by another batch of inmates from the Ostashkov Camp, numbering about 100 men.

Living conditions at the Pavlishtchev Camp proved to be much better than those at Starobyelsk. We were given rooms with a capacity of no more than 8 to 10 men and provided with beds. There was also a special dining room into which we would march three times a day in pairs. Further, there was a lending library and not a bad one too. But what mattered most perhaps was the fact that there was more space and air.

I felt very tired and exhausted by the journey. On the last day I had had nothing to eat because provisions of bread and herrings had run out.

After our arrival at the new camp and after the unavoidable search we were immediately taken to the camp's baths. This was a real treat. The bath installations were excellent, the water was piping hot and there were showers. However, due probably to my extremely weak condition and the high temperature inside the bath-room I suffered for the first time in my life a heart seizure and lost consciousness. With another similar victim, Lieutenant Otto Bisanz, I was carried in a wheelchair to the sick-bay, where we spent three days in the good hands of our doctors, Colonel Szarecki and the brave Doctor Mucho of Warsaw.

During our stay at Pavlishtchev we learned from the radio and from the press about the German invasion of Belgium and France. We could hardly believe it was true. All those daily war bulletins made a most depressing impression on all of us. Poland had fallen under the German onslaught, followed by Norway, Holland and Belgium. It was now the turn of France, generally considered to be a great military power and the only one likely to stand up to the German might. Should France succumb to Germany, this could probably mean but one thing, the end of the war. For it was obvious to us that Great Britain lacked the necessary land forces to fight Germany on her own.

As usual we had endless discussions concerning the latest developments of the war and as usual we were divided between optimists and pessimists. Captain Ginsbert, known as "Jim Poker," the author of popular short stories published before the outbreak of the war by the Warsaw daily *Kurier Warszawski*, kept us informed about the progress of the war as reported in the official war bulletins. Soon we were to learn of France's capitulation and of Great Britain's resolution to carry on to the bitter end. So it seemed to us that our cause was after all not yet totally lost.

After a month's stay at the Pavlishtchev Camp we were suddenly ordered to leave the place forthwith. We had to undergo once more the same procedure of being loaded on trucks and driven to the railway station where the well-known "prisoners' van" was waiting for us. All they would tell us was that we were being transferred to a different camp, but they didn't name it.

And so began a new "journey into the unknown" — travelling in cages like wild beasts. It is only fair to say, though, that this time we were being treated by our guards in a somewhat more civilized manner. The food proved to be better too. The train pulled out in an eastward direction, presumably towards Moscow, which was about 200 kilometres away. It was to take forty-eight hours to get there, but at last we glimpsed the outline of the capital of the Soviet Union and Mecca for all communists in the world. However, we could not see much as there was only a small window and we were unable to leave our "cage". But the train didn't go into the centre of the city anyway. Starting from the goods station on the western side of the city the train went round Moscow to her northern side and after a whole day's halt there proceeded up north. Once more a most unpleasant experience. We kept asking ourselves: "Where are we being taken? Not to the White Sea by any chance?"

Fortunately, however, we were not to go that far. At 6 a.m., after a journey lasting two days and two nights, our train halted at a small station, Gryazovyetz, our ultimate destination. After being detrained we were made to march to a camp about 7 or 8 kilometres away.

The day was the 18th June, 1940. A beautiful warm day too and the first day of Summer in this region where Winter lasts for eight months — from mid-September until mid-May. Spring and Autumn are shortlived and Summer is over in two months.

The one-time *gubernya* (province) of Wologodzk called now the Wologodzk *oblast* (region), bordering on the Archangel "oblast", was known in Tsarist Russia as an area to which people were deported and there were a number of forced labour camps there now. Moscow is about 500 kilometres away.

After a few days spent in the cages, deprived of any light, our march to the new camp seemed like a rather pleasant walk to us. But we had to pass through hamlets on our way which had the appearance of utter misery. Hardly any people could be seen, nor, for that matter, any domestic animals and there was an air of emptiness and great desolation about the places.

On nearing the camp we were able to spot from a distance sentry boxes similar to those we had said goodbye to a few days before, the same barbed wire and inside a large building, once the site of a monastery with a crumbling church close to it. Also, among a cluster of birch and fir trees, there were a few smaller wooden buildings. After we had entered the compound we all lay down on the grass to wait for the promised meal.

The time was 3 p.m. and as we had eaten nothing since morning we were famished. At last, however, the long awaited meal arrived. It was served in the refectory of the ancient cloister, which could seat a hundred men at one time. We therefore needed four sittings for our dinner. The menu consisted of soup and a helping of *kasha* with some bread. To us it seemed very tasty. Next we were taken to other rooms in the same building which contained three-tier bunks with straw mattresses as well as straw pillows and blankets. All this struck us as real luxury. About sixty men were assigned to a room which meant an unavoidable lack of air and foul odour. But we were already well used to this and so we all slept soundly.

At 6 a.m. the next morning we were woken up by reveille. This was followed by ablutions in the river which flowed through the camp. After breakfast we marched four abreast to the camp's square where the Camp Commander's Assistant, an old Lieutenant, addressed us in a few words, reminding us to observe discipline and order, etc. In the course of his speech he used a rather significant and puzzling phrase. He said: "Take care of your uniforms, as they might still come in useful to you." This prophetic sentence, as it proved to be later, appeared rather enigmatic to us then and was widely commented upon in the entire camp. It came after the capitulation of France and at the time when the German offensive against Great Britain was expected. Some "politicians" among us were eagerly prophesying that the Soviet Union would now turn against Germany and would want to form a Polish Red Army. The idea seemed to appeal to some of our men — there were among us a handful of communists and left-wing sympathisers. The great majority,

228

however, was clearly opposed to that kind of contingency. Besides, as further events showed, the Soviet Union not only had no such military inclinations but, on the contrary, was doing everything to avoid a clash with the Germans, hoping that the time would come when the whole of Europe would become worn out by mutual fighting. Only then would the Soviets march against the Western countries in order to impose their rule. Meanwhile they contented themselves with the annexation of Lithuania, Latvia, Estonia and Bessarabia. All this took plce in June and July of 1940. The Soviet press was singing the praises of Stalin the "leader of all peoples," as well the virtues of his uncannily clever and "peace loving" policy which allowed the occupation and incorporation into the Soviets of whole countries without having to resort to any war-like actions. The events of 1941 proved that this "clever policy" was nothing else but very naïve.

We had got off to a good start at Gryazovyetz in settling down to the daily routine of a prisoner of war camp. The time dragged eternally slowly with nothing happening. Events which we were expecting would not materialize. The weather happened to be warm and lovely and we all sunbathed on the meadow by the river.

After two weeks of such an idyllic existence, the Commander of the camp, Major Volkov of the NKVD, unexpectedly descended on us. Putting an end to our easy going ways he started an "iron rod" rule. Regulations were tightened, morning and evening roll calls introduced as well as obligatory work for all the inmates of the camp. The sick were exempted, providing they had a proper doctor's certificate, and so were all officers with the ranks of Major upwards.

Work consisted of demolishing the rest of the church and using the rubble for building a section of a road as well as a dam on the river. We were supposed to work eight hours a day, although it is only fair to say that we didn't put the maximum effort into carrying out our tasks. The "bolshies" just wanted to see something being done. After a while I managed to get a doctor's certificate exempting me from the so-called "hard work" and I was assigned instead to a team of what were called "potato-scrubbers". We peeled potatoes for a few hours every second day in the good company of fellow prisoners, acquiring in this new job a high measure of skill. We felt quite happy. Scrubbing potatoes is undoubtedly a more pleasant occupation than breaking bricks for building a road, or digging clay for a dam.

At the beginning of August ten fellow officers whose families happened to be of German extraction were suddenly summoned and ordered to pack up and get ready to leave. They were outside the gate within an hour. We saw their departure as a sign that we would all be sent home soon.

As it happened, a rather unpleasant incident occurred that day connected with the departure of these men. I was sunbathing in the meadow not far from the path leading to the camp's gate and next to me was a companion of mine, Joseph Czapski. We suddenly saw two of the officers who were about to leave, Captain Kincel and Captain Zinn, carrying their belongings and heading towards the gate. Since we had shared the same room with them, had had our meals together, etc. we thought it natural to bid them goodbye, despite the fact that they were of German origin and might even have considered themselves German. Whatever the situation, they had always behaved loyally towards our country. We therefore went up to them, shook hands and wished them a safe journey. Also, as Captain Kincel came from the city of Lodz in Poland I asked him to pass on a message to my mother who happened to live not so far from the place. And that was all.

What happened next morning was like a bolt from the blue. After having summoned Czapski, myself, Cavalry Captain Slizien and Captain Moszynski, General Wolkowicki, the highest ranking Polish officer in the Camp, gave us a severe "dressing down" because of our "ceremonious farewell" to Germans about to leave the camp. We tried as best we could to explain the facts of the situation to the elderly gentleman but to no avail. He was relying on information obtained from his henchmen, consisting of young Second Lieutenants who were trying to ingratiate themselves with him and a certain Major, Mr. D. a twister and at one time an unsuccessful small time politican in the city of Lwow. His ambition was to become a kind of spiritual leader in the camp, but in fact he kept scheming against some of the officers and confusing things. This whole incident provides a picture of the prevailing conditions which, owing to the said Mr. D. and General Wolkowicki, led to an unfortunate rift among all of us.

There was also a third group of officers – the adherents to communism. They consisted of a dozen or so officers with Captain Rozen-Zawadzki and Flying Lieutenant Wicherkiewicz in Command, plus a few former Police Officers as well as common riff-raff – some fifty men in all. They formed the so-called "krasnyj ugolok" (red corner) and they met in a room especially allocated to them. They even had their own choir who sang Russian songs. We would, of course, have no truck with them and looked on them as traitors to our cause. There was also a Colonel Berling who professed not to belong to the communists but who seemed, however, to have

230

some secret links with them and was regarded as a kind of "guru."

Contrary to what we had hoped there were no more departures after the group of ten had left. The NKVD started a new series of interrogations however. One after another, we were all summoned to the *doprosy* during which they would question us on such personal matters as our military service, our political activities, etc. etc.

The interrogations would sometimes last for a few hours. What the NKVD were really after is hard to say. One had to be very careful not to contradict oneself and to stick always to one's previous statements. This was not always so easy as not everything one would disclose was in fact true. In my first statement whilst still at camp Starobyelsk I said that my profession was that of an employee at an agricultural bureau and that I also owned a few acres of land and a house with a garden. They asked me about everything to do with this, including my family, and I had to give them details regarding my earnings, my income, the exact amount of land in my possession, the number of livestock, etc. Apart from that they asked me many times at Starobyelsk, Pavlishtchev and now Gryazovyetz what my attitude was towards the Soviet Union. To this I always had the same answer: "If the question is: 'Am I provided with a sufficient portion of bread and *kasha*?' then I say Yes – my attitude is positive. The same with the question 'Is the hut where I am housed warm enough?' Briefly, my attitude towards the Soviets who keep me imprisoned can only be defined in these terms." Needless to say my answer did not satisfy the *politruks* who were interested in the political side of the question and not its more down to earth aspects. However, I pretended to be unable to understand what they were after and I also spoke deliberately in very bad Russian with an atrocious accent. This was the best way to prevent oneself being dragged into any political discussions.

One morning at 5 a.m. we were woken up and told to collect our belongings and get outdoors. We thought this meant another journey into the unknown. However it soon proved to be nothing more than an inspection, the first one carried out in the Gryazovyetz Camp. Similar inspections followed at monthly intervals, and always at unexpected times. At first, all the rummaging and poking into our bundles and through our uniform pockets was an unpleasant and unnerving experience. Later on, however, we got used to it and regarded these searches as just routine formalities.

Although we always tried to conceal them, during every check-up and search they would take away from us some document or personal papers as well as money and photographs. After a few days time they would return part of the loot and keep the rest giving us a receipt. In so doing, they at least kept up an appearance of integrity. It was all done, perhaps, to keep the NKVD people busy and to enable the younger soldiers to gain the necessary experience. I succeeded, however, in hiding my officer's identity card. I kept it in a box of toothpowder hidden between two doors and it was never discovered.

Decorations, holy medals and holy pictures were not confiscated but the NKVD soldiers were always intrigued by them and, with a condescending smile, would show surprise that men, apparently intelligent, should believe in such manifestations of superstition. Religious, or rather anti-religious, matters are on the whole a favourite subject for discussions with the "bolshies" and the general standard of these discussions can be summed up by the following "joke" which I have heard time and again. The outstanding Soviet pilot Tchvalov – after whom the city of Orenburg had been named – when asked whether God existed answered: "I have been flying at an altitude of 2, 3, 5, and 10 thousand metres but I have never seen God, so obviously he does not exist!"

Summer with its sweltering, torrid days and chilly nights did not last long. Autumn soon set in, cold and wet, and by the end of September the first snow fell. Real winter began about mid-October, although it was only around Christmas time that temperatures fell below 20 centigrade.

At the end of August some of the officers were transferred from the ancient monastery building to two detached houses situated by the river. House number 6 was assigned to senior officers: a General, some Colonels and Lieutenant-Colonels, thirty men in all. House number 7 was to accommodate junior officers. Our group formed the first company of prisoners of the Gryazovyetz Camp. Lieutenant-Colonel Morawski, an old acquaintance of mine from the time when he was deputy to the Commander of the 10th Infantry Regiment in the town of Lowicz, was made the Senior Elder of our company. He would settle all matters with the Soviet authorities, was responsible for preparing the time-table of work to be done by us, and so on. The Polish Commander of the Camp, Captain Tadeusz Czerny, took great pains to make our life in the camp as bearable as possible. Amongst other things he was responsible for the running of the kitchen, public baths, the barber's shop, laundry, and all workshops. No wonder he was an extremely busy man.

After a few months time, however, he had had enough of all this and, besides, he had incurred the displeasure of the Soviet authorities. This led to a new person being appointed in his place. The new man was Second Lieutenant Szczypiorski. He was one of the "red circle" and boasted of having once belonged to the

Communist Party when in Poland. But this was doubtful – he was probably a member of the Polish Socialist Party.* On his appointment as Polish Commander he filled all posts in the kitchen, in the workshops, as well as those of the elders of the companies of which there were four in the camp, with communists or communist-sympathisers.

The only exception was Cavalry Captain Olgierd Slizien. He became the leader of our company in October after Lieutenant-Colonel Morawski and seven other officers had been taken to some unknown destination. Much to our satisfaction Slizien remained in his post until the end of our captivity. An officer of the 1st Lancer Regiment and an ADC to General Anders during the German-Polish campaign in 1939, he was a big landowner in the Slonim Region. He was a brave and most likeable man, although a bit hot-tempered. We shared room number 3 with him on the first floor of our house – the best and warmest of all.

There were seven of us in that room during our stay in the camp and we all became very close friends. So let me describe them. Apart from Slizien and myself, there was Cavalry Captain, Count Joseph Hutten-Czapski, who, however, dropped the "Hutten" and never used it. A true aristocrat, not only by birth but also by nature, he was a most uncommon man. Highly intelligent, he had many interests, including painting and writing. Nevertheless he was a man of simplicity and warm-heartedness, and was respected and liked by everybody. Owing to his height (over six feet) he was also a conspicuous figure in the camp.

Captain Adam Moszynaski had been Assistant Director of one of the banks in Lwow. He was the best of companions, a man of a most amiable disposition, without any guile, always good-natured, full of life and at the same time deeply religious. Every Sunday morning, throughout our whole stay at the camp, he could call us together and read the gospel for the day as well as other prayers which, on our knees, we repeated after him. This was a proper religious service held with the greatest precautions as religious meetings were banned by the authorities and there were spies amongst us.

---

* It should be remembered that owing to Stalin's mistrust of Polish communists the Polish Communist Party was disbanded on his orders in 1938. Most Polish communists who had the misfortune of finding themselves at that time in the Soviet Union were savagely persecuted and finally exterminated. It is therefore doubtful that Lieutenant Szczypiorski would have boasted about his pre-war membership of that party. On the other hand the Polish Socialist Party was always considered by the Russian communists as traitors to the cause of socialism and consequently treated as one of their worst enemies. – Trs.

Lieutenant Bronislaw Mlynarski, Assistant Director of the Gdynia-American Line, was an extremely likeable man, intelligent and well travelled. He had a wide general knowledge and a well-developed talent for relating his experiences. He spoke excellent English and taught the language to a number of his companions. He was the son of the well-known musician Emil Mlynarski, Director of the Warsaw Opera.

Lieutenant Konstanty Cierpinski – Counsel at the Office of the State Attorney of Wilno and a landowner in that region – was a very upright and most respected man but a real chatter-box who delighted in talking politics, sometimes boring us to distraction in the process. A model husband and family man he had a wife and three children in Wilno and was pining for them.

Lieutenant Otton Bisanz came from Lwow and was deeply attached to that city. Up to the ware he had been Manager of the Savings Bank in Rawa Ruska. Basically he was a good man, but in everyday life he was a bit difficult to get on with. Such was our "group of seven" among which I spent one and a half years in a small room crammed tightly with beds.

Since leaving Starobyelsk we had been unable to correspond with out families in Poland. The Soviets kept promising that we would be able to write again soon, but weeks and months went by and we were still not allowed to write letters or receive any correspondence addressed to us. It was only in October 1940 that they allowed us to send postcards home.

This was announced to us by the Commander of the Camp himself after he had arrived from Moscow, stressing that it was a mark of the authorities, real concern for our well-being. He also announced that as from October we would be receiving monthly pay amounting to twenty roubles for officers and ten for privates. Although this in itself was a very small sum it was of considerable value to those of us, myself included, who were without any means at all. In the summer I borrowed five roubles from my good friend Joseph Czapski which I succeeded in making last a fairly long time, but I was now at the end of my tether. With the monthly pay it was now possible to purchase from time to time some necessities from the little shop in the camp, such as tooth powder, needle and thread, shoe polish and sometimes even some sugar or sweets (between 200 and 300 grammes but only one item at a time). It was impossible to spend a great deal of money in the shop as it had a very small stock and only opened once a week, or sometimes once a fortnight. In December my financial position had improved to such an extent that I could afford to order a pair of warm slippers. They were manufactured by one of our men by the name of Zuk. He had once done a stretch in prison in Poland for some trivial offences and had learned the craft there. I paid fifteen roubles for the pair and they proved to be of great use to me.

After posting our letters in October and later at the beginning of November we awaited replies with great trepidation. The first communication to reach us was a telegram for Joseph Czapski from his sister in Warsaw. After that, some of our companions received letters. We all shared the news contained in them for it was the only link connecting us to the world outside.

At last my turn came too. A telegram – a real Christmas present – arrived shortly before Christmas Eve followed later by some postcards from my mother and my sister Sophie. I was overjoyed. There was such a sense of yearning in their words that I would go over them again and again with great emotion. I wished that they could detect in my letters the same feeling towards them. While taking long walks in the mornings and evenings through the picturesque alleys and roads of the camp compound I prayed for them ardently, and standing on the high hill on the site of the old monastery, looking to the west over the endless, dark, forbidding forests, I made the sign of the cross.

For the second time we were to celebrate Christmas in captivity and despite the official ban we assembled in room number 4 to hear Christmas Eve prayers. They were read by the Reverend Kantak, Professor at the Seminary of Pinsk, who was arrested in 1939 and kept in prison in Moscow from where ultimately he was sent to our camp. In the evening in our room, we ate the traditional Polish Christmas Eve meal, consisting of fish and potatoes as well as a cake, baked in our oven by Lieutenant Bisanz, and tea. We also had a small Christmas tree, brought from the forest by our men who used to go up there to fetch some wood for heating. We then sang Christmas carols so loudly that the guards heard us. However, we got away with it without any incidents occurring. After two *politruks* had appeared and listened to our singing we pretended that the songs were just ordinary folk songs and not religious ones. This explanation satisfied them and they left. As for Christmas trees, for three years these had been officially permitted for children in accordance with Stalin's slogan "zhit stalo lutche, zhit stalo vyesyelye" (life has become better and more cheerful). So we got away with our tree as well. Needless to say, the officially-approved trees are topped by red communist stars.

On Christmas Day we were allowed to organise a Chopin recital in the camp's cinema. This was a converted wooden Greek Orthodox church with a capacity of three hundred people and in which films, most of them of a crude propaganda character, were shown from time to time. Also, on two or three occasions, we had been visited by a repertory company from Vologda which put on some foul, anti-religious plays. The great majority of our men left the hall after the first act. The same would happen during the film performances. Our concert, on the other hand, was a great success and made a great impact on all of us. Lieutenant Grzybowski, a concert pianist from Warsaw and one of the prize-winners at the Chopin competition, was the soloist. At the end of the recital he inserted the motif of the well-known Polish carol "The Lord is born" in Chopin's *Fantasy*.

Summoned later to the Command of the Camp he had a most unpleasant conversation with the Soviet officers. Some of our "music loving" spies must have reported his piece of camouflaged religious propaganda.

While any political activity amongst the prisoners was sternly suppressed the authorities did their best to propagate the tenets of the communist faith through meetings, lectures, films, periodicals and the radio. All this was supposed to capture the attention of the prisoners and lead them towards embracing communism. On the whole all their endeavourings were of little avail. Apart from a few dozen scoundrels who right from the beginning proved to be traitors and fraternized with the "bolshies" it seemed to me that the communists failed to enrol a single adherent. On the contrary, the prisoners reacted by strongly asserting their hostile and uncompromisingly negative attitude towards the communist regime. Even some of those among us who professed or pretended to profess a favourable attitude lost heart and became disillusioned. An encouraging and characteristic thing was that our non-commissioned officers and privates, many of whom were of proletarian origin, were among those most opposed to communism.

We listened attentively to the news bulletins on the radio. Sensational things were happening in the autumn and winter of 1940. In Greece and Ethiopia the Italians were getting a good thrashing, and this news filled us with delight and lifted our morale. On the other hand, it seemed to us that Molotov's visit to Berlin pointed to a strengthening of the German-Soviet alliance and we did not like this at all. We feared for the future of Poland. These two demoniac regimes had, after all conspired between themselves to finish us off for good. Such was our fear. As it turned out, however, Molotov's Berlin visit did not lead at all to the tightening of the German-Soviet alliance.

During the winter of 1941 relations between the two countries began to cool and despite the Soviets' compliant disposition and reluctance to fight the Germans, war finally broke out.

Shortly before Christmas freezing cold weather set in. Temperatures fell and would often reach 40 centigrade below zero.

But this never lasted very long. After a few days of heavy frost it would be snowing again and the temperatures would rise to 20 centigrade below zero or less.

The worst thing about winters in the north of Russia is the winds which keep blowing even during heavy frost. The climate, therefore, is considered to be worse than the continental climate of Siberia where winds hardly ever occur. Fortunately we had been issued with padded jackets and pants, the so called *fufayki,* which are very warm and also very light, so I had no reason to complain about feeling cold. Neither did we lack wood for heating purposes. Apart from what we were supplied we used to steal wood whenever we could and store it under our beds so that we could use it later when it became really cold and we most needed it. And so we managed to survive our second winter in captivity.

In March and April I received two parcels from home and what a great joy they were to me! I particularly appreciated the small pillow which my dear mother, guessing what I most lacked in the camp, sent me.

But my God, what had become of all our companions with whom, a year previously, we had spent winter at Camp Starobyelsk? We knew nothing about them and we had no means of knowing anything. We only learned from the letters we received from our families that it was only us, that is, the inmates of the Gryazovyetz Camp, who were corresponding with them. Why us only? Why were all the others not writing? This was a riddle we were unable to solve.

We only learned the truth later — after we had been released from captivity. Since April 1940 our camp had been the only one in the Soviet Union where Polish prisoners of war were treated more or less according to the rules of the Geneva Convention, or, rather, the Soviet interpretation of them. This was probably made for the sake of the outside world, to show that Polish prisoners of war in Soviet Russia were kept in normal conditions.

Our fellow-prisoners had probably been deported to forced labour camps in the far north or in Siberia where they would have had to work as common law convicts, unable to enjoy any of the privileges that are supposed to be granted to prisoners of war. But we couldn't be sure that this had happened. Despite all our endeavours to try and establish their whereabouts their fate was still unknown. And who knows, the Soviets might have disposed of them in some treacherous way of which only they are capable. Providence had indeed protected our group and it was due to a real miracle that we were saved.

Winter was dragging on and the amount of snow seemed to increase all the time. It was still in full swing when Easter arrived. But the evenings were drawing in. The magnificent sunsets of winter which are characteristic of the north had ceased by now to impress us. We became really fed up with the unending whiteness of the landscape and longed for the advent of spring and for a bit of warmth. But it was only in May that spring set in and it proved to be very cold indeed.

We followed the news of the German campaigns in Greece and Yugoslavia with great interest. We expected a swift German defeat as we had a high opinion of the Greek and Yugoslav forces, and, to a lesser extent, the Turkish force too. But our optimism was to be proved groundless. The occupation by the Germans of Yugoslavia, of Greece and later of the island of Crete proved not only that Germany's military strength was in no way impaired but that it constituted a threat to the whole world, including the Soviet Union. All this could not fail to make a strong impact on the country. We could sense it even in our camp, in conversations with our "protectors." Their attitude towards us took a turn for the better. All officers became exempt from manual work and we were allowed to hold lectures and meetings, formerly something strictly prohibited. Our shop also became better stocked with various "delicacies," such as sweets, preserves, etc. When speaking to us Soviet officers would now stress that now we were in no way considered as enemies. "Vy nashi druzhya. Razvye my nye ukhazhivayem za vami?" (You are our friends. Don't we take proper care of you?)

In May came an important announcement – Stalin was to become the head of the Government. Several articles of a rather unusual nature appeared in *Pravda*. Great stress was laid on the patriotic feelings of the Russian people as well as on their readiness to take up arms against "any enemy" who dared to raise a hand against the Soviets. It was easy to guess whom they had in mind when mentioning a "possible enemy." We became convinced that war with Germany was imminent and we awaited this moment with the greatest longing.

II "AMNESTY"

War did indeed come. A special address by Molotov was broadcast at mid-day on the 22nd June. We all assembled in front of the loudspeaker in anticipation of some news of great importance. In fact we heard Molotov informing the people of the Soviet Union that she had been treacherously attacked by the Germans and that a fight for life or death had begun. God be praised. Let them slaughter each other.

As a result of the war our conditions as prisoners of war deteriorated visibly. Food rations were cut – 700 grammes of bread instead of 800 – and we also received less meat and fish, as well as *kasha*. Camp regulations were also tightened and a warning given that any infringements would be dealt with by a court martial. In fact a young Second Lieutenant was committed for trial for having on the first day of the German attack shouted in a state of acute excitement at the Soviet Commander on duty. "You'll now get the punishment you deserve – a good beating from the Germans."

After a few days we were told to expect the arrival of a party of Polish prisoners of war from other camps. Then one morning we saw in the distance a long stream of men approaching us from the railway station. When they were close to us we noticed that they were dressed partly in khaki and partly in blueish uniforms. We stood along the road or in the meadow to get a better look at the newcomers, and some of us went up to the barbed wire. They all looked somewhat different from our men. When we fired some questions at them they answered in French. Was it possible they were French? If so how did they get here? All this seemed strange to us. The distance was too far away to allow us to communicate properly. They passed along the barbed wire fences only to disappear among the buildings housing the Camp Command. They were billeted separately in the cinema, which had been fenced off from the proper camp. So only wires divided them from us.

They were French officers and privates – as it turned out – who after having escaped from the Germans were captured immediately by the Soviets and found themselves in this camp. They cursed both the Germans and the Russians. Mutual relations between them and ourselves proved to be very good. There were under three hundred of them and the majority were followers of General de Gaulle. They sang French military songs for us in the evenings, and we reciprocated by singing Polish ones. We fraternized and held long conversations with them. The "bolshies" behaved in a suprisingly passive way and only when the singing got out of hand or

239

became too loud would a Soviet officer on duty appear and tell us to disperse.

An hour later on the same day that the French arrived we saw another procession of men moving towards us, this time a much longer one. We instantly recognized the Polish uniforms – they were our men without any doubt. They marched into the camp's compound soon after and what passed for accommodation in various sheds, corridors or lofts. The majority had nowhere to sleep and had to bed down in the camp's parade square. Fortunately it was now summer time and the weather happened to be fine.

The newly-arrived party of Polish prisoners numbered some 1,200 men with about 800 officers among them. All of them had been originally interned in Lithuania, Latvia and Estonia after they had crossed the frontiers of those countries at the end of the Polish-German Campaign in 1939. Later, after those countries were annexed by the Soviet Union, they were taken to the Kozyelsk Camp and kept there for a year. Their arrival in our camp was most probably connected with the advance of German troops and the evacuation of Russia's Western provinces.*

The influx of so many prisoners led to chaos in the camp. There wasn't enough space in our dining room for all the newcomers and we had to have our breakfast and dinner in our living quarters. The quality of food deteriorated too. On the other hand as there were now more of us we felt in a way safer and more sure of ourselves and we were looking forward eagerly to further developments.

The German offensive was making great strides. Although Moscow Radio would only indicate the direction of German thrusts, namely those of Wilno, Brest Litovsk, Lwow at the beginning, later Minsk, Dynaburg, Rowno and later still Pskov, Smolensk and Byala Cerkyev, we were, however, able to deduce from the war bulletins that the forces of our hosts were retreating eastwards in great haste. On the 31st July came a bomb-shell. At 6 a.m. we heard a report on the radio that an agreement had been signed between the Polish Government in Exile in London and the Government of the Soviet Union regarding the establishment of diplomatic relations between

---

* The above point requires elucidaton. The Polish prisoners of war – former internees in Lithuania, Estonia and Latvia – mentioned here by the author arrived at the Kozyelsk Camp to find it empty. All its original inmates (about 4,500) sent there in 1939 – except for some 200 men allowed by the Soviets to survive – were already dead, massacred in April 1940 in the nearby Katyn Woods. Their bodies were found three years later by the Germans and this gave rise to the famous case of the Katyn Woods murders. Nearly all of the inmates of the Starobyelsk and Ostaschkov Camps were also massacred, but the sites where these despicable crimes took place have not been revealed or discovered.–Trs.

the two countries. This happened two weeks after an Anglo-Soviet agreement on mutual assistance had been signed and was of course a logical sequel to it. From that moment on the attitude of the Soviet camp authorities towards us underwent a basic change. Our food rations were restored to their previous size and camp regulations were loosened up.

So after a hungry period of around five weeks things improved again. We now looked forward every day to a visit by our Ambassador and we made bets as to who would fill the new post. Soon we learned of the arrival in Moscow from London of our new Chargé d'Affaires, Jozef Retinger as well as of General Szyszko-Bohusz, Chief of the Polish Military Mission. And on the 14th August the radio at last announced the signing of a Military Convention between the two governments and a decision to form a Polish Army in the Soviet Union under the Command of General Wladyslaw Anders. The choice of this person, a well-known military leader, a brilliant Cavalry man and former member of General Dowbor-Musnicki's Corps,* seemed to guarantee that the new army would come up to our expectations. We were not sure and had many doubts about whether the new army would be independent or subordinated to the Soviet Command, along what lines it would be organized, from whom it would get its armaments and uniforms and finally in what region of the Soviet Union it would be formed and concentrated. We were soon to learn the answers to these questions.

On the 20th August the only two Polish Generals in the Camp – Przezdziecki and Wolkowicki – were summoned to Moscow. They left amidst great cheers from their fellow prisoners. We formed two lanes along the road leading from hut number 6 to the camp gate so that the Generals had to pass us to reach the car which was waiting for them. There was no end to shouts and other manifestations of sympathy. Although they were not particularly popular amongst us, we all wished them a safe journey and much success in their mission. Two days later they were followed by a dozen or so officers and an announcement was made at the same time that a mixed Polish-Soviet Commission would soon be arriving from Moscow to settle all necessary formalities connected with our release from the camp as well as our recruitment to the army which was about to be formed.

On the 21st August a memorable ceremony took place. The Soviet

---

* An army corps recruited from Poles serving in the Russian Army and formed in 1917 in Bobruysk (Byelorussia). It was later disbanded by the Germans after their troops, unopposed by the Red Army, had advanced far to the East, occupying vast stretches of land held by the Russians.–Trs.

Commander of the Camp, a Lieutenant-Colonel, called a parade of all our companies and after we had lined up read out a decree of the Council of the People's Commissars granting us the so called "amnesty." He finished by extending his good wishes to all of us. Soviet sentries were removed and on the orders of Colonel Boleslawowicz, the now highest ranking Polish officer in the camp and recently made its Commander, they were replaced by our sentries, who were former Polish Police Officers. To cross the gate of the camp a special permit was required from Colonel Boleslawowicz but no one seemed eager to apply for it.

The long expected Commission from Moscow arrived on the 25th August. After we had assembled in lines on the meadow along the river we saw a mixed group of officers coming towards us from the side of the buildings near the Camp Command. It was headed by a tall, slim man in a civilian light overcoat, wearing a hat, with Colonel Boleslawowicz at his side. This was Lieutenant-Colonel Stanislaw Pstrokonski, who had arrived from Moscow with three Soviet officers. He stepped into the centre of the square formed by us and announced that he was here on the orders of General Anders to receive us on his behalf into the new Polish Army. He then gave us a brief account of the fighting by Polish troops on various fronts since the downfall of our country in 1939, after which he called out "Long live Poland!" This was repeated loudly by us three times. He also announced that General Anders himself would be arriving later in the day after travelling by air from Moscow.

General Anders arrived at 4 p.m., having travelled by car from the Vologda airport. He was in the company of General Szyszko-Bohusz, who had flown in from London a few days earlier, as well as a few Soviet officers, among them General Zhukov, a plenipotentiary of the Soviet Government regarding all matters connected with the organizing of the Polish Army in the Soviet Union.

Once more we lined up, forming a square on the meadow by the river. As General Anders and his retinue approached the command "Attention" resounded. Tall and looking pale – he had been released from a Soviet prison after a two year detention – he was, as the result of a wound received in the Polish-German Campaign in 1939, limping slightly and had to lean on a stout walking stick. He did the rounds, saluting each officer and private and looking into their eyes intently. All this was deeply moving and was carried out in complete silence. He then halted in the centre of the square and welcomed us on behalf of the Commander in Chief of all Polish forces, General Sikorski in London. Further, he declared that he would be proceeding to form a Polish Army in the Soviet Union of which we were to be its nucleus. This was followed by raising the shout "LONG LIVE POLAND" and "LONG LIVE OUR ALLIES", "GREAT BRITAIN AND THE SOVIET UNION." We then sang one of our patriotic songs "Boze co Polske." Our new allies – oh irony! – were standing to attention, saluting. Only a few weeks before, anyone found guilty of singing a Polish song would have been thrown into the cooler and put on a strict diet of bread and water.

After the ceremony was over we surrounded our Generals who welcomed cordially all their acquaintances and told us news from the outside world. General Szyszko-Bohusz, a veteran of the Narvik Campaign, was the object of great ovations. They later attended a reception in their honour given for them by the Camp Commander and left in the evening.

After this unforgettable day we awaited our departure from the camp with great impatience. We were no longer prisoners but we still lived behind wires, although the sentries were Polish. On Sunday, for the first time in the history of the camp, a mass was said with official approval. We found ourselves once more standing four abreast in front of a specially constructed camp altar. On the next day registration commenced for the new Polish Army. Our officers, appointed by the new Commander, Colonel Boleslawowicz, began their duties in a number of rooms of the former Soviet Command of the camp, known to all of us only too well from the many interrogations which were once held there in the daytime as well as during the night.

At last, on the 28th August, came the announcement of our forthcoming departure. We were told to get up at 4 a.m. on the next morning, pack up our belongings and bring them outside to the meadow from where trucks would take them to the railway station. We were to leave on foot before noon.

Although the plan had been well worked out as usual in the Soviet Union nothing came of it. The train from Vologda on which we were to travel not only did not arrive on time, it failed to arrive at all that day. We had to spend the night once again in the huts to which we had already said goodbye. The same happened next morning. No train, all our nerves on edge and our questions answered stoically by our new friends with habitual "Vagonov yeshcho nyet" (The box-cars have not arrived yet.) Since, however, our luggage was being transported all day long to the station this seemed to indicate that our friends really meant us to leave the camp. There were nevertheless some pessimists among us who kept saying: "All this is bluff, nothing but bluff, simply a Soviet joke. We shall never get out of the damned camp."

We left it, however, at 6 p.m. on the 30th August. As we marched four abreast through the wide-open gate, our former guards saluted us and bid us farewell in a friendly manner. Not surprisingly, we covered the eight kilometres separating us from the station in a much better mood than a year ago, when carrying our miserable bundles, we had trudged along in the opposite direction.

Soon, however, it started to drizzle and then eventually the rain poured down. The road turned into quagmire and became almost impassable. Although partly paved, the many pot holes were filled with water. On top of this it became quite dark. Numbering some 1,600 men our column was moving at a very slow pace. We were soaked to the skin and water was lapping over the tops of our boots.

We reached the station at 9 p.m. As it turned out there were still no box-cars and as there was not enough room for us in the station buildings we had to wait outside in the wind and rain. After an hour of waiting I realized that if I didn't find some shelter soon I would succumb to a severe chill. Adam Moszynski and I eventually forced our way into some shed already filled to capacity with people and later we even managed to squeeze ourselves into the station building. We had to stay there until the train arrived from Vologda. This happened at 2 a.m.

We started to entrain. There were no coaches of course, box-cars only but they were provided with twenty-five bunks to a car which was considered a luxury. During our journey from Shepetovka to Starobyelsk, almost two years ago, we had been crammed fifty-five men to a car. Since we had had our bunks assigned to us whilst still in the camp the operation was soon over so that at 4 a.m. we set off for Yaroslav on our way south. Colonel Kunstler was the officer in charge of the transport and was helped by a Soviet Officer.

As the train halted at various railway stations for long periods at a time our progress was very slow. On the afternoon of the next day we finally reached Yaroslav, an old city on the Volga river. A dinner a the Red Army canteen was waiting for us. These are huge halls with space for 1,000-2,000 men. The meals consist of soup, *kasha* and goulash and are served to members of the forces in transit. The standard of these meals is good, the portions are adequate and the canteens are well organized and well run. It is hard to believe that all this is possible in the Soviet Union, the more so as everything is spotlessly clean. But the Soviet Union is, after all, a country of paradoxes.

From Yaroslav we moved farther on to the east by way of Ivanovo, Nokvi, Murom, Arzamas and Ruzhayevka. At this last station the train divided into two parts. One was to go to Totzkoye through

Penza the other to Tatishchev near Saratov. Unlike our previous journeys across the Soviet Union we now knew where we were going and what our itinerary would be. How very different we felt during this journey compared with our previous experience. No one was locked in and we were allowed to get off the train when it halted (although there were some restrictions to this.) Further, it was possible, although not always easy, to buy some food. We were able to get, at very high prices, milk, eggs and even roast chicken.

We were all well provided with money. Before leaving our camp we were paid a so-called indemnity, although we did not know whether it was damages for moral suffering or compensation for various belongings pinched from us. Generals received 10,000 roubles, Colonels 5,000, Lieutenant-Colonels and Majors 3,000, Captains and lower ranks 2,000, Privates 500 roubles. In September 1941 this was still a sizeable amount of money to each rank. The price of an egg was 1 rouble, a litre of milk $1\frac{1}{2}$ roubles. It was only later, during the winter, that prices soared considerably. At more important railway junctions such as Arzamas, Ruzhayvka and Samara we would be taken to the railway canteens for meals. Bread, conserves, sugar and tea were shared out in our box-cars. All in all we could no longer complain about lack of food.

We were crossing the immense stretches of Russia. Up to Arzamas there was nothing but woods, but later on the scenery changed. Woods were superseded by fairly fertile arable land. From Samara it was again different — enormous, scarcely-populated areas, mostly steppes, only rarely tilled. Across the River Volga there were more vast stretches of excellent black soil. Railway station buildings were overcrowded with refugees and people evacuated from the war zones.

Trains filled with those people would often stand for a few days at a station. All of their passengers, hungry and dressed in rags, were trying to get further eastwards. However, trains carrying troops — and we saw quite a number of them — were moving in the opposite direction. Our train was creating quite a sensation. Our uniforms were different from the Soviet ones and the local population had no idea to what forces we belonged. Despite our two years in captivity our uniforms were still in relatively good condition and anyway they looked better than the tatty ones of the Red Army.

We were often asked whether we were "Germancy" (Germans) and when told we were Poles people would shake their heads with incredulity. On the whole the public at the railway stations looked unbelievably poor and shabby. During the twenty years of its existence the Soviet regime had brought the country to the brink of utter destitution, except of course the class of government and party officials who were considerably better off than the rest of the population. People, generally speaking, looked down-trodden and kept silent. They feared to say what they thought and to show their real feelings.

However, exceptions do occur sometimes. One man, a member of a nearby *kholkhoz*, came up to me at one of the stations and started a conversation. He told me openly of the conditions under which peasants have to live in the *kholkhoz* and said finally: "We have been holding out for a long time, but should things go on like this and not change, we shall all starve to death. We simply have nothing to eat."

Not far from Kuybyshev (the former Samara) we had to pass enormous, newly constructed complexes for the war industry. These works had been completed within the last two years through the efforts of convicts and political prisoners. They were so vast that they stretched for about thirty kilometres and it took our train the better part of an hour to cover the distance. They were all fenced off by barbed wire, interspersed every few hundred metres with special watch towers and illuminated by electric lamps. Altogether it was a most impressive sight.

This was not the only industrial complex of that kind. During the last few years similar ones had been constructed in the Ural Region and farther to the east. Preparations for war had been going on for a long time and, as one could see, on a very large and comprehensive scale. Today, after losing to the Germans the south of Russia with all her industry, the Soviet Union is in a position to continue the war thanks only to the industrial areas of the Ural Region.

Our train reached its final destination — the railway station of Totzkoye — on the 9th September. We didn't take long to detrain. After lining up four abreast on the station square we marched off to the military camp of Totzkoye, situated about 3 kilometres away. To do this we had to cross a steppe-like country. Night had fallen when we reached the ramparts surrounding the camp and its gate on top of which a Polish flag was fluttering in the wind. Here at Totzkoye the sovereign Polish Army in the Soviet Union was to be formed and we happened to be one of the first detachments of Polish soldiers to arrive on the spot.

We had been preceded by only a handful of Polish officers from Moscow — members of a special commission whose task was to take over the camp from the Soviet military authorities and organize it. After two years of captivity I was going to serve again in the Polish Army. I was going back to life.

Buzuluk
October-November, 1941.